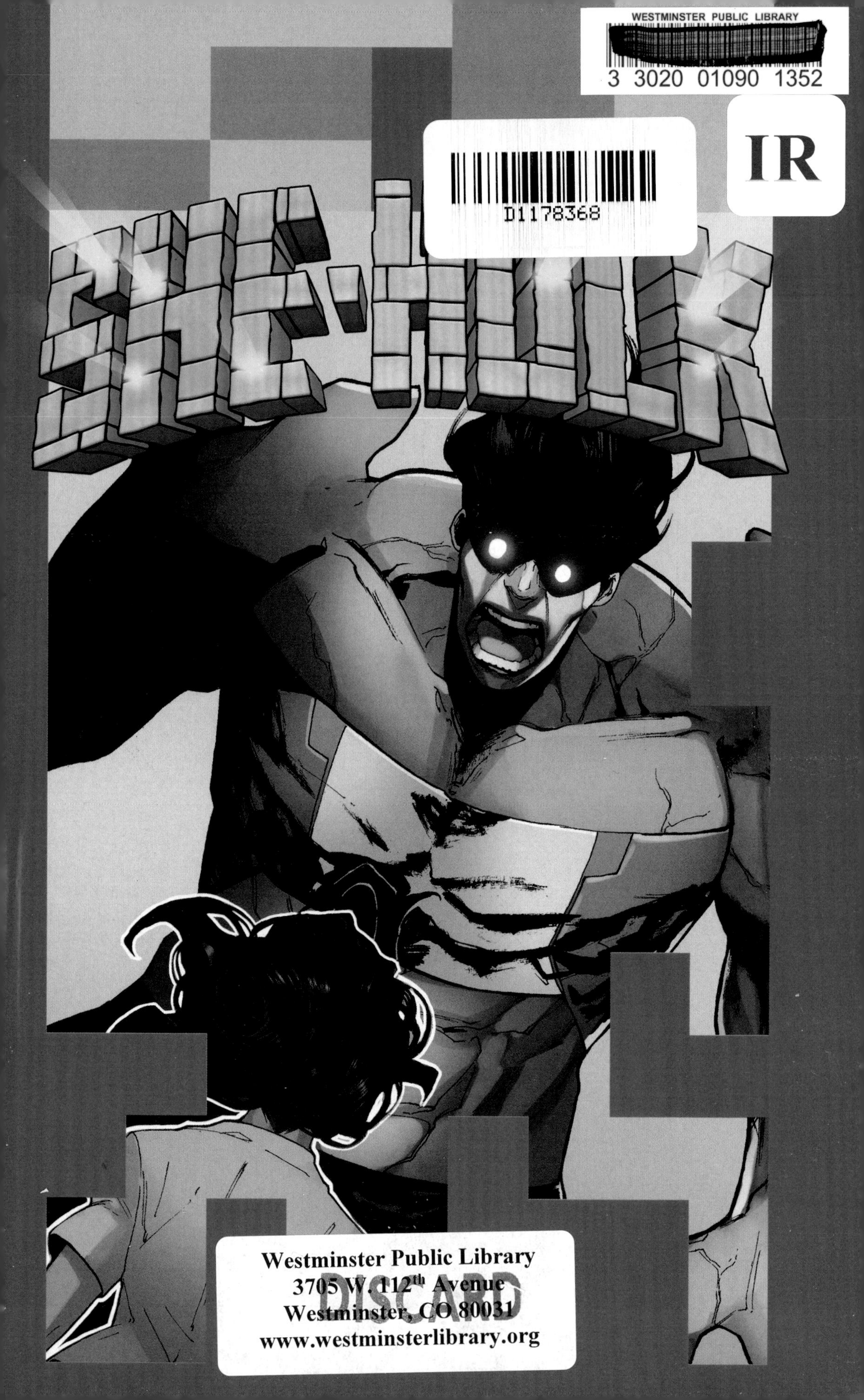
SHE-HULK

SHE-HULK VOL. 3: JEN WALTERS MUST DIE. Contains material originally published in magazine form as SHE-HULK #159-163. First printing 2018. ISBN 978-1-302-90569-9. Published by MARVEL WORLDWIDE, INC., a subsidiary of MARVEL ENTERTAINMENT, LLC. OFFICE OF PUBLICATION: 135 West 50th Street, New York, NY 10020. Copyright © 2018 MARVEL No similarity between any of the names, characters, persons, and/or institutions in this magazine with those of any living or dead person or institution is intended, and any such similarity which may exist is purely coincidental. **Printed in Canada.** DAN BUCKLEY, President, Marvel Entertainment; JOHN NEE, Publisher; JOE QUESADA, Chief Creative Officer; TOM BREVOORT, SVP of Publishing; DAVID BOGART, SVP of Business Affairs & Operations, Publishing & Partnership; DAVID GABRIEL, SVP of Sales & Marketing, Publishing; JEFF YOUNGQUIST, VP of Production & Special Projects; DAN CARR, Executive Director of Publishing Technology; ALEX MORALES, Director of Publishing Operations; SUSAN CRESPI, Production Manager; STAN LEE, Chairman Emeritus. For information regarding advertising in Marvel Comics or on Marvel.com, please contact Vit DeBellis, Custom Solutions & Integrated Advertising Manager; at vdebellis@marvel.com. For Marvel subscription inquiries, please call 888-511-5480. **Manufactured between 3/9/2018 and 4/10/2018 by SOLISCO PRINTERS, SCOTT, QC, CANADA.**

10 9 8 7 6 5 4 3 2 1

JENNIFER WALTERS HAS ALWAYS BATTLED FOR JUSTICE, BOTH AS A LAWYER AND AS THE SUPER HERO SHE-HULK. BUT DURING THE LAST SUPER HERO CIVIL WAR, JEN WAS CRITICALLY INJURED. AT THE SAME TIME, JEN'S COUSIN, BRUCE BANNER, A.K.A. THE ORIGINAL HULK, WAS MURDERED. SINCE THE INCIDENT, JEN'S HULK PERSONA HAS BECOME GRAY, SCARRED AND MUDDIED BY RAGE.

NOW JEN MUST SEARCH FOR A WAY TO BECOME

SHE-HULK

JEN WALTERS MUST DIE

WRITER **MARIKO TAMAKI**

ARTISTS **JAHNOY LINDSAY** (#159-162)
& **DIEGO OLORTEGUI** (#163)

COLOR ARTISTS **FEDERICO BLEE**
WITH **CHRIS SOTOMAYOR** (#159)

LETTERER **VC's TRAVIS LANHAM**

COVER ART **MIKE DEODATO JR.**
& **MARCELO MAIOLO** (#159)
AND **RAHZZAH** (#160-163)

ASSISTANT EDITOR **CHRISTINA HARRINGTON**
EDITOR **MARK PANICCIA**

COLLECTION EDITOR **JENNIFER GRÜNWALD** | ASSISTANT EDITOR **CAITLIN O'CONNELL**
ASSOCIATE MANAGING EDITOR **KATERI WOODY** | EDITOR, SPECIAL PROJECTS **MARK D. BEAZLEY**
VP PRODUCTION & SPECIAL PROJECTS **JEFF YOUNGQUIST** | SVP PRINT, SALES & MARKETING **DAVID GABRIEL**
BOOK DESIGNER **JAY BOWEN**

EDITOR IN CHIEF **C.B. CEBULSKI** | CHIEF CREATIVE OFFICER **JOE QUESADA**
PRESIDENT **DAN BUCKLEY** | EXECUTIVE PRODUCER **ALAN FINE**

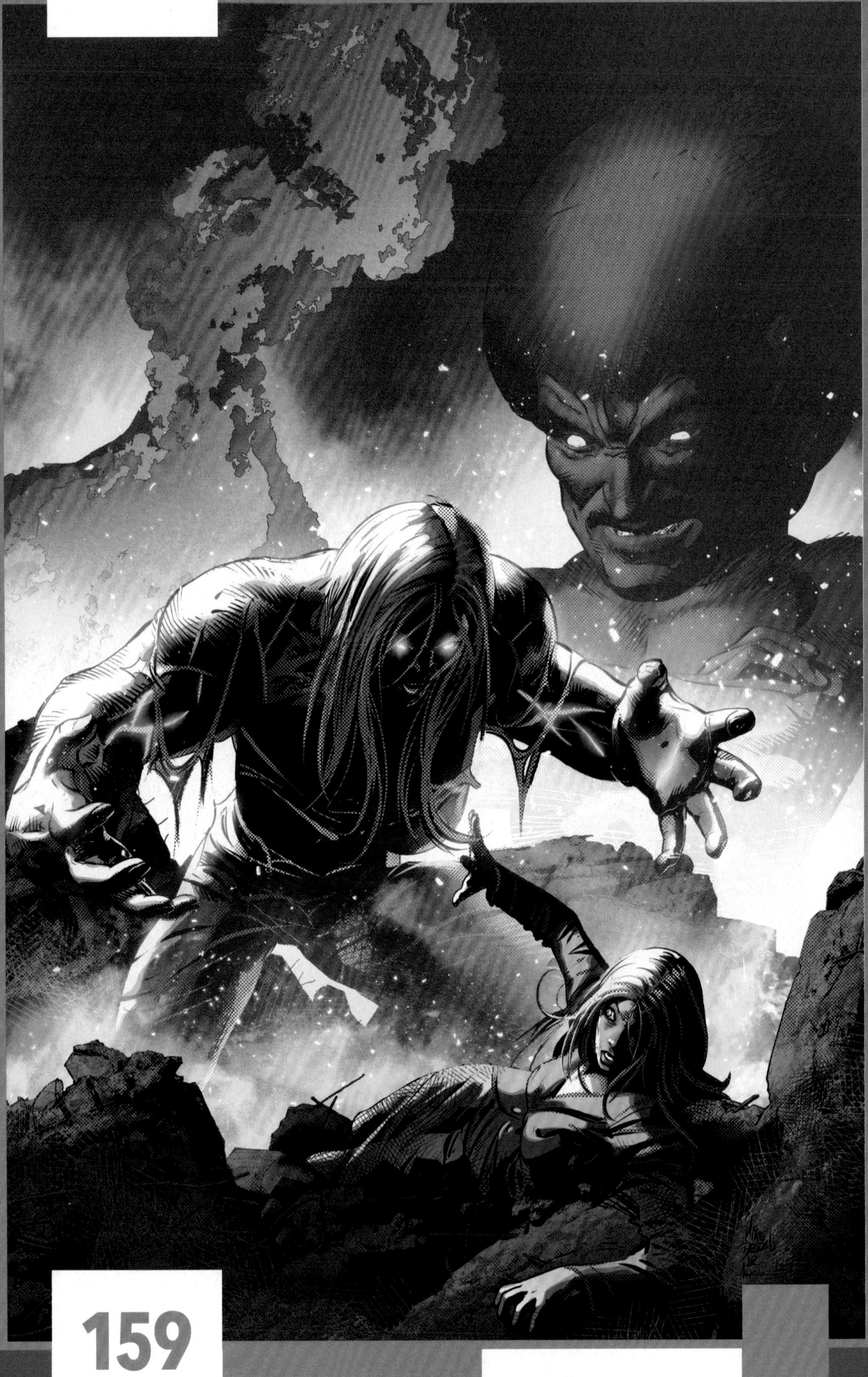

159

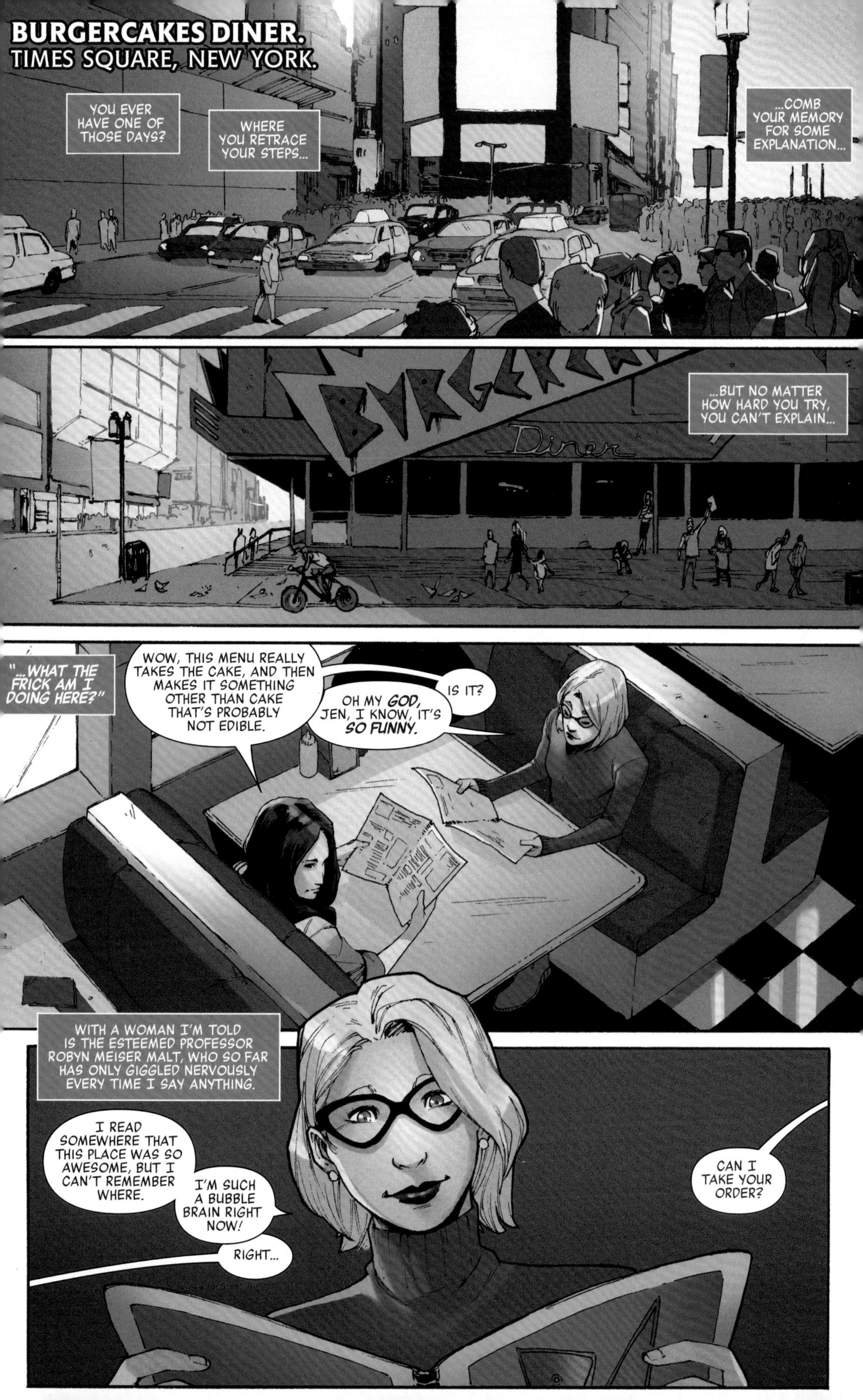
BURGERCAKES DINER.
TIMES SQUARE, NEW YORK.
YOU EVER HAVE ONE OF THOSE DAYS?
WHERE YOU RETRACE YOUR STEPS...
...COMB YOUR MEMORY FOR SOME EXPLANATION...
...BUT NO MATTER HOW HARD YOU TRY, YOU CAN'T EXPLAIN...
"...WHAT THE FRICK AM I DOING HERE?"
WOW, THIS MENU REALLY TAKES THE CAKE, AND THEN MAKES IT SOMETHING OTHER THAN CAKE THAT'S PROBABLY NOT EDIBLE.
IS IT?
OH MY GOD, JEN, I KNOW, IT'S SO FUNNY.
WITH A WOMAN I'M TOLD IS THE ESTEEMED PROFESSOR ROBYN MEISER MALT, WHO SO FAR HAS ONLY GIGGLED NERVOUSLY EVERY TIME I SAY ANYTHING.
I READ SOMEWHERE THAT THIS PLACE WAS SO AWESOME, BUT I CAN'T REMEMBER WHERE.
I'M SUCH A BUBBLE BRAIN RIGHT NOW!
RIGHT...
CAN I TAKE YOUR ORDER?

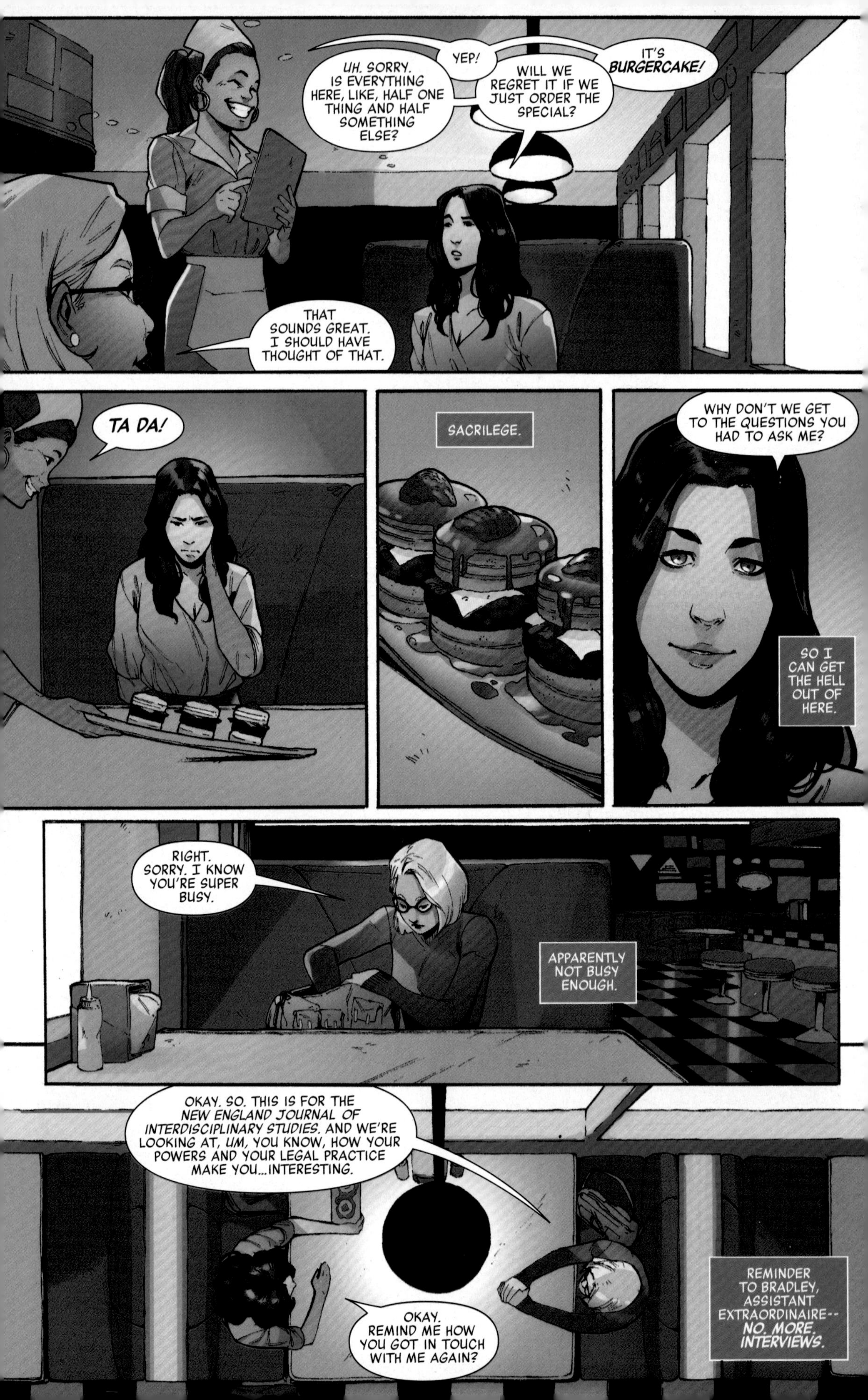
UH. SORRY. IS EVERYTHING HERE, LIKE, HALF ONE THING AND HALF SOMETHING ELSE?
YEP!
IT'S BURGERCAKE!
WILL WE REGRET IT IF WE JUST ORDER THE SPECIAL?
THAT SOUNDS GREAT. I SHOULD HAVE THOUGHT OF THAT.
TA DA!
SACRILEGE.
WHY DON'T WE GET TO THE QUESTIONS YOU HAD TO ASK ME?
SO I CAN GET THE HELL OUT OF HERE.
RIGHT. SORRY. I KNOW YOU'RE SUPER BUSY.
APPARENTLY NOT BUSY ENOUGH.
OKAY. SO. THIS IS FOR THE NEW ENGLAND JOURNAL OF INTERDISCIPLINARY STUDIES. AND WE'RE LOOKING AT, UM, YOU KNOW, HOW YOUR POWERS AND YOUR LEGAL PRACTICE MAKE YOU...INTERESTING.
OKAY. REMIND ME HOW YOU GOT IN TOUCH WITH ME AGAIN?
REMINDER TO BRADLEY, ASSISTANT EXTRAORDINAIRE-- NO. MORE. INTERVIEWS.

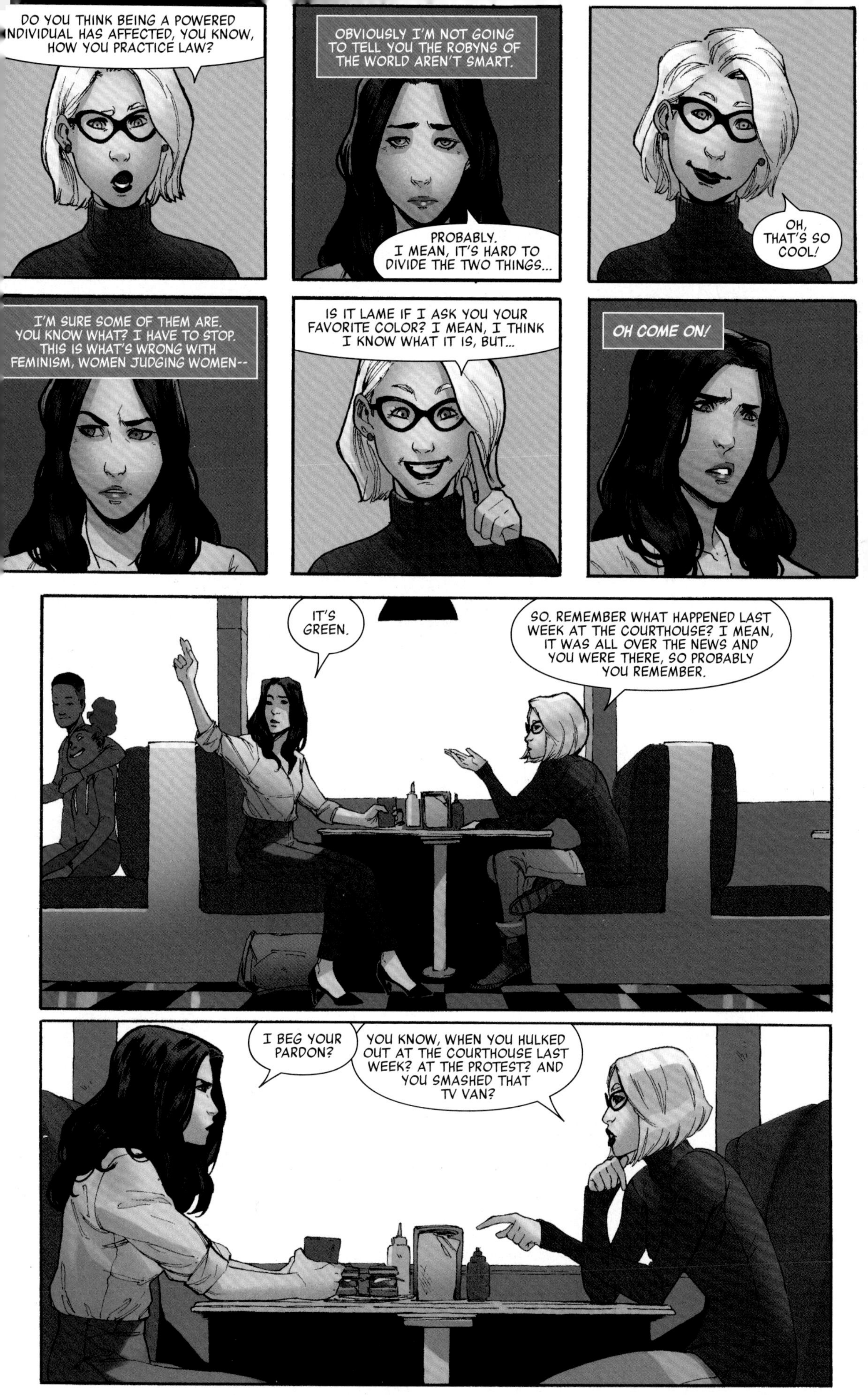
DO YOU THINK BEING A POWERED INDIVIDUAL HAS AFFECTED, YOU KNOW, HOW YOU PRACTICE LAW?
OBVIOUSLY I'M NOT GOING TO TELL YOU THE ROBYNS OF THE WORLD AREN'T SMART.
PROBABLY. I MEAN, IT'S HARD TO DIVIDE THE TWO THINGS...
OH, THAT'S SO COOL!
I'M SURE SOME OF THEM ARE. YOU KNOW WHAT? I HAVE TO STOP. THIS IS WHAT'S WRONG WITH FEMINISM, WOMEN JUDGING WOMEN--
IS IT LAME IF I ASK YOU YOUR FAVORITE COLOR? I MEAN, I THINK I KNOW WHAT IT IS, BUT...
OH COME ON!
IT'S GREEN.
SO. REMEMBER WHAT HAPPENED LAST WEEK AT THE COURTHOUSE? I MEAN, IT WAS ALL OVER THE NEWS AND YOU WERE THERE, SO PROBABLY YOU REMEMBER.
I BEG YOUR PARDON?
YOU KNOW, WHEN YOU HULKED OUT AT THE COURTHOUSE LAST WEEK? AT THE PROTEST? AND YOU SMASHED THAT TV VAN?

MY CLIENT WAS ACQUITTED. HE IS INNOCENT. HIS MUTATION DOES NOT MAKE HIM--

SO YOU'RE SAYING THAT MUTANTS AREN'T INHERENTLY DANGEROUS?

PROTECT AMERICA!

Mutants WILL ALWAYS BE WEAPONS

A PERSON is NOT A WEAPON

GO HOME!

"I AM NOT HERE TO ANSWER THOSE QUESTIONS."

OH, I THOUGHT IT WAS JUST A REGULAR QUESTION. IT'S NOT A REGULAR QUESTION?

NO, IT'S NOT. AND YOUR TIME IS **UP**, PROFESSOR.

WAS THAT A STUPID QUESTION?

I DON'T KNOW WHERE MY HEAD IS SOMETIMES.

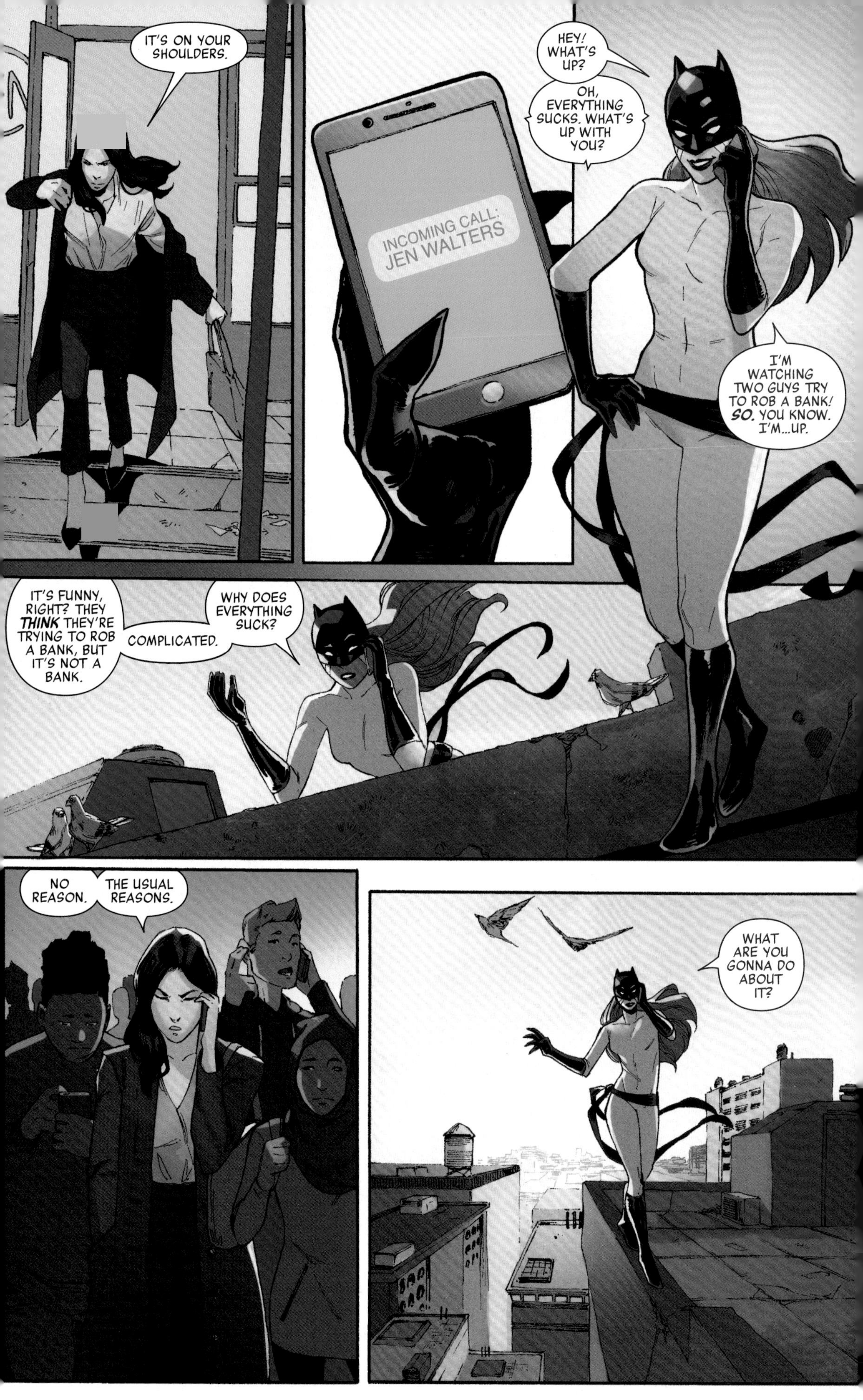
IT'S ON YOUR SHOULDERS.
INCOMING CALL: JEN WALTERS
HEY! WHAT'S UP?
OH, EVERYTHING SUCKS. WHAT'S UP WITH YOU?
I'M WATCHING TWO GUYS TRY TO ROB A BANK! **SO.** YOU KNOW. I'M...UP.
WHY DOES EVERYTHING SUCK?
COMPLICATED.
IT'S FUNNY, RIGHT? THEY ***THINK*** THEY'RE TRYING TO ROB A BANK, BUT IT'S NOT A BANK.
NO REASON.
THE USUAL REASONS.
WHAT ARE YOU GONNA DO ABOUT IT?

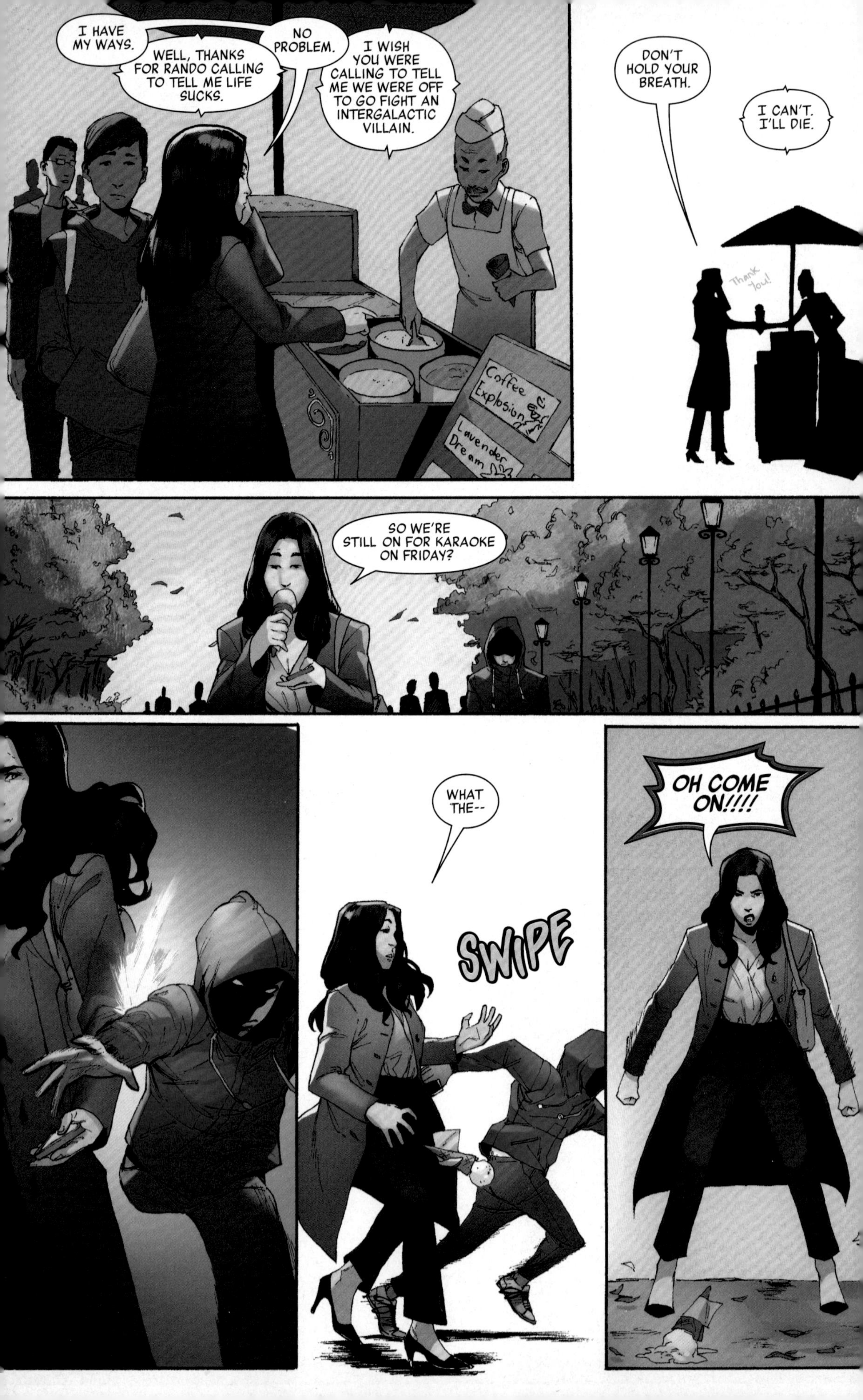
I HAVE MY WAYS.
WELL, THANKS FOR RANDO CALLING TO TELL ME LIFE SUCKS.
NO PROBLEM.
I WISH YOU WERE CALLING TO TELL ME WE WERE OFF TO GO FIGHT AN INTERGALACTIC VILLAIN.
Coffee Explosion
Lavender Dream
DON'T HOLD YOUR BREATH.
I CAN'T. I'LL DIE.
Thank You!
SO WE'RE STILL ON FOR KARAOKE ON FRIDAY?
WHAT THE--
SWIPE
OH COME ON!!!!

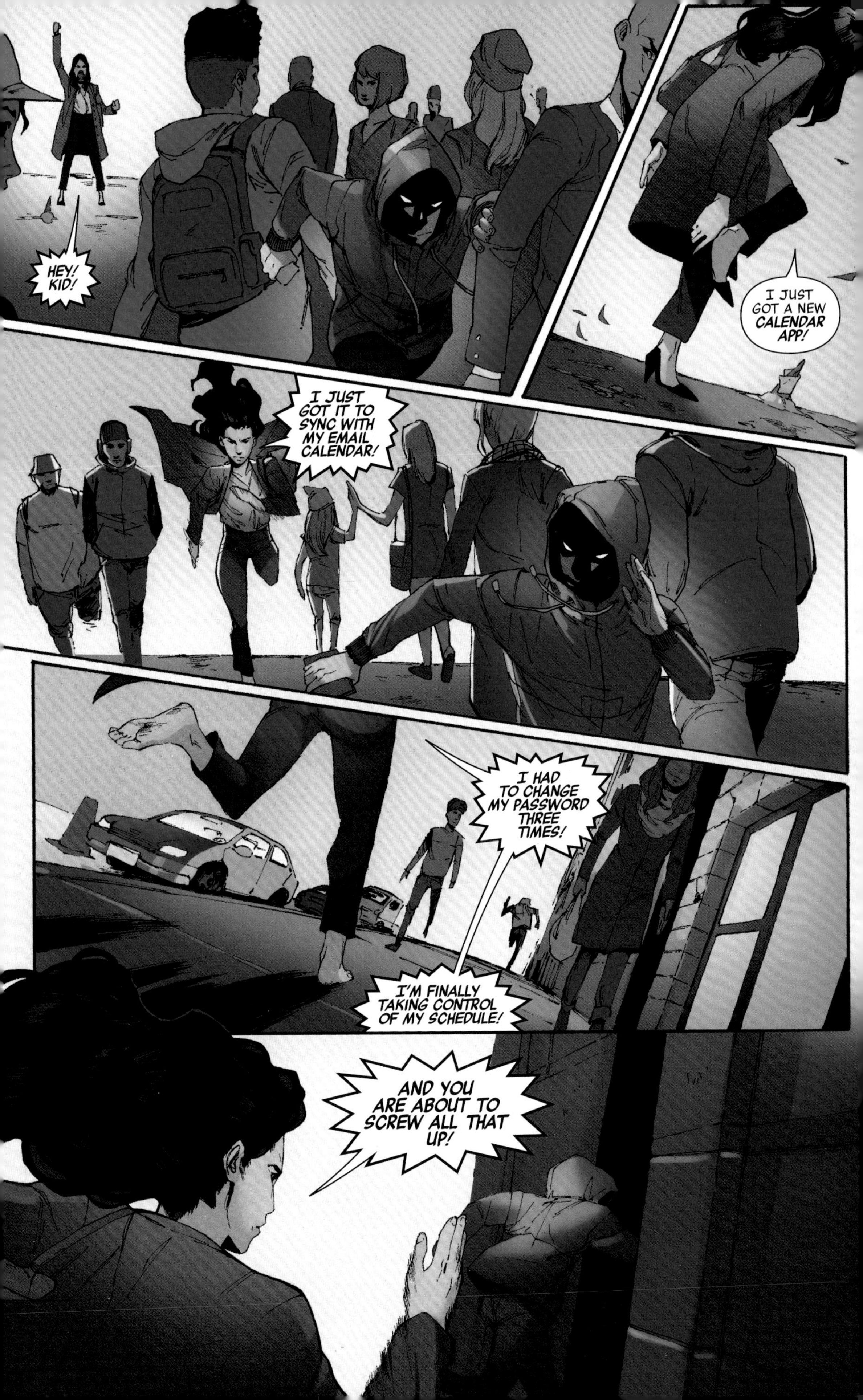
HEY! KID!
I JUST GOT A NEW CALENDAR APP!
I JUST GOT IT TO SYNC WITH MY EMAIL CALENDAR!
I HAD TO CHANGE MY PASSWORD THREE TIMES!
I'M FINALLY TAKING CONTROL OF MY SCHEDULE!
AND YOU ARE ABOUT TO SCREW ALL THAT UP!

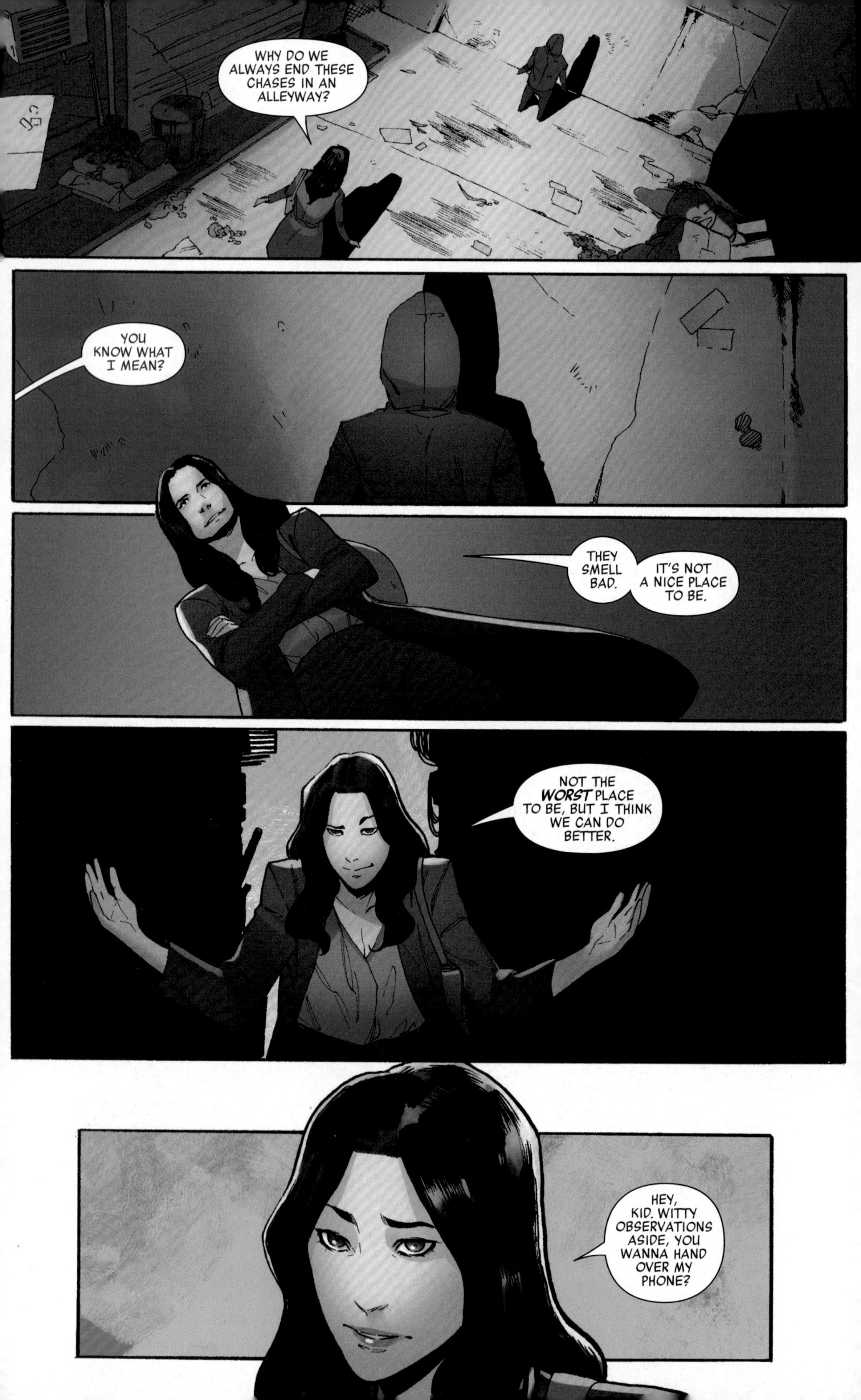
WHY DO WE ALWAYS END THESE CHASES IN AN ALLEYWAY?
YOU KNOW WHAT I MEAN?
THEY SMELL BAD.
IT'S NOT A NICE PLACE TO BE.
NOT THE WORST PLACE TO BE, BUT I THINK WE CAN DO BETTER.
HEY, KID. WITTY OBSERVATIONS ASIDE, YOU WANNA HAND OVER MY PHONE?

OUT OF BREATH?

YEAH, HA HA, KID. JUST GIVE ME MY PHONE BA--

JENNIFER WALTERS.

YOU LOOK CHANGED, FOR CERTAIN. SOMETHING IN THE EYES, YES?

I KNOW YOU?

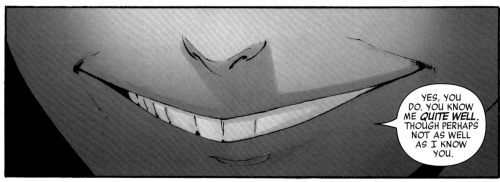

YES, YOU DO. YOU KNOW ME QUITE WELL. THOUGH PERHAPS NOT AS WELL AS I KNOW YOU.

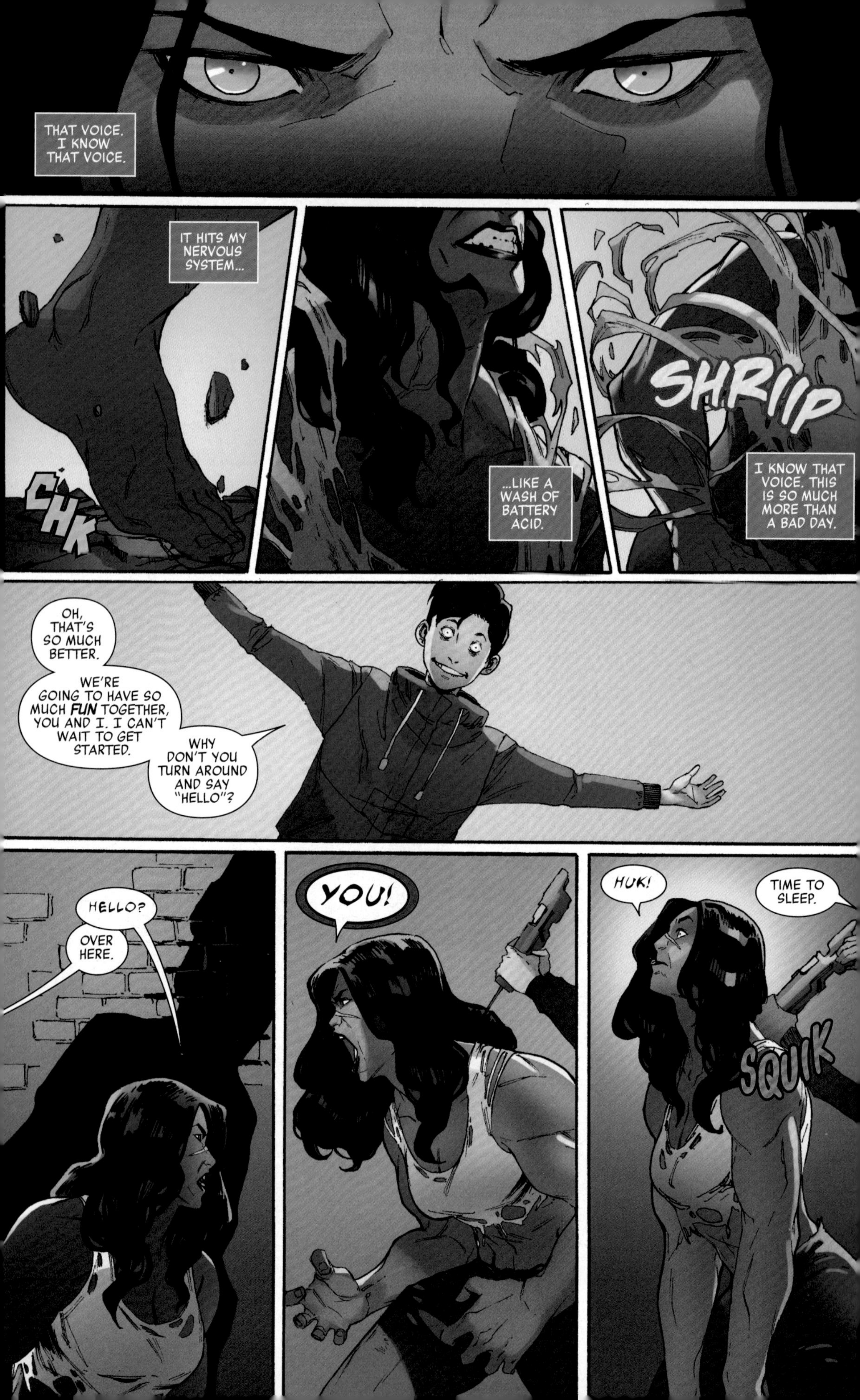
THAT VOICE. I KNOW THAT VOICE.
IT HITS MY NERVOUS SYSTEM...
CHK
...LIKE A WASH OF BATTERY ACID.
SHRIIP
I KNOW THAT VOICE. THIS IS SO MUCH MORE THAN A BAD DAY.
OH, THAT'S SO MUCH BETTER.
WE'RE GOING TO HAVE SO MUCH FUN TOGETHER, YOU AND I. I CAN'T WAIT TO GET STARTED.
WHY DON'T YOU TURN AROUND AND SAY "HELLO"?
HELLO?
OVER HERE.
YOU!
HUK!
TIME TO SLEEP.
SQUIK

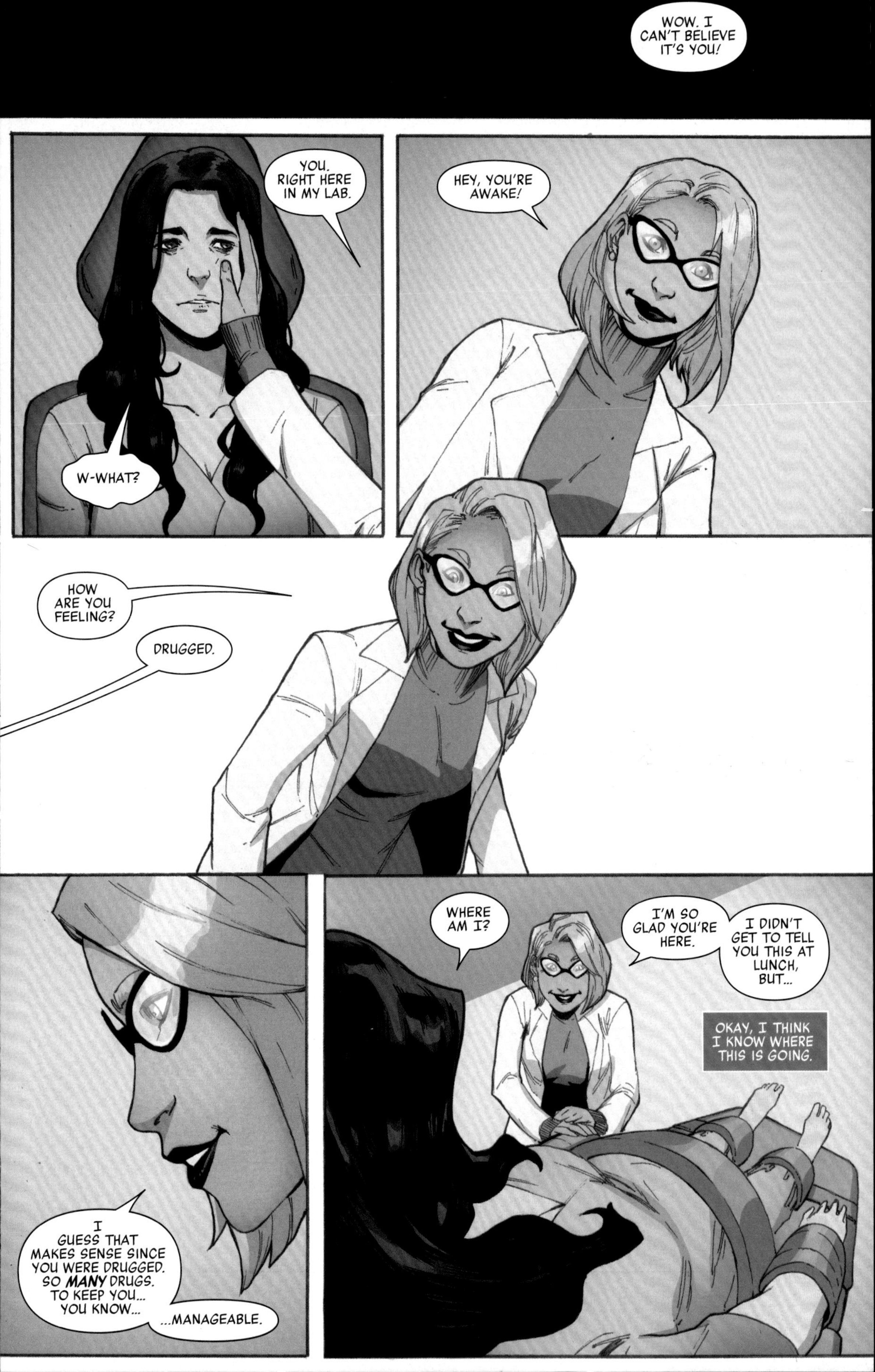
WOW. I CAN'T BELIEVE IT'S YOU!
YOU. RIGHT HERE IN MY LAB.
W-WHAT?
HEY, YOU'RE AWAKE!
HOW ARE YOU FEELING?
DRUGGED.
I GUESS THAT MAKES SENSE SINCE YOU WERE DRUGGED. SO MANY DRUGS. TO KEEP YOU... YOU KNOW...
...MANAGEABLE.
WHERE AM I?
I'M SO GLAD YOU'RE HERE.
I DIDN'T GET TO TELL YOU THIS AT LUNCH, BUT...
OKAY, I THINK I KNOW WHERE THIS IS GOING.

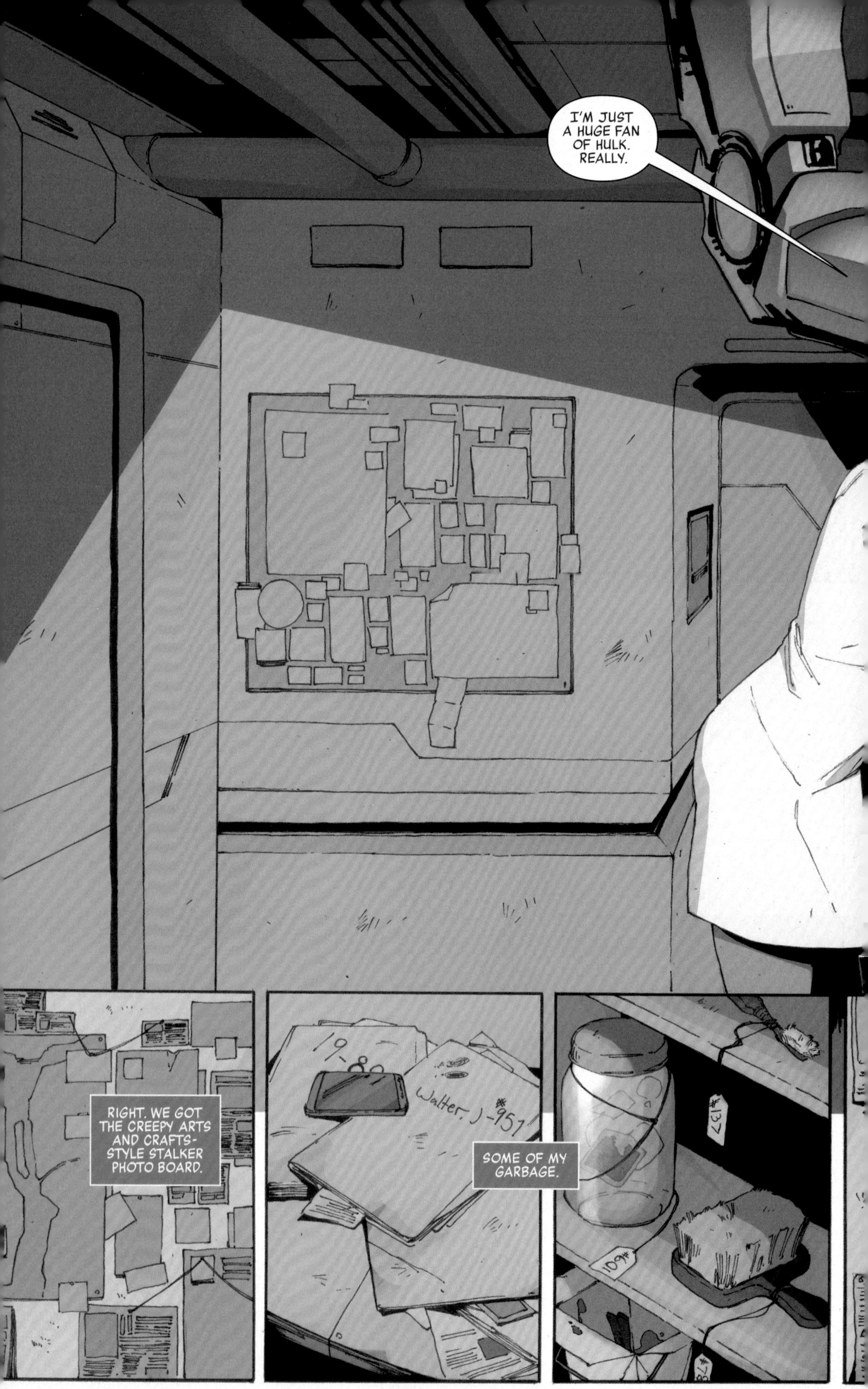
I'M JUST A HUGE FAN OF HULK. REALLY.
RIGHT. WE GOT THE CREEPY ARTS AND CRAFTS-STYLE STALKER PHOTO BOARD.
Walter, J-951
SOME OF MY GARBAGE.

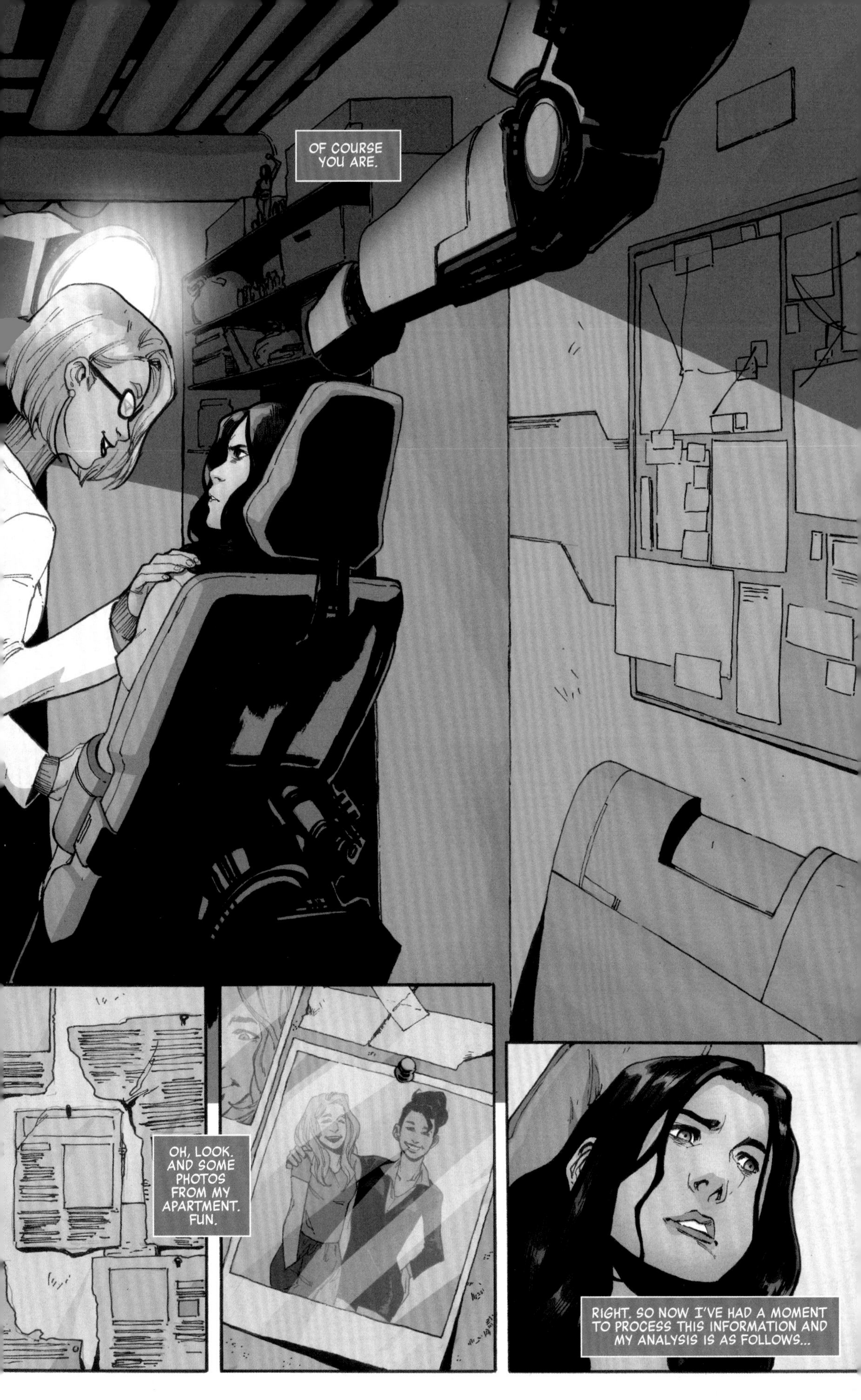
OF COURSE YOU ARE.
OH, LOOK. AND SOME PHOTOS FROM MY APARTMENT. FUN.
RIGHT. SO NOW I'VE HAD A MOMENT TO PROCESS THIS INFORMATION AND MY ANALYSIS IS AS FOLLOWS...

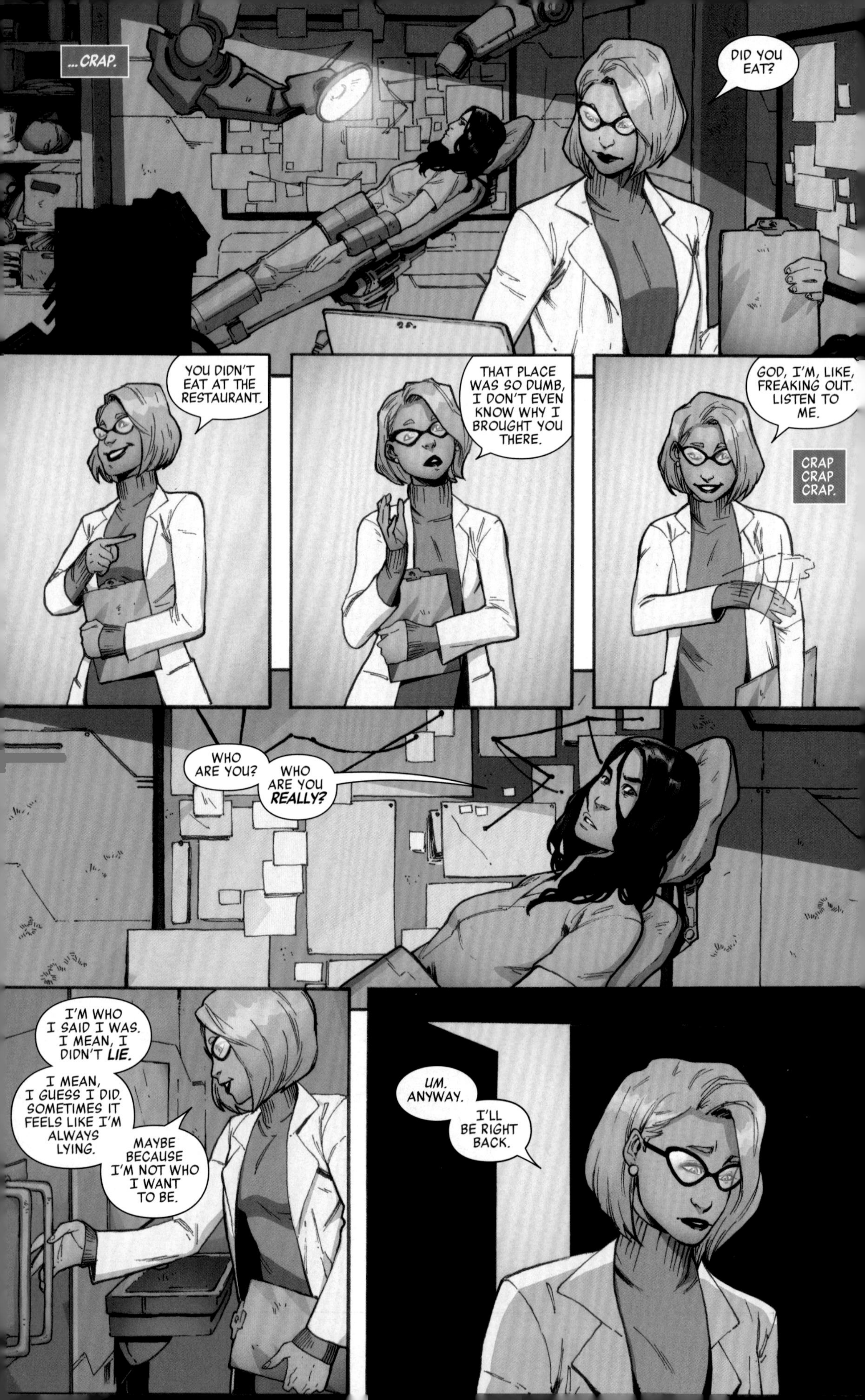
...CRAP.
DID YOU EAT?
YOU DIDN'T EAT AT THE RESTAURANT.
THAT PLACE WAS SO DUMB, I DON'T EVEN KNOW WHY I BROUGHT YOU THERE.
GOD, I'M, LIKE, FREAKING OUT. LISTEN TO ME.
CRAP CRAP CRAP.
WHO ARE YOU?
WHO ARE YOU *REALLY?*
I'M WHO I SAID I WAS. I MEAN, I DIDN'T *LIE.*
I MEAN, I GUESS I DID. SOMETIMES IT FEELS LIKE I'M ALWAYS LYING.
MAYBE BECAUSE I'M NOT WHO I WANT TO BE.
UM. ANYWAY.
I'LL BE RIGHT BACK.

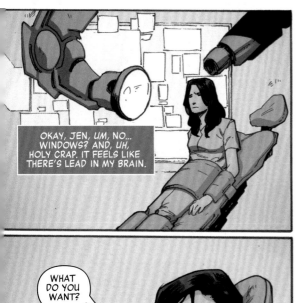

OKAY, JEN, UM, NO... WINDOWS? AND, *UH,* HOLY CRAP. IT FEELS LIKE THERE'S LEAD IN MY BRAIN.

RIGHT. SO. WHAT WAS I SAYING? MAN, MY BRAIN IS SO EVERYWHERE SOMETIMES!

WHAT DO YOU WANT?

ISN'T IT OBVIOUS?

I MEAN, SO YOU'RE SO SMART. YOU CAN PROBABLY GUESS.

UH. RESEARCH?

NOOO*WAH!*

GUESS AGAIN!

SORRY. CAN'T TALK. JUST TAKING A MOMENT TO TRY AND MENTALLY TRANSPORT MYSELF SOMEWHERE VERY FAR AWAY.

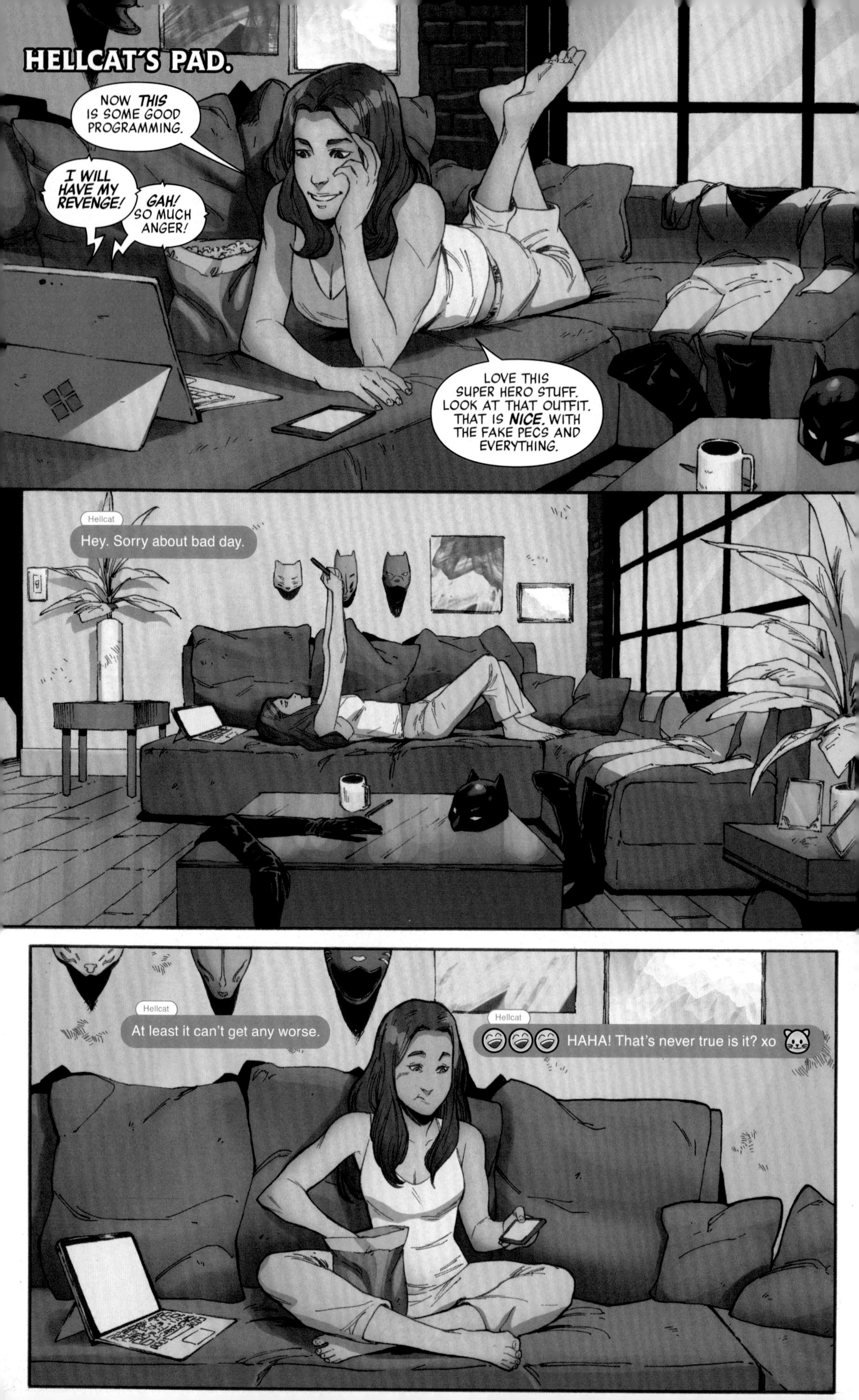
HELLCAT'S PAD.
NOW THIS IS SOME GOOD PROGRAMMING.
I WILL HAVE MY REVENGE!
GAH! SO MUCH ANGER!
LOVE THIS SUPER HERO STUFF. LOOK AT THAT OUTFIT. THAT IS NICE. WITH THE FAKE PECS AND EVERYTHING.
Hellcat
Hey. Sorry about bad day.
Hellcat
At least it can't get any worse.
Hellcat
HAHA! That's never true is it? xo

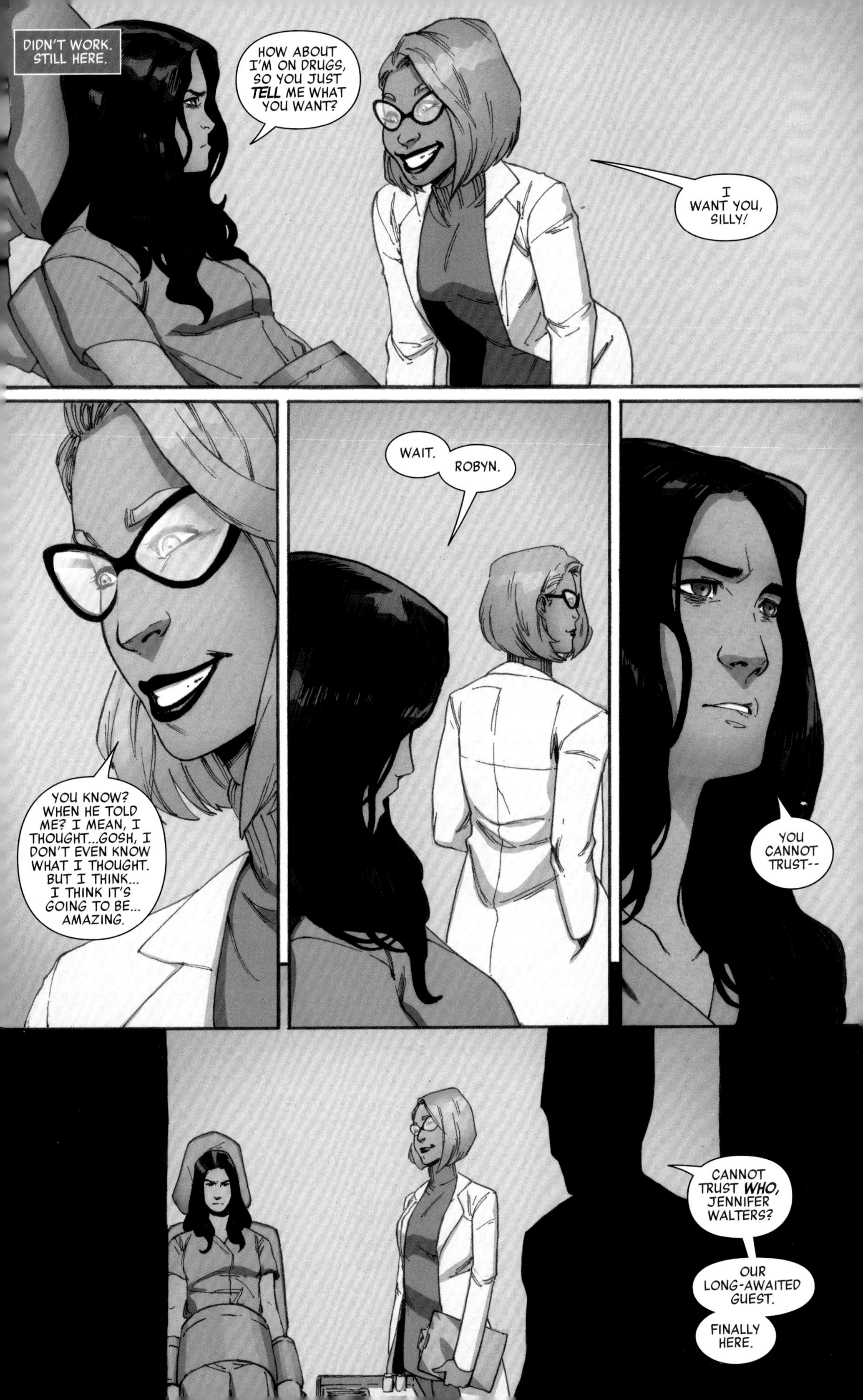
DIDN'T WORK. STILL HERE.
HOW ABOUT I'M ON DRUGS, SO YOU JUST TELL ME WHAT YOU WANT?
I WANT YOU, SILLY!
YOU KNOW? WHEN HE TOLD ME? I MEAN, I THOUGHT...GOSH, I DON'T EVEN KNOW WHAT I THOUGHT. BUT I THINK... I THINK IT'S GOING TO BE... AMAZING.
WAIT.
ROBYN.
YOU CANNOT TRUST--
CANNOT TRUST WHO, JENNIFER WALTERS?
OUR LONG-AWAITED GUEST.
FINALLY HERE.

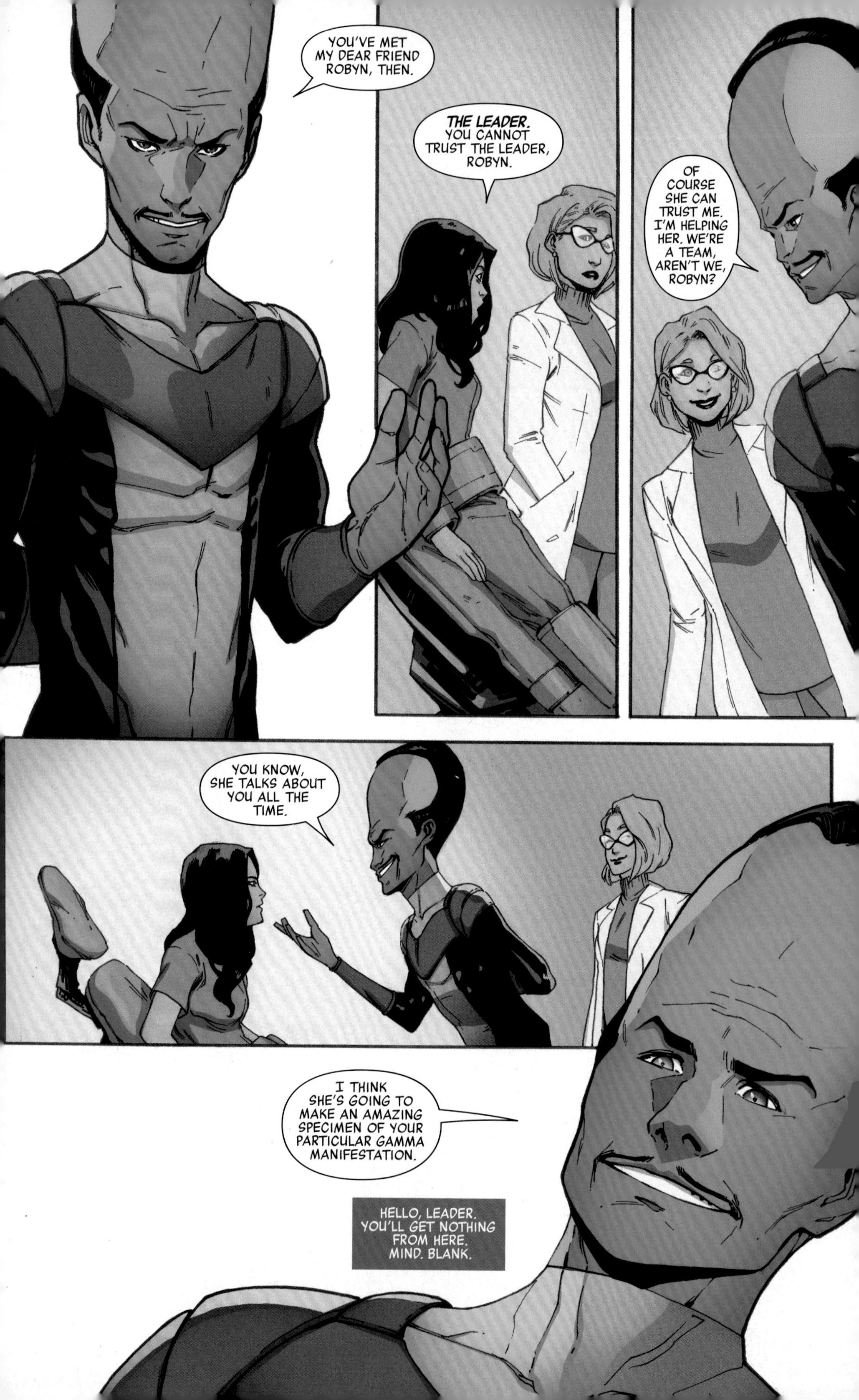
YOU'VE MET MY DEAR FRIEND ROBYN, THEN.
THE LEADER. YOU CANNOT TRUST THE LEADER, ROBYN.
OF COURSE SHE CAN TRUST ME. I'M HELPING HER. WE'RE A TEAM, AREN'T WE, ROBYN?
YOU KNOW, SHE TALKS ABOUT YOU ALL THE TIME.
I THINK SHE'S GOING TO MAKE AN AMAZING SPECIMEN OF YOUR PARTICULAR GAMMA MANIFESTATION.
HELLO, LEADER. YOU'LL GET NOTHING FROM HERE. MIND. BLANK.

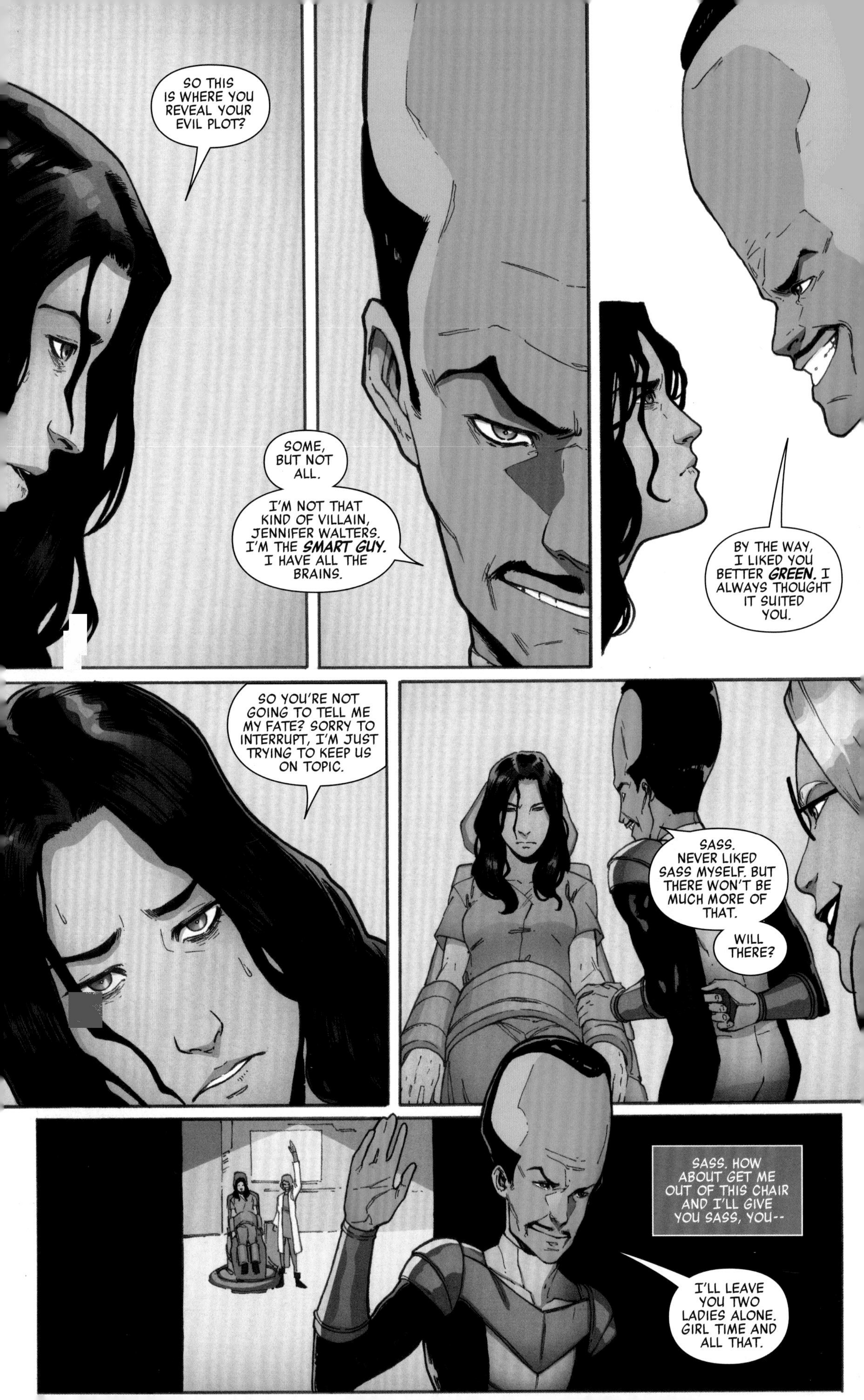
SO THIS IS WHERE YOU REVEAL YOUR EVIL PLOT?
SOME, BUT NOT ALL.
I'M NOT THAT KIND OF VILLAIN, JENNIFER WALTERS. I'M THE SMART GUY. I HAVE ALL THE BRAINS.
BY THE WAY, I LIKED YOU BETTER GREEN. I ALWAYS THOUGHT IT SUITED YOU.
SO YOU'RE NOT GOING TO TELL ME MY FATE? SORRY TO INTERRUPT, I'M JUST TRYING TO KEEP US ON TOPIC.
SASS. NEVER LIKED SASS MYSELF. BUT THERE WON'T BE MUCH MORE OF THAT.
WILL THERE?
SASS. HOW ABOUT GET ME OUT OF THIS CHAIR AND I'LL GIVE YOU SASS, YOU--
I'LL LEAVE YOU TWO LADIES ALONE. GIRL TIME AND ALL THAT.

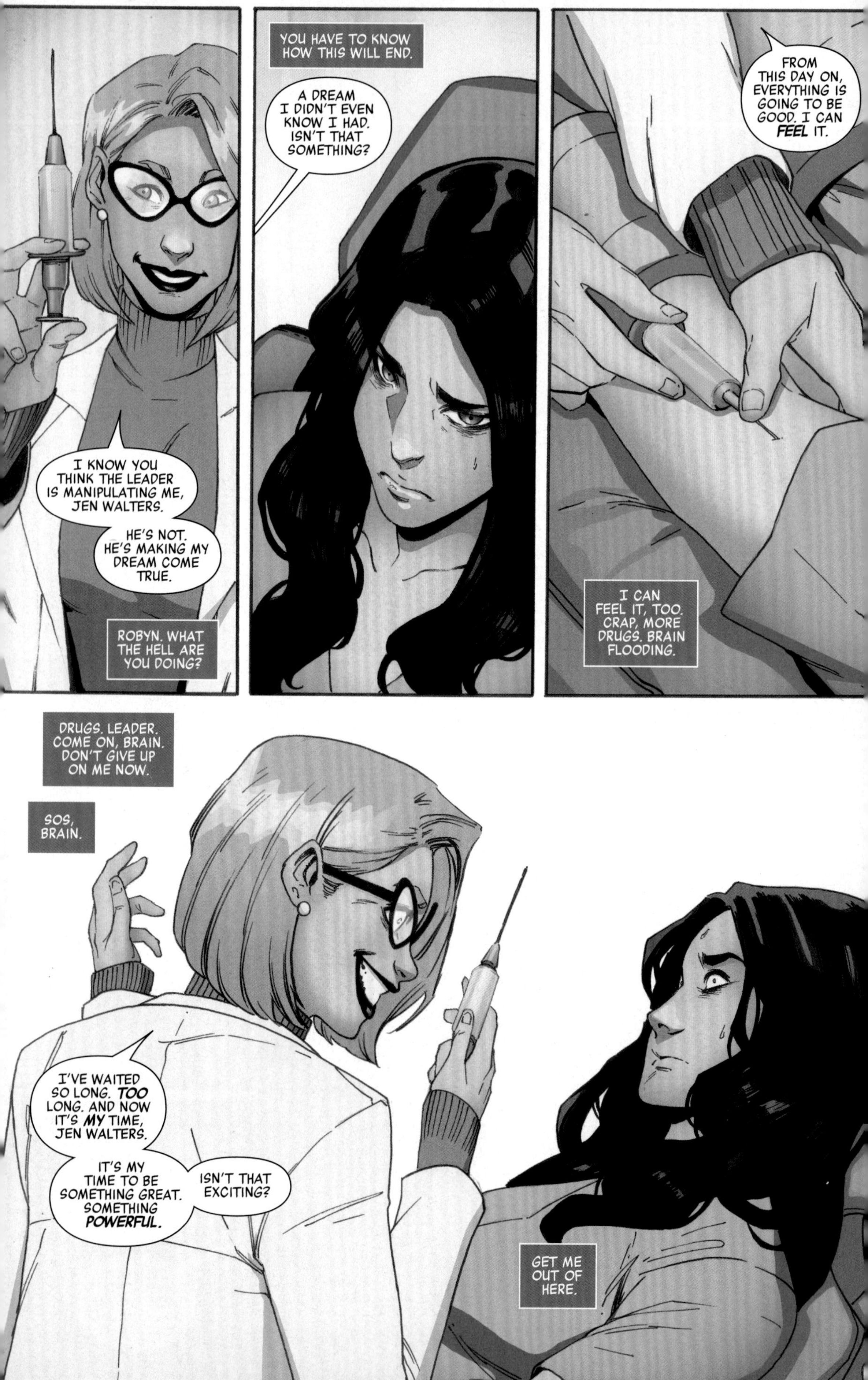
I KNOW YOU THINK THE LEADER IS MANIPULATING ME, JEN WALTERS.
HE'S NOT. HE'S MAKING MY DREAM COME TRUE.
ROBYN. WHAT THE HELL ARE YOU DOING?
YOU HAVE TO KNOW HOW THIS WILL END.
A DREAM I DIDN'T EVEN KNOW I HAD. ISN'T THAT SOMETHING?
FROM THIS DAY ON, EVERYTHING IS GOING TO BE GOOD. I CAN FEEL IT.
I CAN FEEL IT, TOO. CRAP, MORE DRUGS. BRAIN FLOODING.
DRUGS. LEADER. COME ON, BRAIN. DON'T GIVE UP ON ME NOW.
SOS, BRAIN.
I'VE WAITED SO LONG. TOO LONG. AND NOW IT'S MY TIME, JEN WALTERS.
IT'S MY TIME TO BE SOMETHING GREAT. SOMETHING POWERFUL.
ISN'T THAT EXCITING?
GET ME OUT OF HERE.

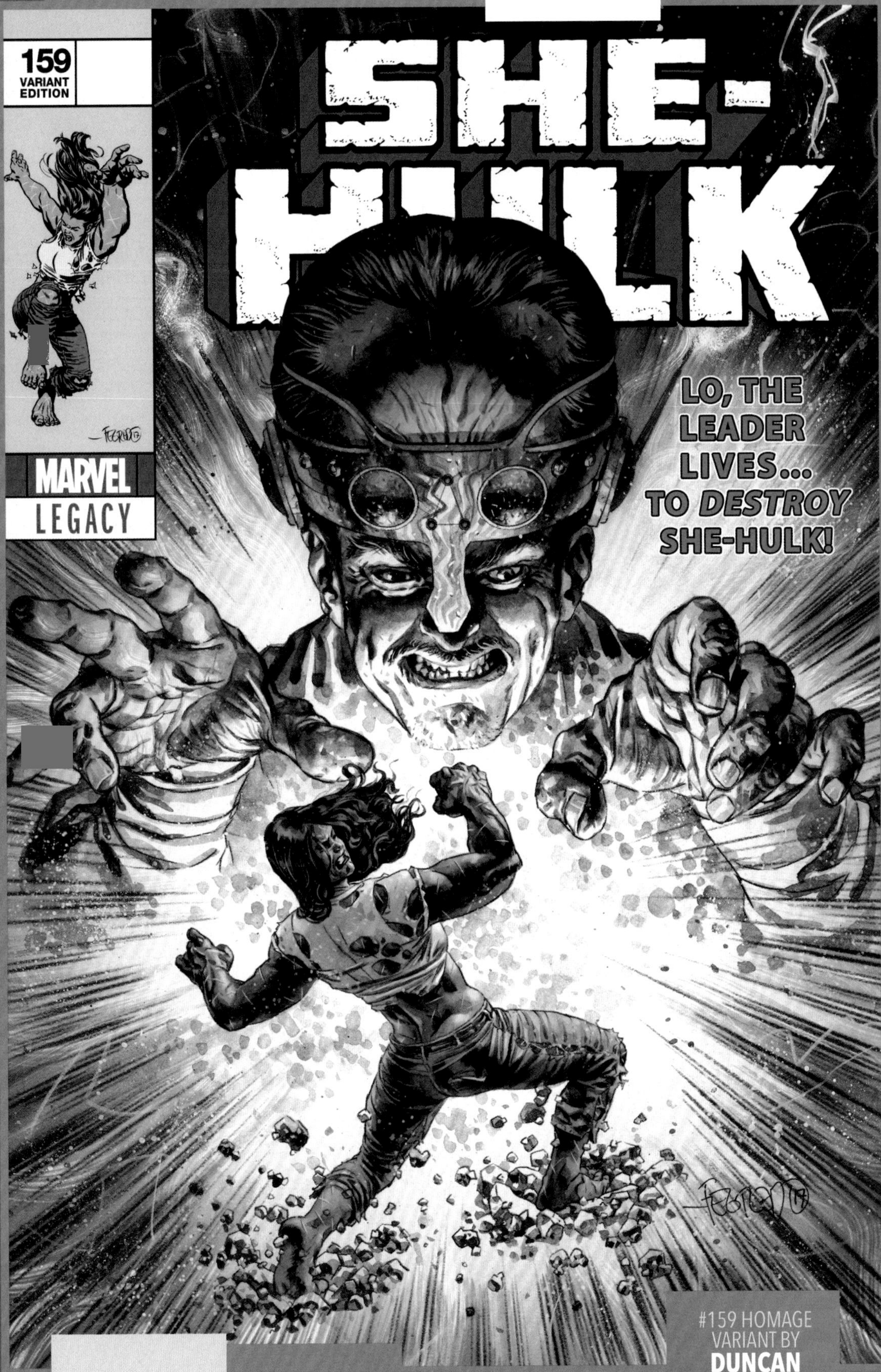
159
VARIANT EDITION
SHE-HULK
LO, THE LEADER LIVES... TO *DESTROY* SHE-HULK!
MARVEL
LEGACY

#159 HOMAGE VARIANT BY **DUNCAN FEGREDO**

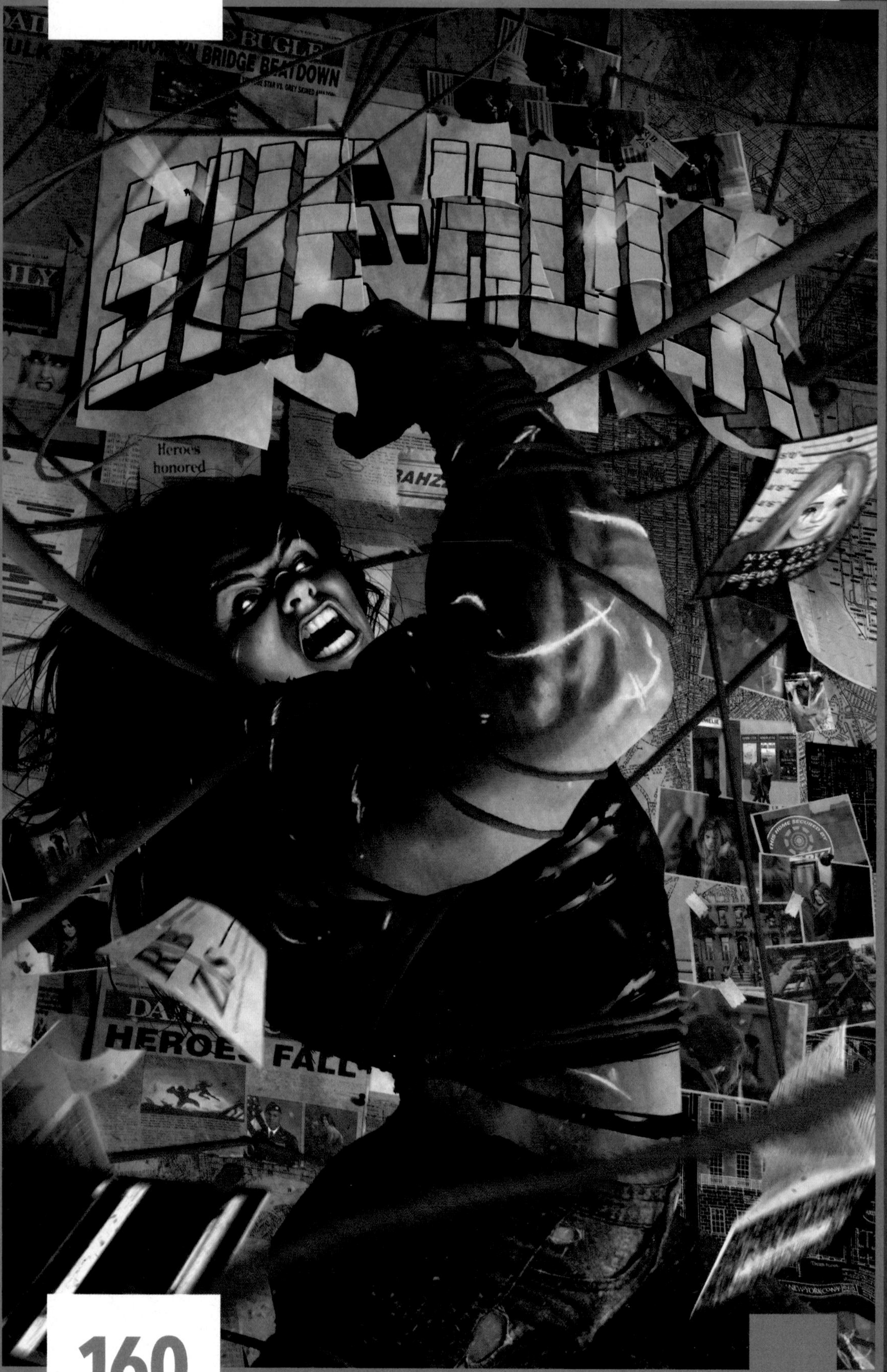
SHE-HULK
BUGLE
BRIDGE BEATDOWN
Heroes
honored
HEROES FALL

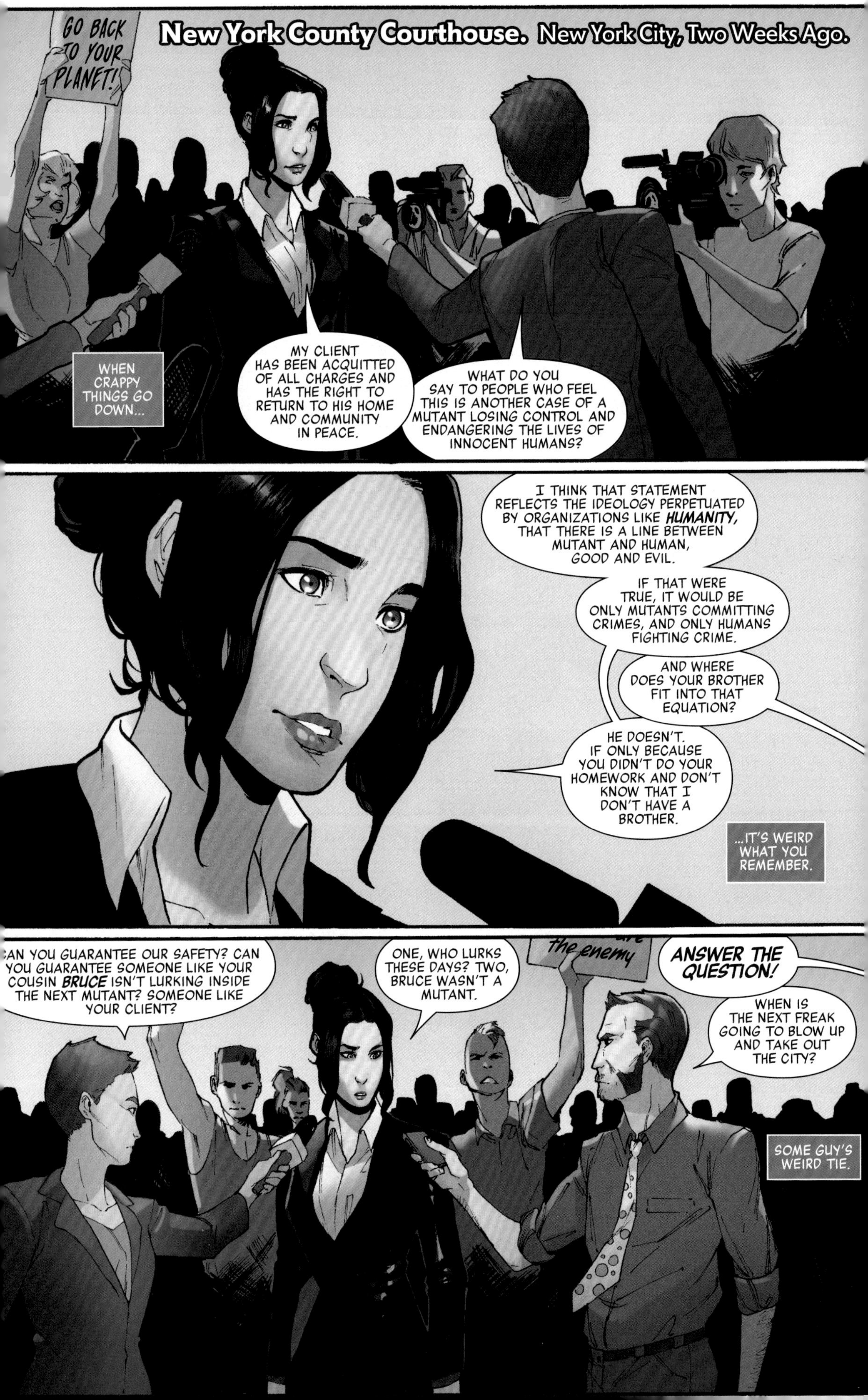
GO BACK TO YOUR PLANET!
New York County Courthouse. New York City, Two Weeks Ago.
WHEN CRAPPY THINGS GO DOWN...
MY CLIENT HAS BEEN ACQUITTED OF ALL CHARGES AND HAS THE RIGHT TO RETURN TO HIS HOME AND COMMUNITY IN PEACE.
WHAT DO YOU SAY TO PEOPLE WHO FEEL THIS IS ANOTHER CASE OF A MUTANT LOSING CONTROL AND ENDANGERING THE LIVES OF INNOCENT HUMANS?
I THINK THAT STATEMENT REFLECTS THE IDEOLOGY PERPETUATED BY ORGANIZATIONS LIKE HUMANITY, THAT THERE IS A LINE BETWEEN MUTANT AND HUMAN, GOOD AND EVIL.
IF THAT WERE TRUE, IT WOULD BE ONLY MUTANTS COMMITTING CRIMES, AND ONLY HUMANS FIGHTING CRIME.
AND WHERE DOES YOUR BROTHER FIT INTO THAT EQUATION?
HE DOESN'T. IF ONLY BECAUSE YOU DIDN'T DO YOUR HOMEWORK AND DON'T KNOW THAT I DON'T HAVE A BROTHER.
...IT'S WEIRD WHAT YOU REMEMBER.
CAN YOU GUARANTEE OUR SAFETY? CAN YOU GUARANTEE SOMEONE LIKE YOUR COUSIN BRUCE ISN'T LURKING INSIDE THE NEXT MUTANT? SOMEONE LIKE YOUR CLIENT?
ONE, WHO LURKS THESE DAYS? TWO, BRUCE WASN'T A MUTANT.
the enemy
ANSWER THE QUESTION!
WHEN IS THE NEXT FREAK GOING TO BLOW UP AND TAKE OUT THE CITY?
SOME GUY'S WEIRD TIE.

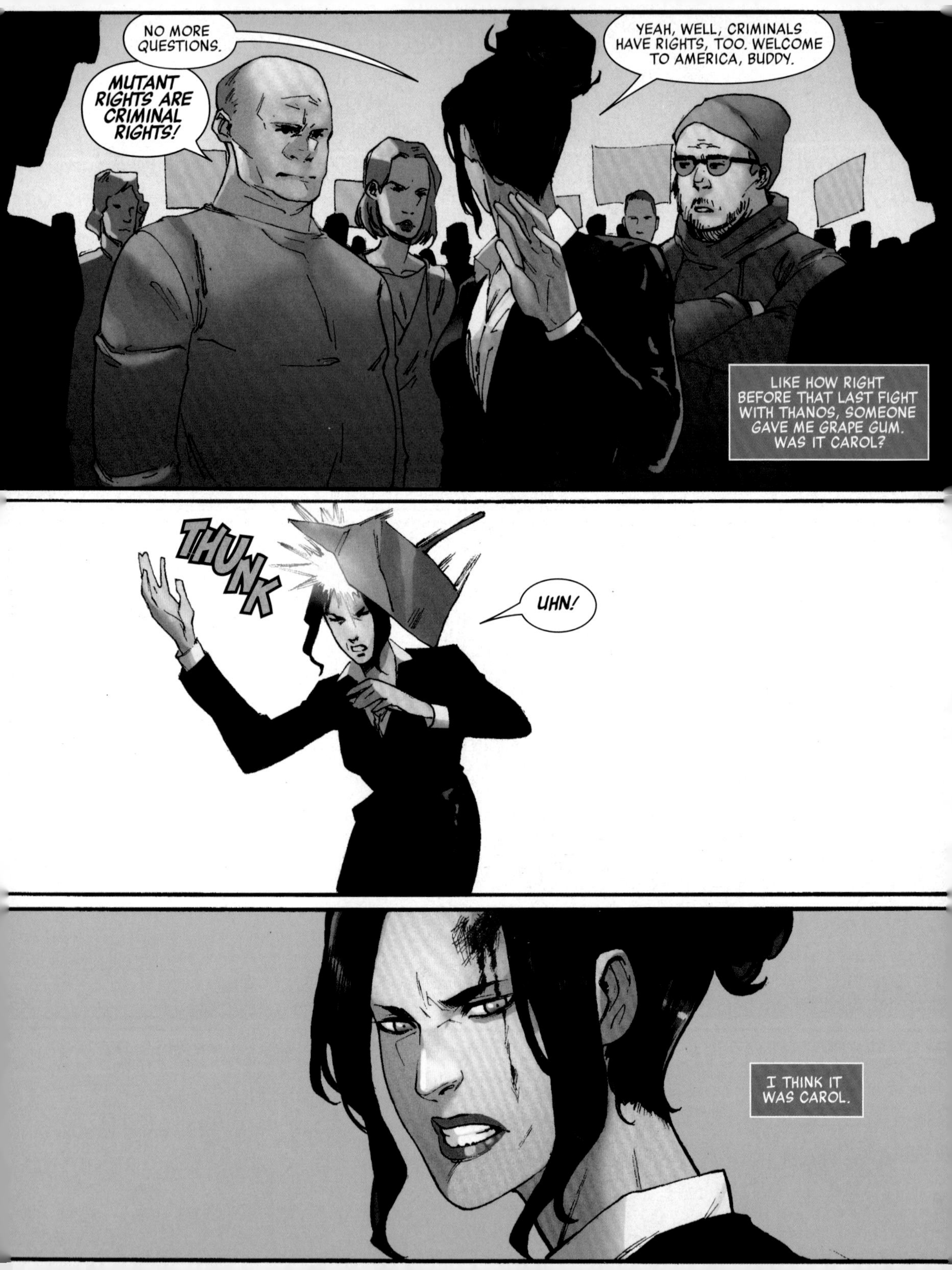
NO MORE QUESTIONS.
MUTANT RIGHTS ARE CRIMINAL RIGHTS!
YEAH, WELL, CRIMINALS HAVE RIGHTS, TOO. WELCOME TO AMERICA, BUDDY.
LIKE HOW RIGHT BEFORE THAT LAST FIGHT WITH THANOS, SOMEONE GAVE ME GRAPE GUM. WAS IT CAROL?
THUNK
UHN!
I THINK IT WAS CAROL.

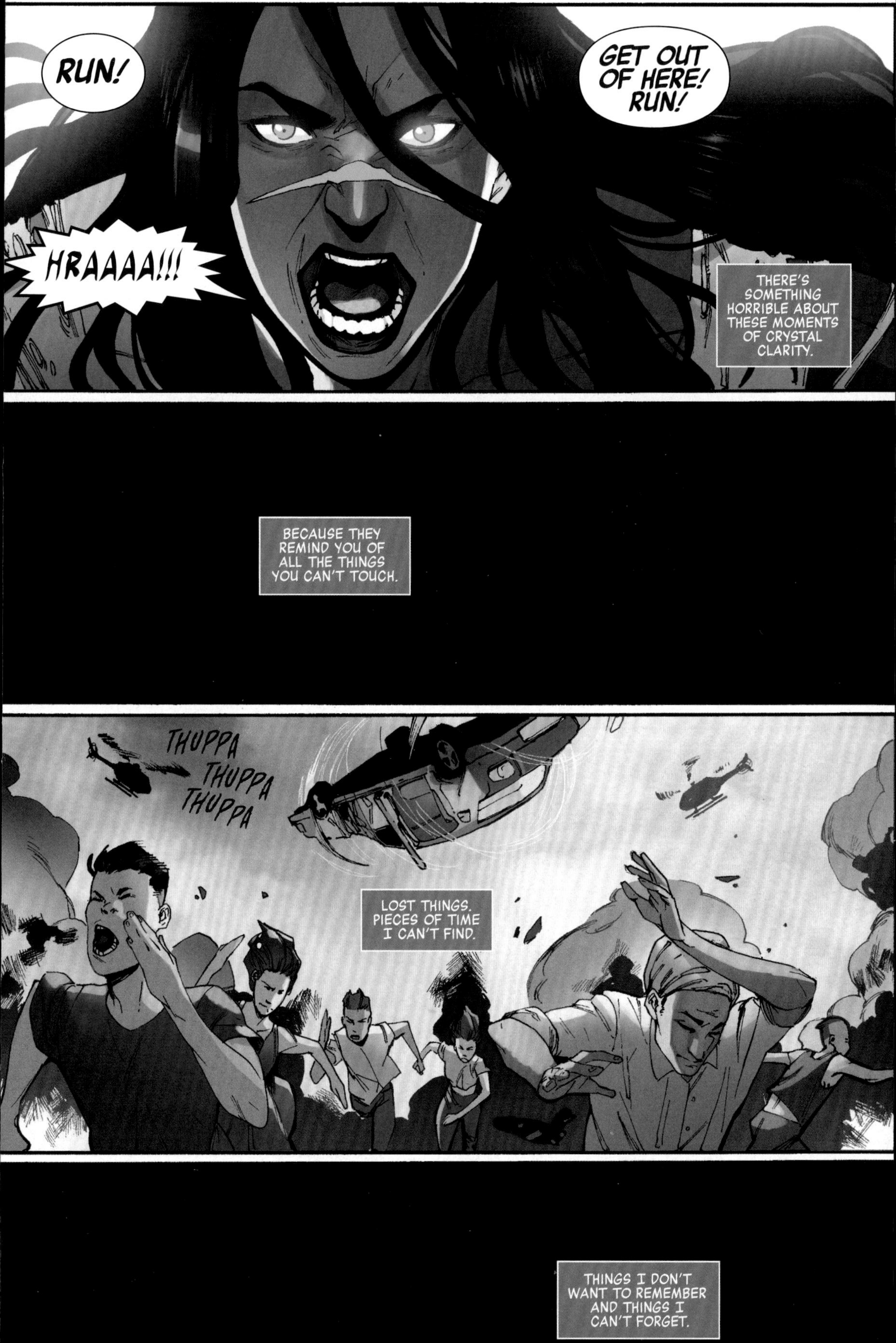
RUN!
GET OUT OF HERE! RUN!
HRAAAA!!!
THERE'S SOMETHING HORRIBLE ABOUT THESE MOMENTS OF CRYSTAL CLARITY.
BECAUSE THEY REMIND YOU OF ALL THE THINGS YOU CAN'T TOUCH.
THUPPA THUPPA THUPPA
LOST THINGS. PIECES OF TIME I CAN'T FIND.
THINGS I DON'T WANT TO REMEMBER AND THINGS I CAN'T FORGET.

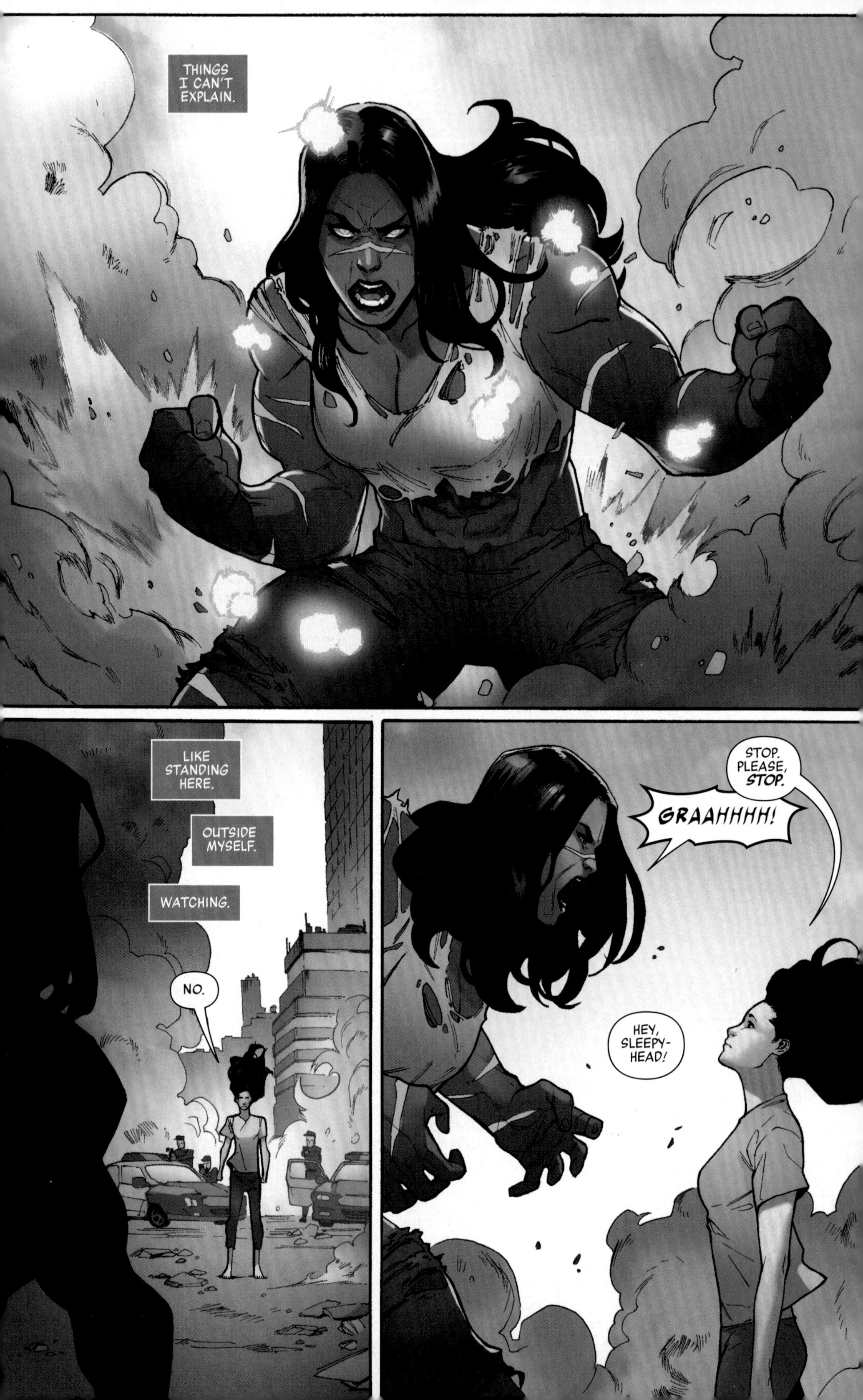
THINGS I CAN'T EXPLAIN.
LIKE STANDING HERE.
OUTSIDE MYSELF.
WATCHING.
NO.
STOP. PLEASE, STOP.
GRAAHHHH!
HEY, SLEEPY-HEAD!

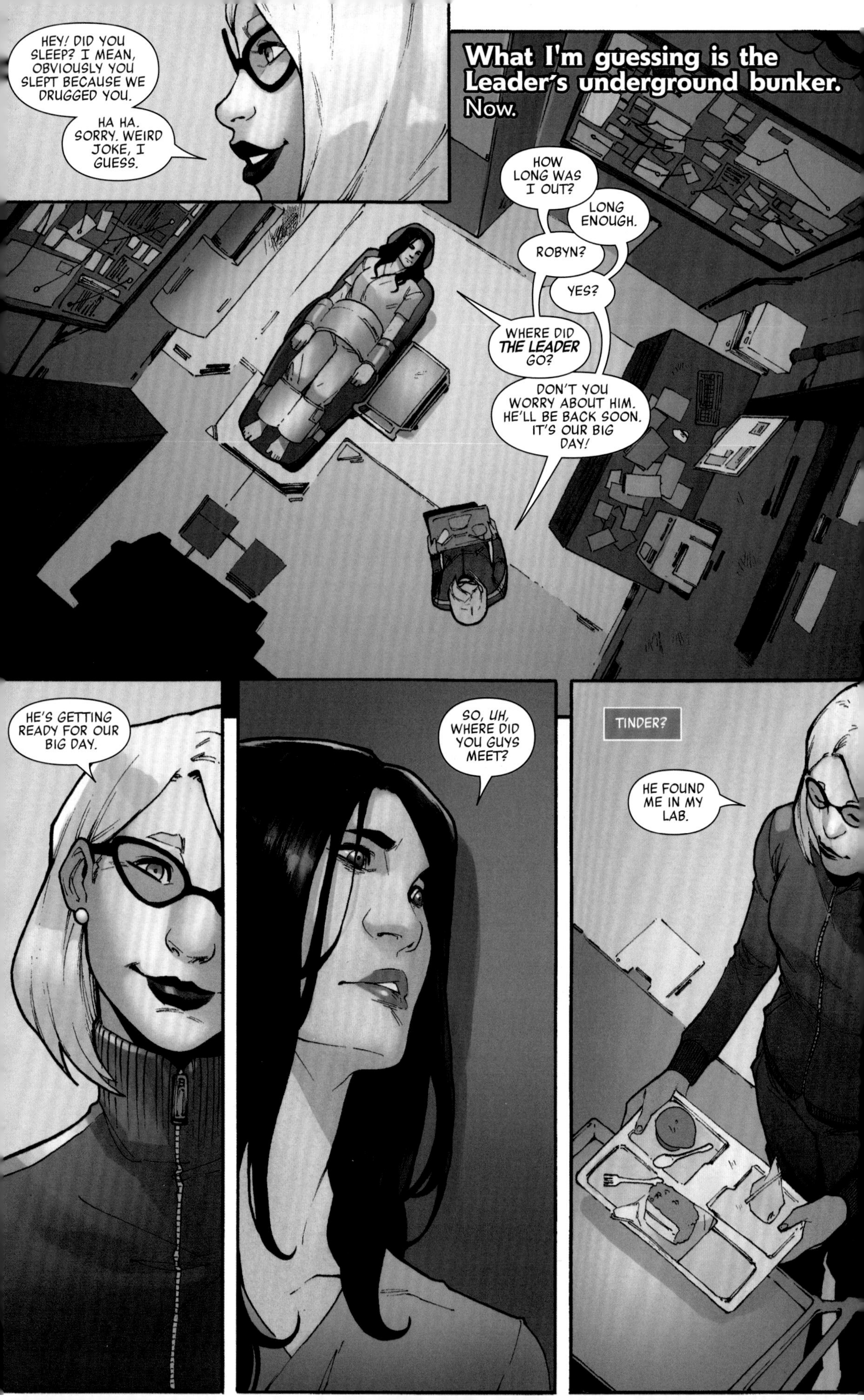
HEY! DID YOU SLEEP? I MEAN, OBVIOUSLY YOU SLEPT BECAUSE WE DRUGGED YOU.
HA HA. SORRY. WEIRD JOKE, I GUESS.
What I'm guessing is the Leader's underground bunker. Now.
HOW LONG WAS I OUT?
LONG ENOUGH.
ROBYN?
YES?
WHERE DID THE LEADER GO?
DON'T YOU WORRY ABOUT HIM. HE'LL BE BACK SOON. IT'S OUR BIG DAY!
HE'S GETTING READY FOR OUR BIG DAY.
SO, UH, WHERE DID YOU GUYS MEET?
TINDER?
HE FOUND ME IN MY LAB.

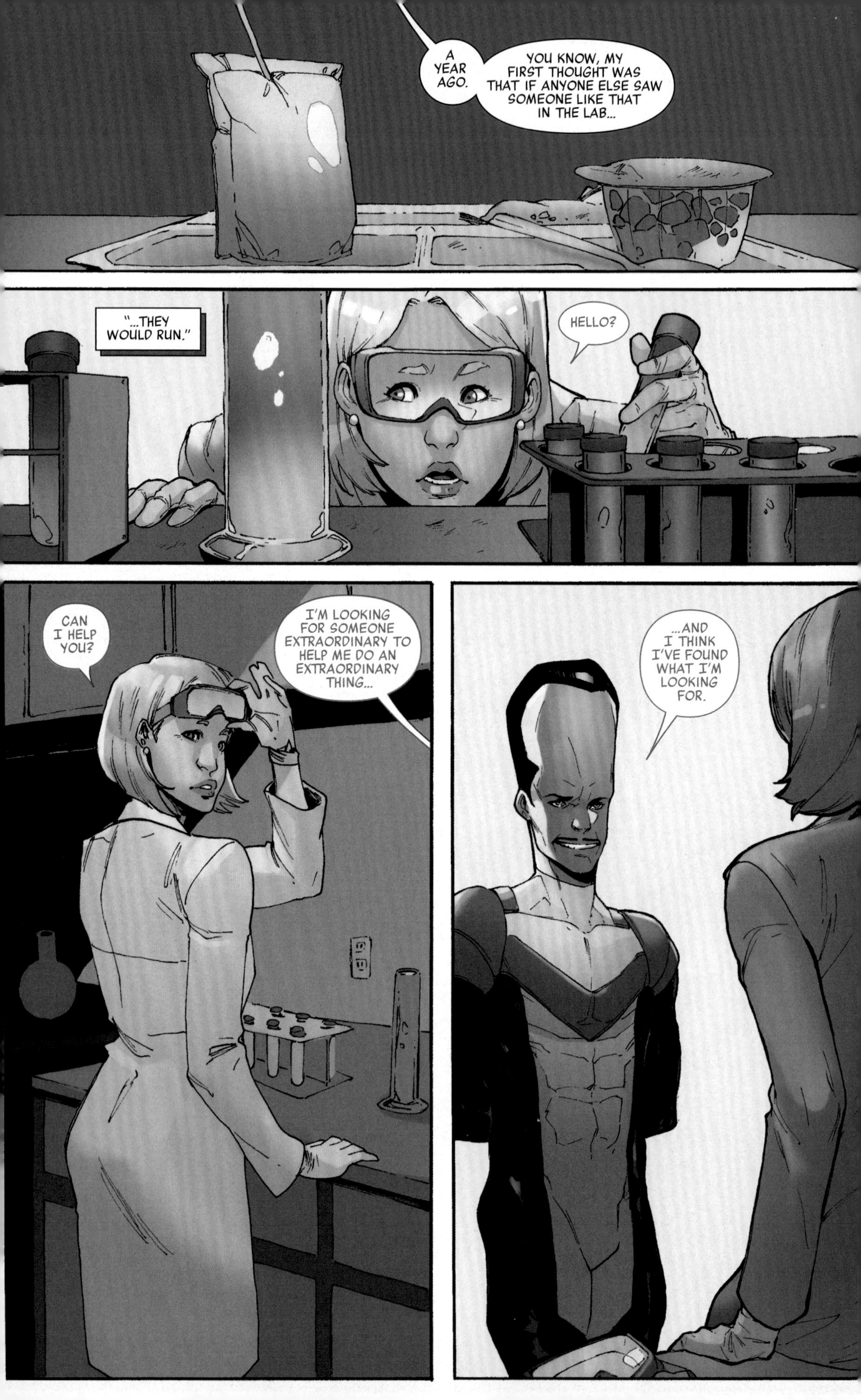
A YEAR AGO.
YOU KNOW, MY FIRST THOUGHT WAS THAT IF ANYONE ELSE SAW SOMEONE LIKE THAT IN THE LAB...
"...THEY WOULD RUN."
HELLO?
CAN I HELP YOU?
I'M LOOKING FOR SOMEONE EXTRAORDINARY TO HELP ME DO AN EXTRAORDINARY THING...
...AND I THINK I'VE FOUND WHAT I'M LOOKING FOR.

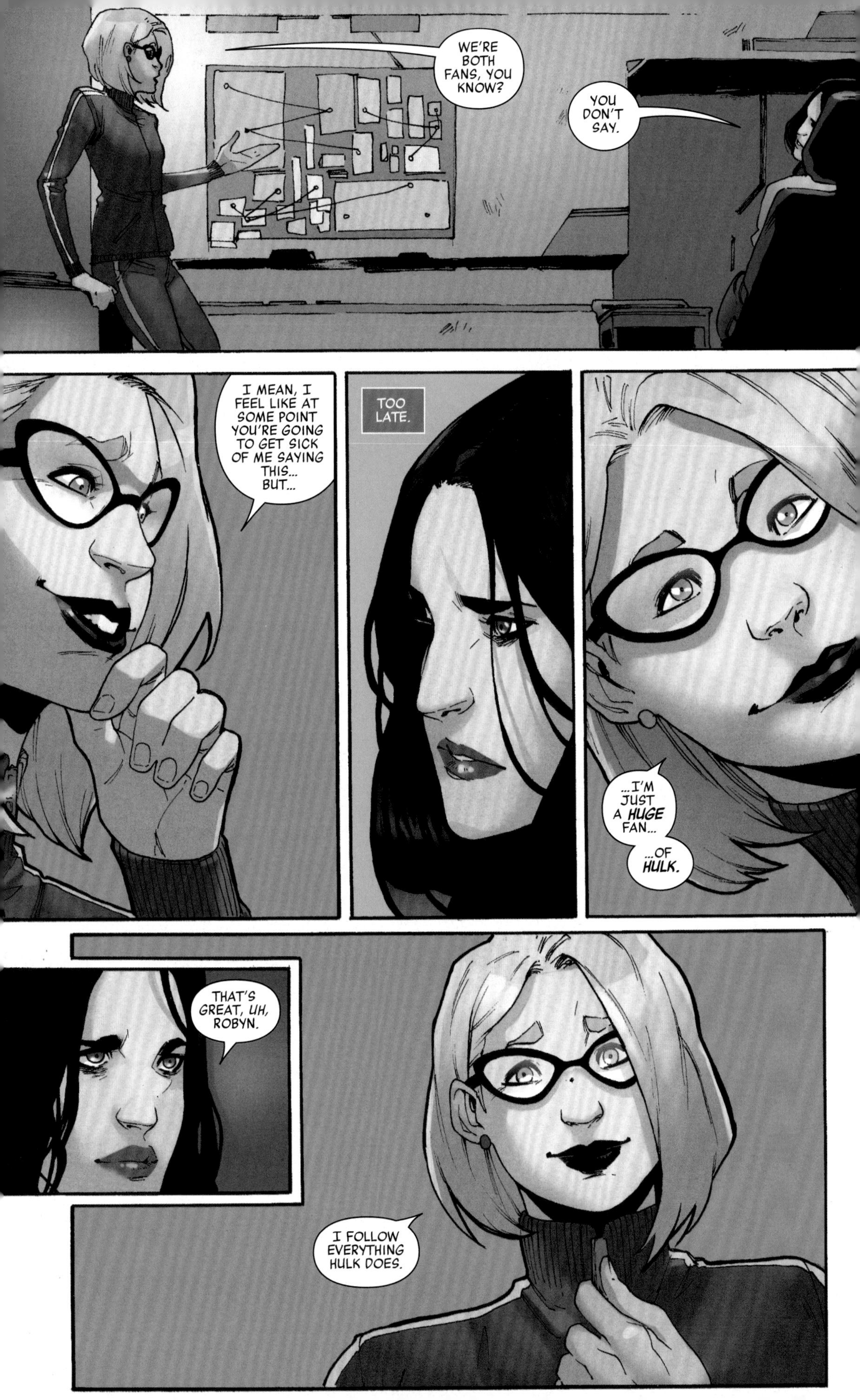
WE'RE BOTH FANS, YOU KNOW?
YOU DON'T SAY.
I MEAN, I FEEL LIKE AT SOME POINT YOU'RE GOING TO GET SICK OF ME SAYING THIS... BUT...
TOO LATE.
...I'M JUST A *HUGE* FAN...
...OF *HULK*.
THAT'S GREAT, *UH*, ROBYN.
I FOLLOW EVERYTHING HULK DOES.

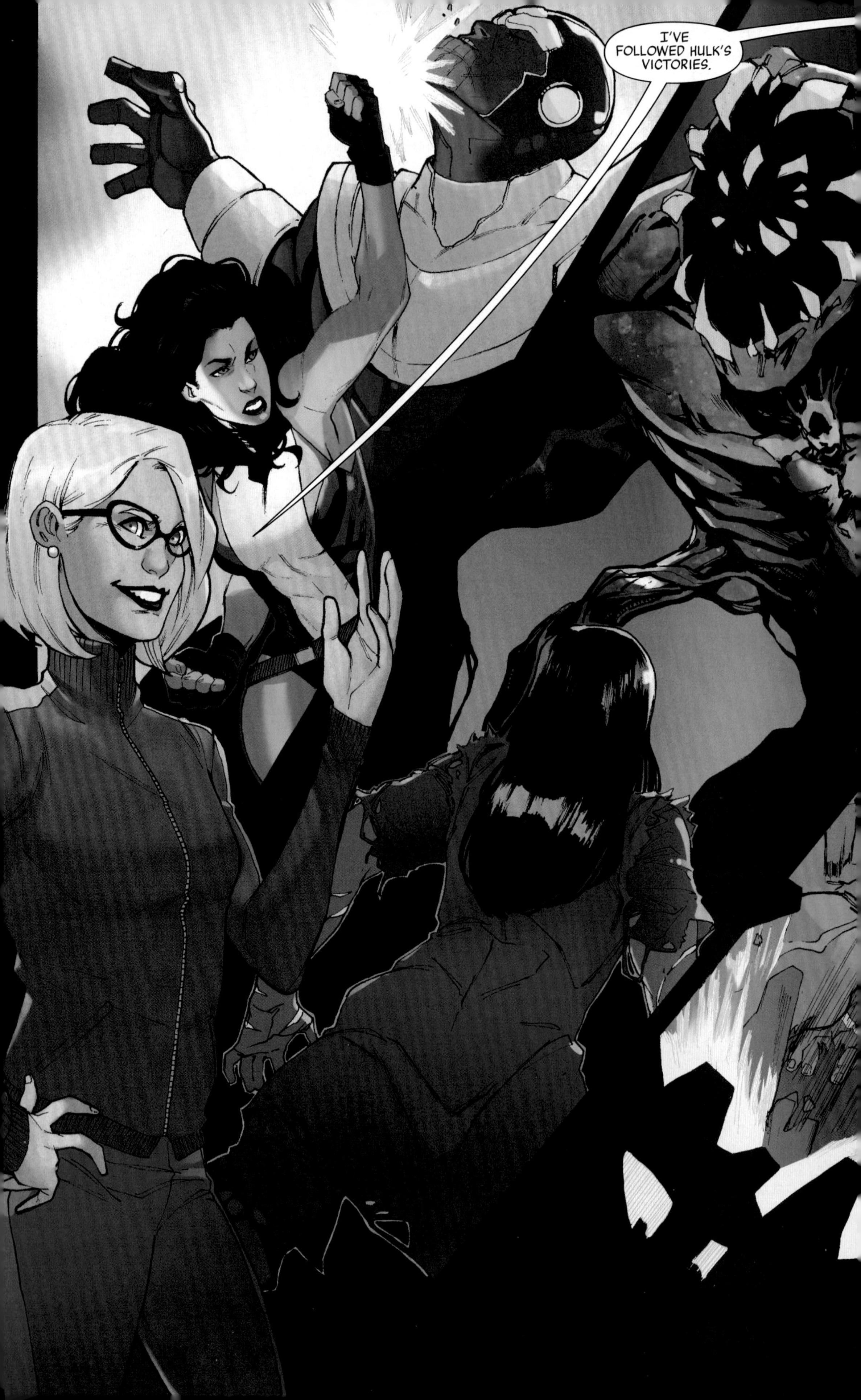
I'VE FOLLOWED HULK'S VICTORIES.

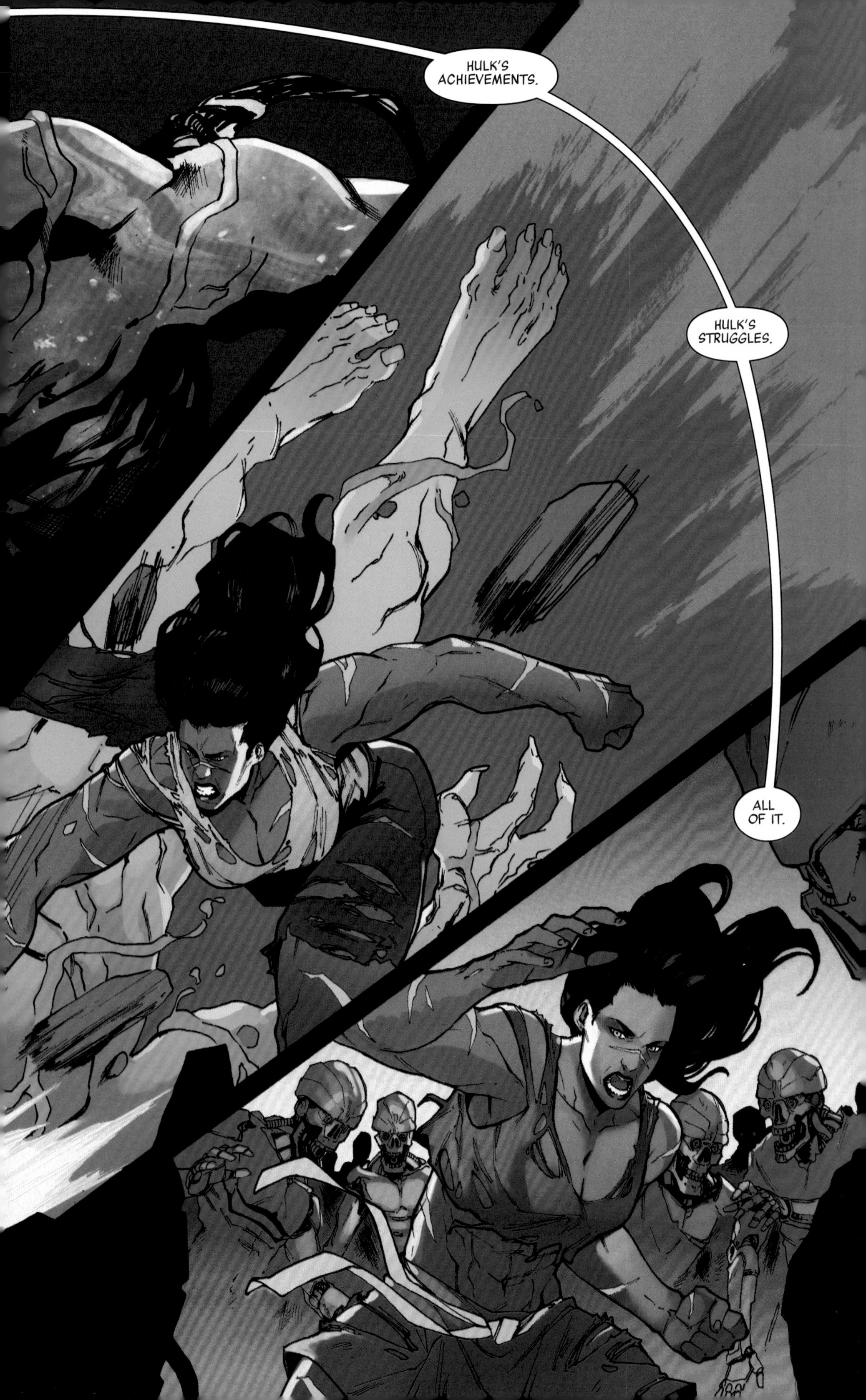
HULK'S ACHIEVEMENTS.
HULK'S STRUGGLES.
ALL OF IT.

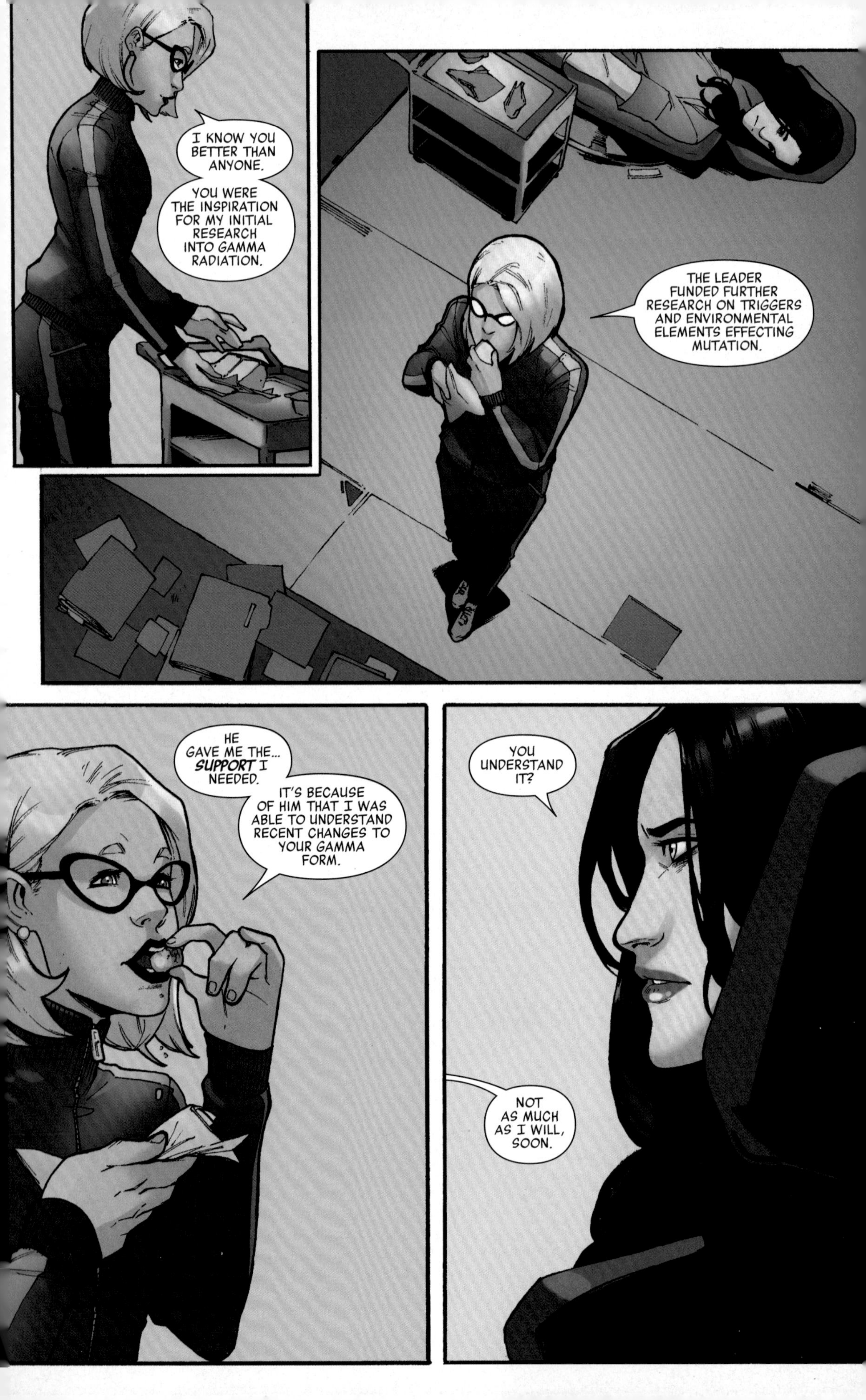
I KNOW YOU BETTER THAN ANYONE.
YOU WERE THE INSPIRATION FOR MY INITIAL RESEARCH INTO GAMMA RADIATION.
THE LEADER FUNDED FURTHER RESEARCH ON TRIGGERS AND ENVIRONMENTAL ELEMENTS EFFECTING MUTATION.
HE GAVE ME THE... *SUPPORT* I NEEDED.
IT'S BECAUSE OF HIM THAT I WAS ABLE TO UNDERSTAND RECENT CHANGES TO YOUR GAMMA FORM.
YOU UNDERSTAND IT?
NOT AS MUCH AS I WILL, SOON.

"AT FIRST I THOUGHT IT WAS JUST THAT HULK HAD CHANGED HER STRIPES, SO TO SPEAK.

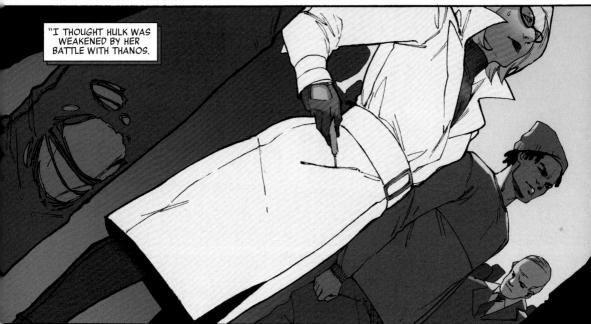

"I THOUGHT HULK WAS WEAKENED BY HER BATTLE WITH THANOS.

"IT WAS THE LEADER'S SUGGESTION TO PUT MY RESEARCH TO THE TEST. HE GAVE ME THE COURAGE... TO SEE FOR MYSELF.

Sorry.

"THANKS TO HIM, I KNOW NOW.

WELCOME TO AMERICA, BUDDY.

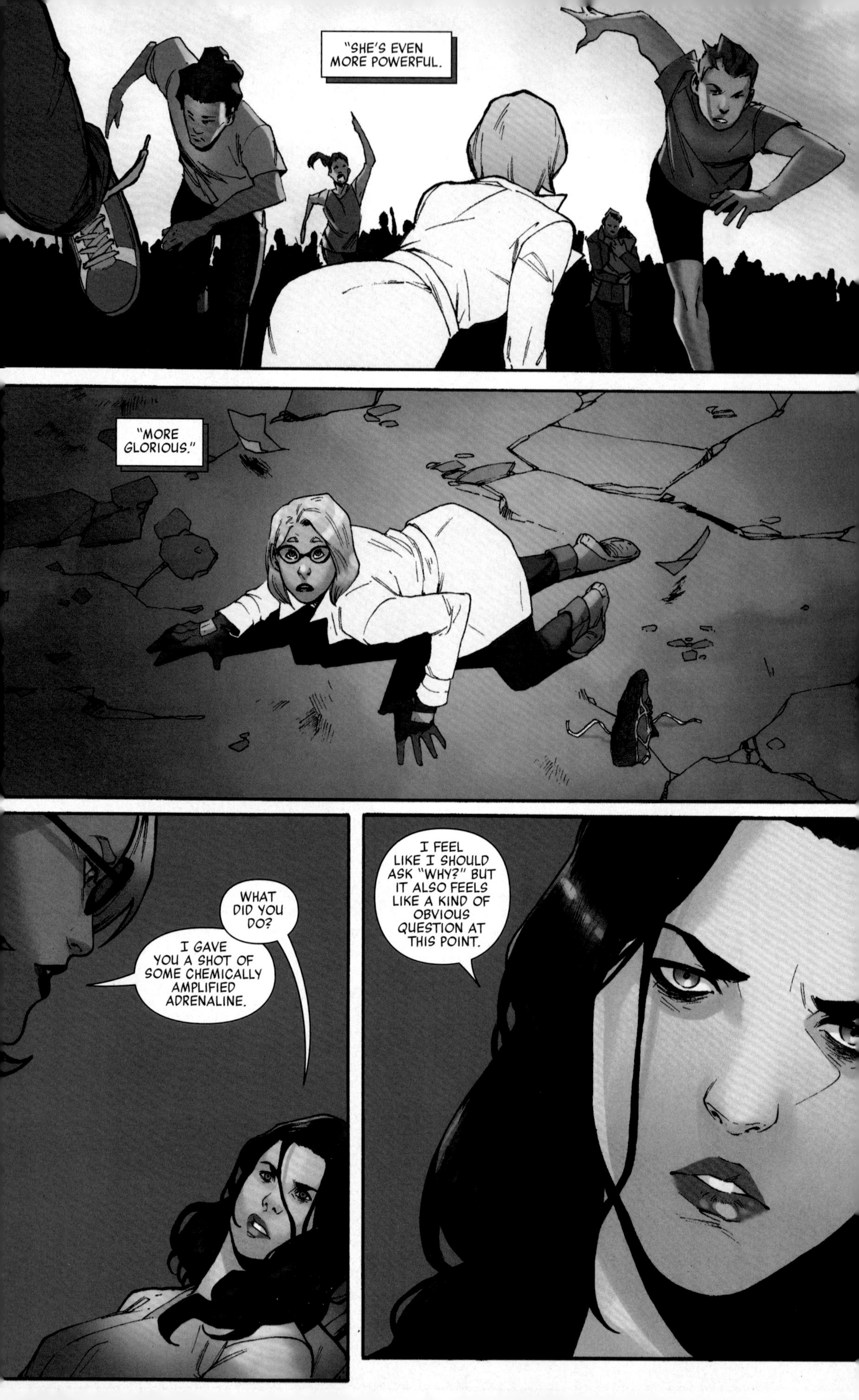
"SHE'S EVEN MORE POWERFUL.
"MORE GLORIOUS."
WHAT DID YOU DO?
I GAVE YOU A SHOT OF SOME CHEMICALLY AMPLIFIED ADRENALINE.
I FEEL LIKE I SHOULD ASK "WHY?" BUT IT ALSO FEELS LIKE A KIND OF OBVIOUS QUESTION AT THIS POINT.

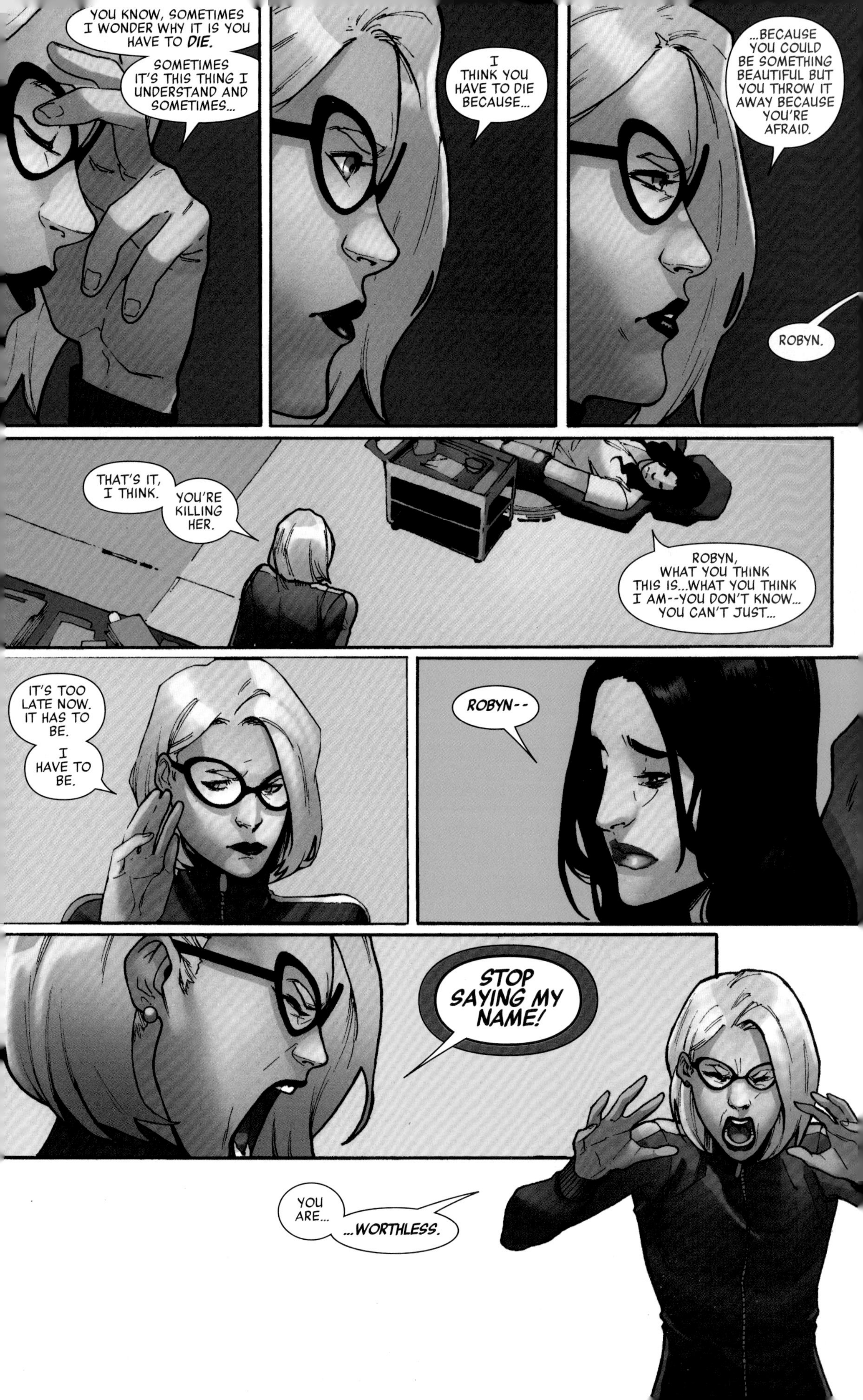
YOU KNOW, SOMETIMES I WONDER WHY IT IS YOU HAVE TO DIE.
SOMETIMES IT'S THIS THING I UNDERSTAND AND SOMETIMES...
I THINK YOU HAVE TO DIE BECAUSE...
...BECAUSE YOU COULD BE SOMETHING BEAUTIFUL BUT YOU THROW IT AWAY BECAUSE YOU'RE AFRAID.
ROBYN.
THAT'S IT, I THINK.
YOU'RE KILLING HER.
ROBYN, WHAT YOU THINK THIS IS...WHAT YOU THINK I AM--YOU DON'T KNOW... YOU CAN'T JUST...
IT'S TOO LATE NOW. IT HAS TO BE.
I HAVE TO BE.
ROBYN--
STOP SAYING MY NAME!
YOU ARE...
...WORTHLESS.

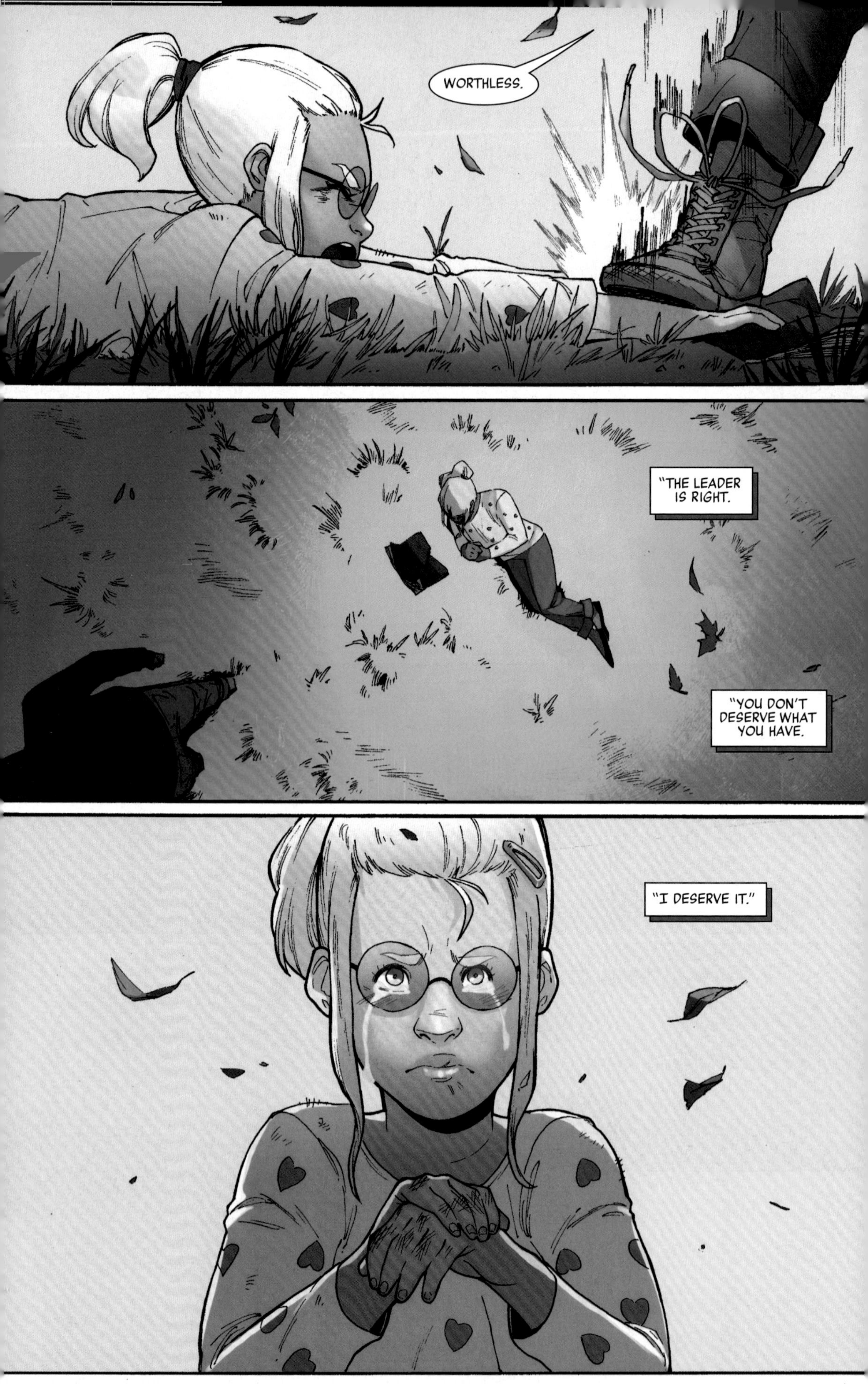
WORTHLESS.
"THE LEADER IS RIGHT.
"YOU DON'T DESERVE WHAT YOU HAVE.
"I DESERVE IT."

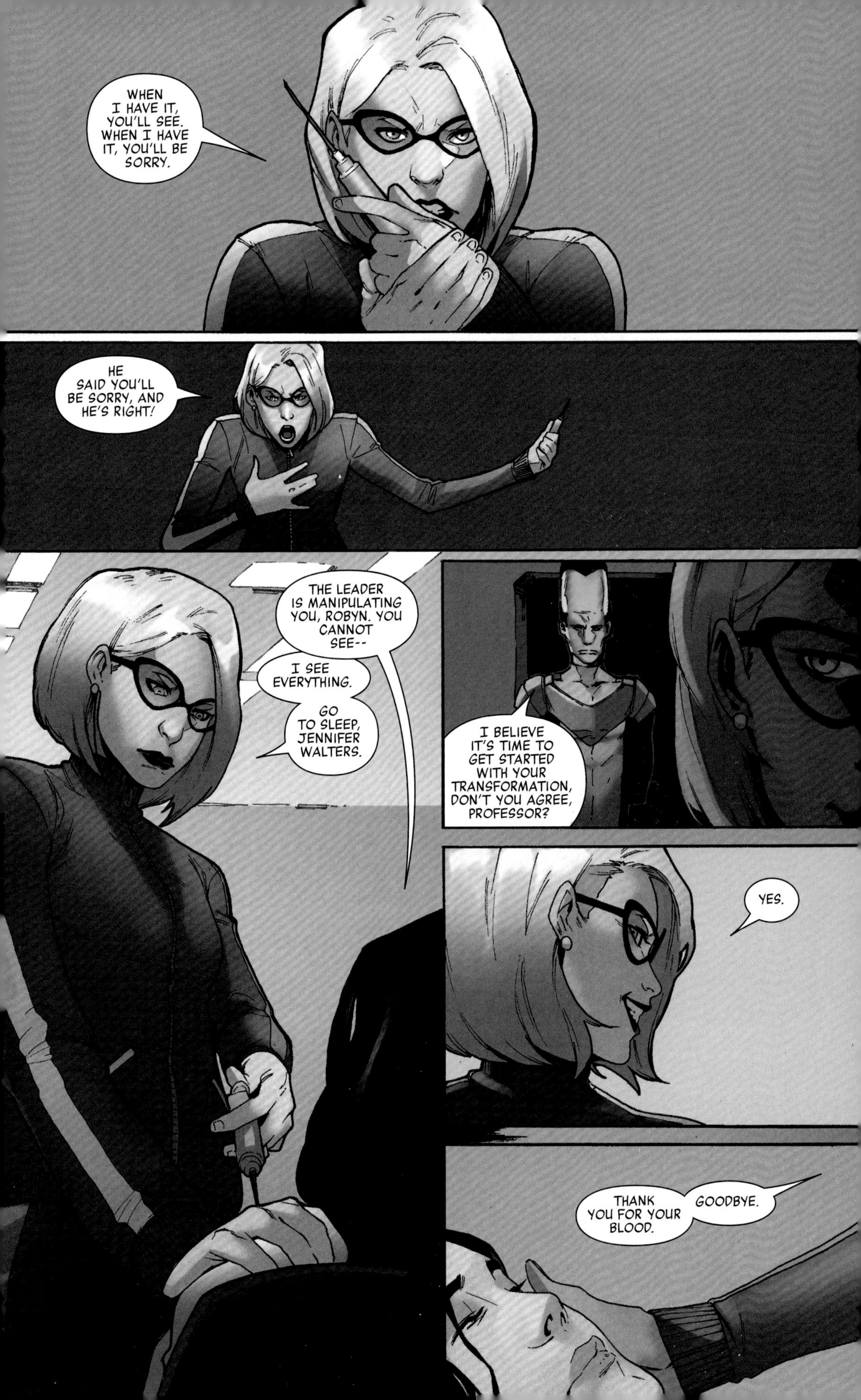
WHEN I HAVE IT, YOU'LL SEE. WHEN I HAVE IT, YOU'LL BE SORRY.
HE SAID YOU'LL BE SORRY, AND HE'S RIGHT!
THE LEADER IS MANIPULATING YOU, ROBYN. YOU CANNOT SEE--
I SEE EVERYTHING.
GO TO SLEEP, JENNIFER WALTERS.
I BELIEVE IT'S TIME TO GET STARTED WITH YOUR TRANSFORMATION, DON'T YOU AGREE, PROFESSOR?
YES.
THANK YOU FOR YOUR BLOOD.
GOODBYE.

"JENNIFER WALTERS.

"YOU KNOW, YOU DEFENDED A FRIEND OF MINE RECENTLY. IN COURT.

"HE WAS VERY PLEASED WITH YOUR SERVICES.

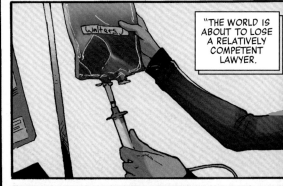

"THE WORLD IS ABOUT TO LOSE A RELATIVELY COMPETENT LAWYER.

"ALTHOUGH I SUPPOSE THERE IS THAT JOKE ABOUT LAWYERS AT THE BOTTOM OF THE OCEAN.

"WAKE UP, MS. WALTERS. IT'S ALMOST TIME."

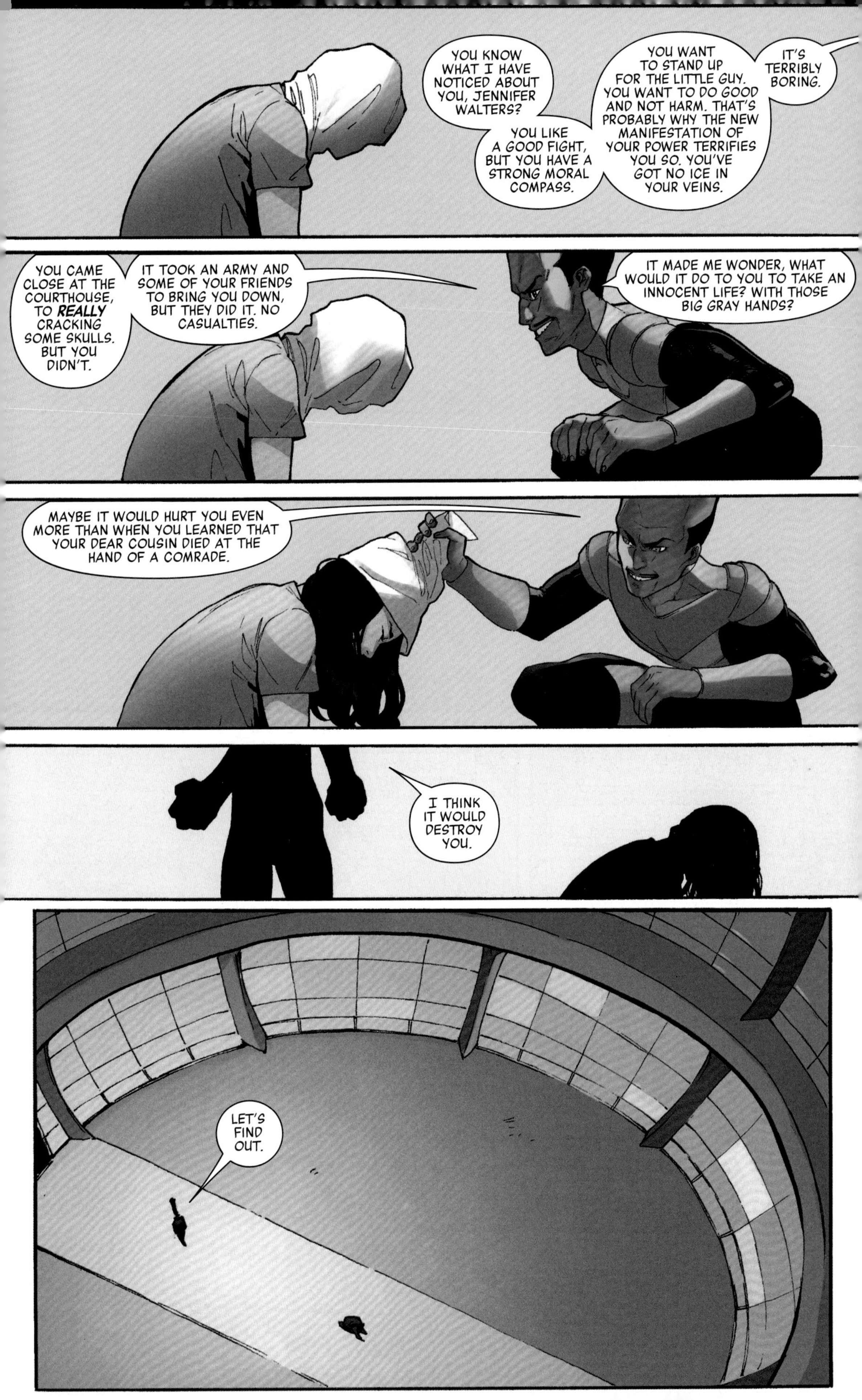
YOU KNOW WHAT I HAVE NOTICED ABOUT YOU, JENNIFER WALTERS?
YOU LIKE A GOOD FIGHT, BUT YOU HAVE A STRONG MORAL COMPASS.
YOU WANT TO STAND UP FOR THE LITTLE GUY. YOU WANT TO DO GOOD AND NOT HARM. THAT'S PROBABLY WHY THE NEW MANIFESTATION OF YOUR POWER TERRIFIES YOU SO. YOU'VE GOT NO ICE IN YOUR VEINS.
IT'S TERRIBLY BORING.
YOU CAME CLOSE AT THE COURTHOUSE, TO REALLY CRACKING SOME SKULLS. BUT YOU DIDN'T.
IT TOOK AN ARMY AND SOME OF YOUR FRIENDS TO BRING YOU DOWN, BUT THEY DID IT. NO CASUALTIES.
IT MADE ME WONDER, WHAT WOULD IT DO TO YOU TO TAKE AN INNOCENT LIFE? WITH THOSE BIG GRAY HANDS?
MAYBE IT WOULD HURT YOU EVEN MORE THAN WHEN YOU LEARNED THAT YOUR DEAR COUSIN DIED AT THE HAND OF A COMRADE.
I THINK IT WOULD DESTROY YOU.
LET'S FIND OUT.

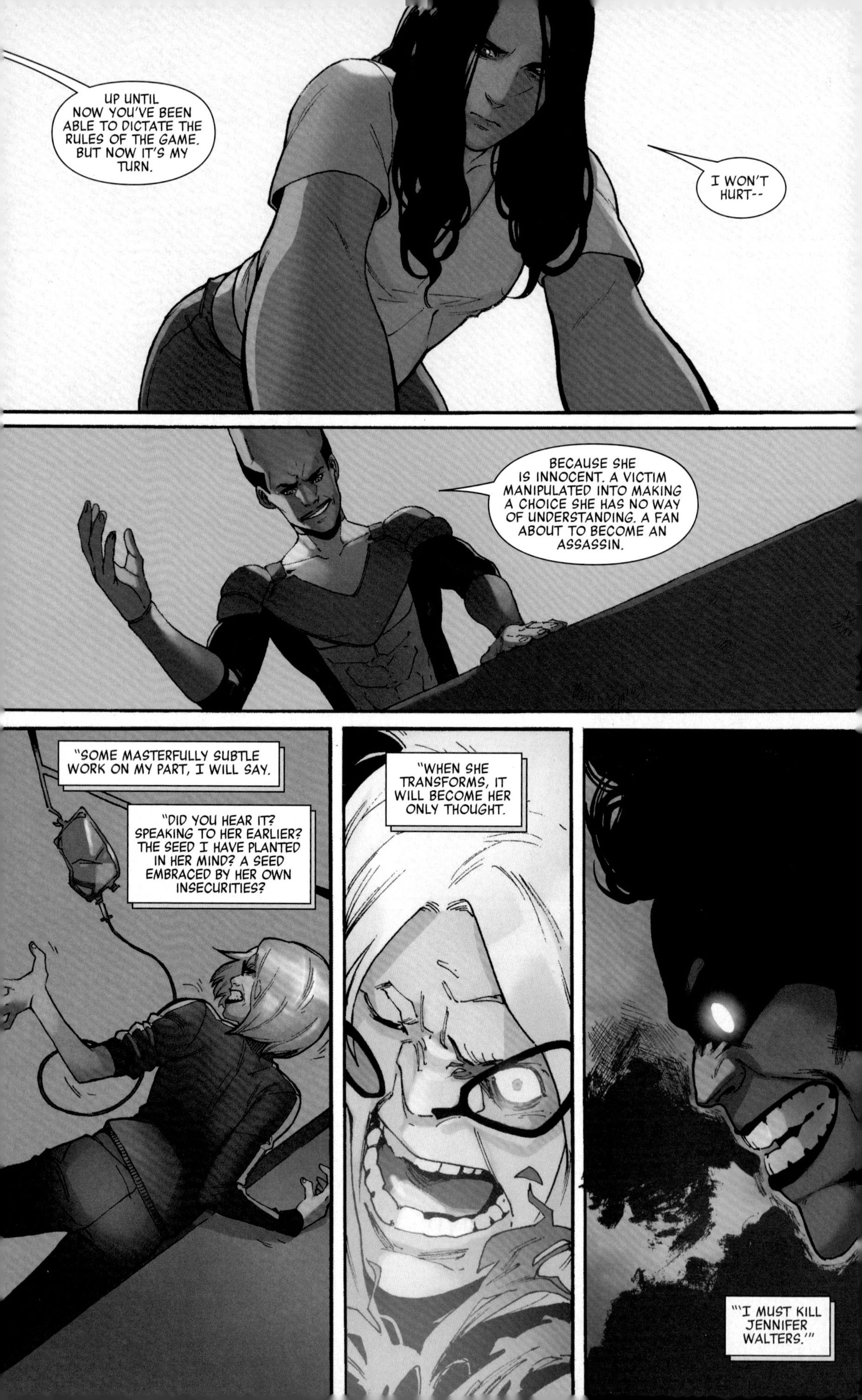
UP UNTIL NOW YOU'VE BEEN ABLE TO DICTATE THE RULES OF THE GAME. BUT NOW IT'S MY TURN.
I WON'T HURT--
BECAUSE SHE IS INNOCENT. A VICTIM MANIPULATED INTO MAKING A CHOICE SHE HAS NO WAY OF UNDERSTANDING. A FAN ABOUT TO BECOME AN ASSASSIN.
"SOME MASTERFULLY SUBTLE WORK ON MY PART, I WILL SAY.
"DID YOU HEAR IT? SPEAKING TO HER EARLIER? THE SEED I HAVE PLANTED IN HER MIND? A SEED EMBRACED BY HER OWN INSECURITIES?
"WHEN SHE TRANSFORMS, IT WILL BECOME HER ONLY THOUGHT.
"'I MUST KILL JENNIFER WALTERS.'"

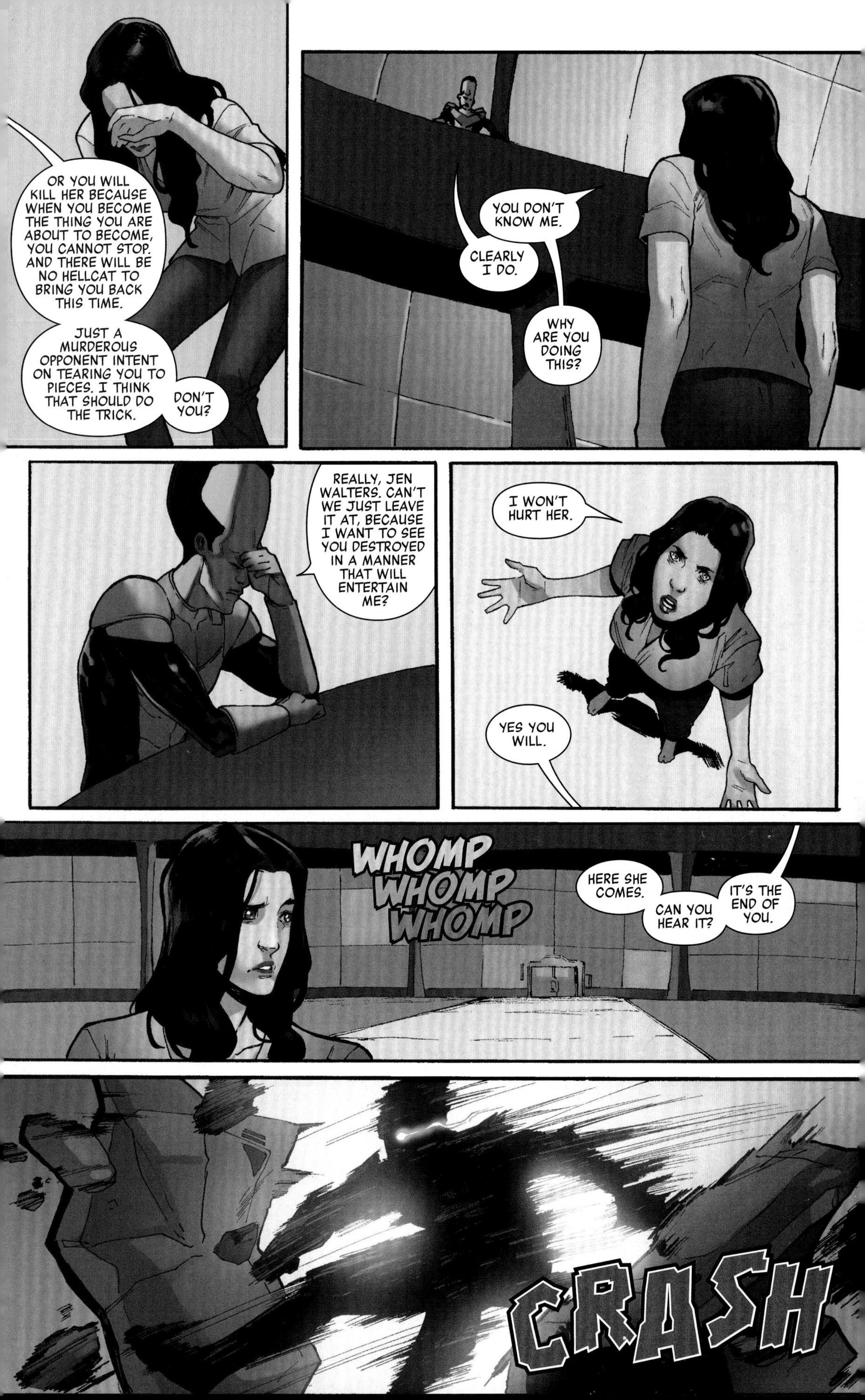
OR YOU WILL KILL HER BECAUSE WHEN YOU BECOME THE THING YOU ARE ABOUT TO BECOME, YOU CANNOT STOP. AND THERE WILL BE NO HELLCAT TO BRING YOU BACK THIS TIME.
JUST A MURDEROUS OPPONENT INTENT ON TEARING YOU TO PIECES. I THINK THAT SHOULD DO THE TRICK.
DON'T YOU?
YOU DON'T KNOW ME.
CLEARLY I DO.
WHY ARE YOU DOING THIS?
REALLY, JEN WALTERS. CAN'T WE JUST LEAVE IT AT, BECAUSE I WANT TO SEE YOU DESTROYED IN A MANNER THAT WILL ENTERTAIN ME?
I WON'T HURT HER.
YES YOU WILL.
WHOMP
WHOMP
WHOMP
HERE SHE COMES.
CAN YOU HEAR IT?
IT'S THE END OF YOU.
CRASH

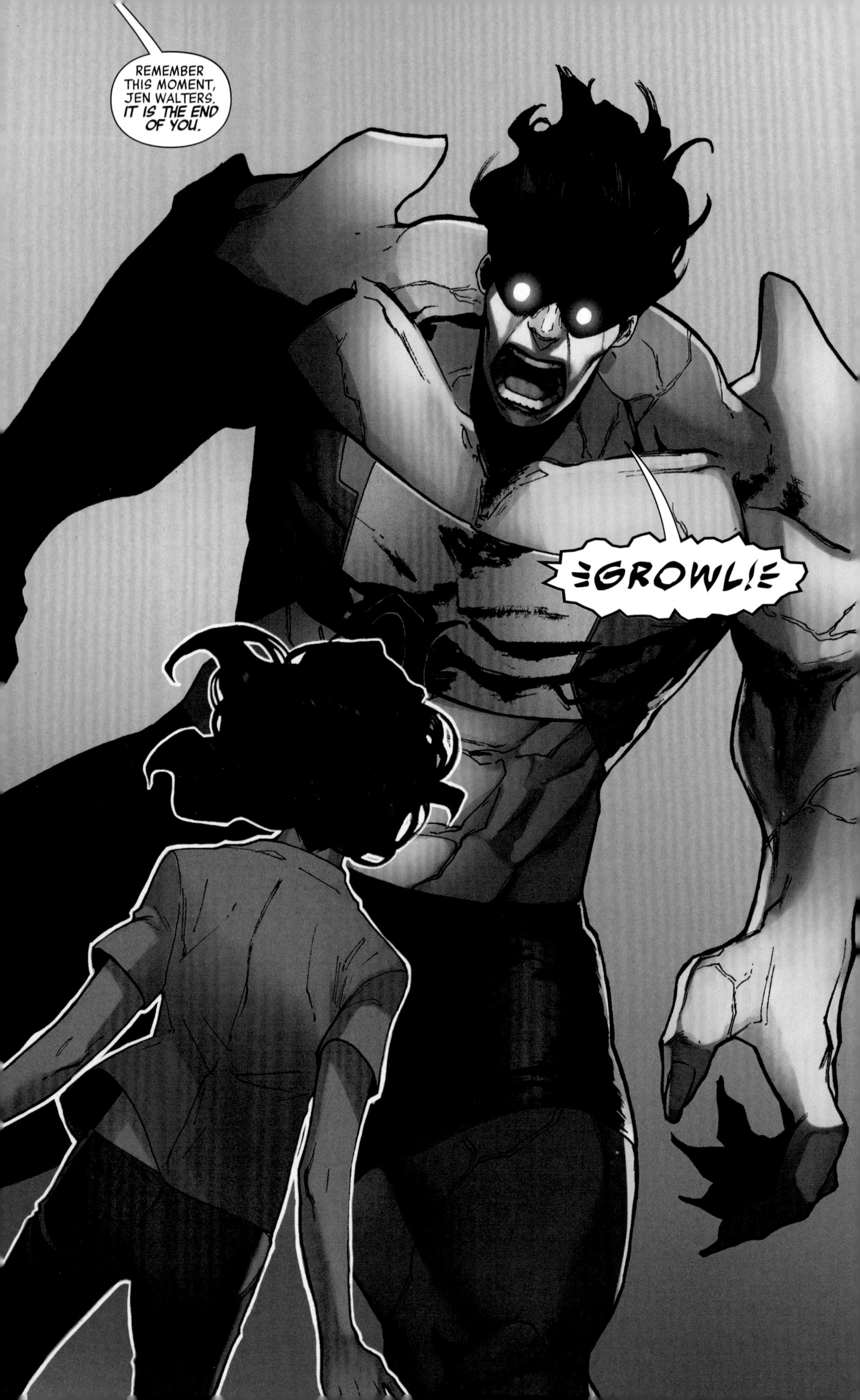
REMEMBER THIS MOMENT, JEN WALTERS. IT IS THE END OF YOU.
GROWL!

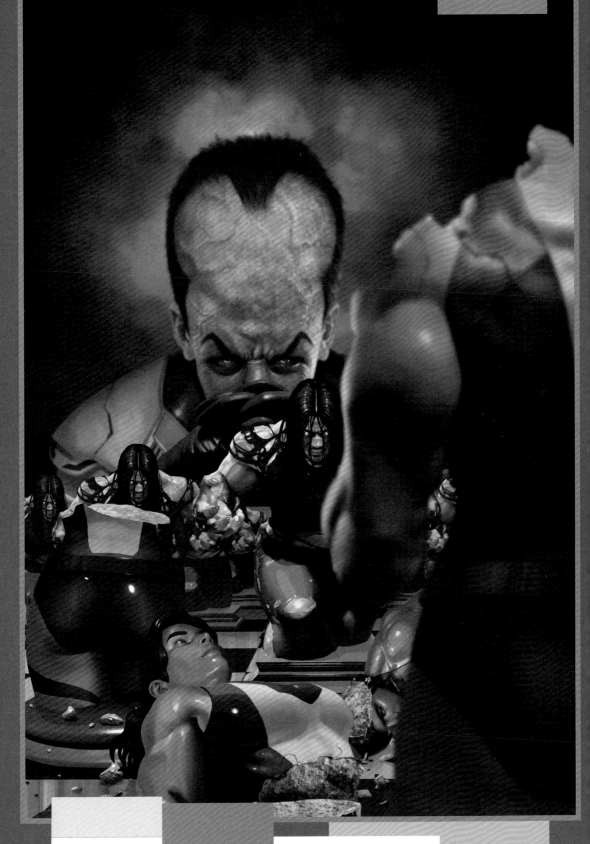

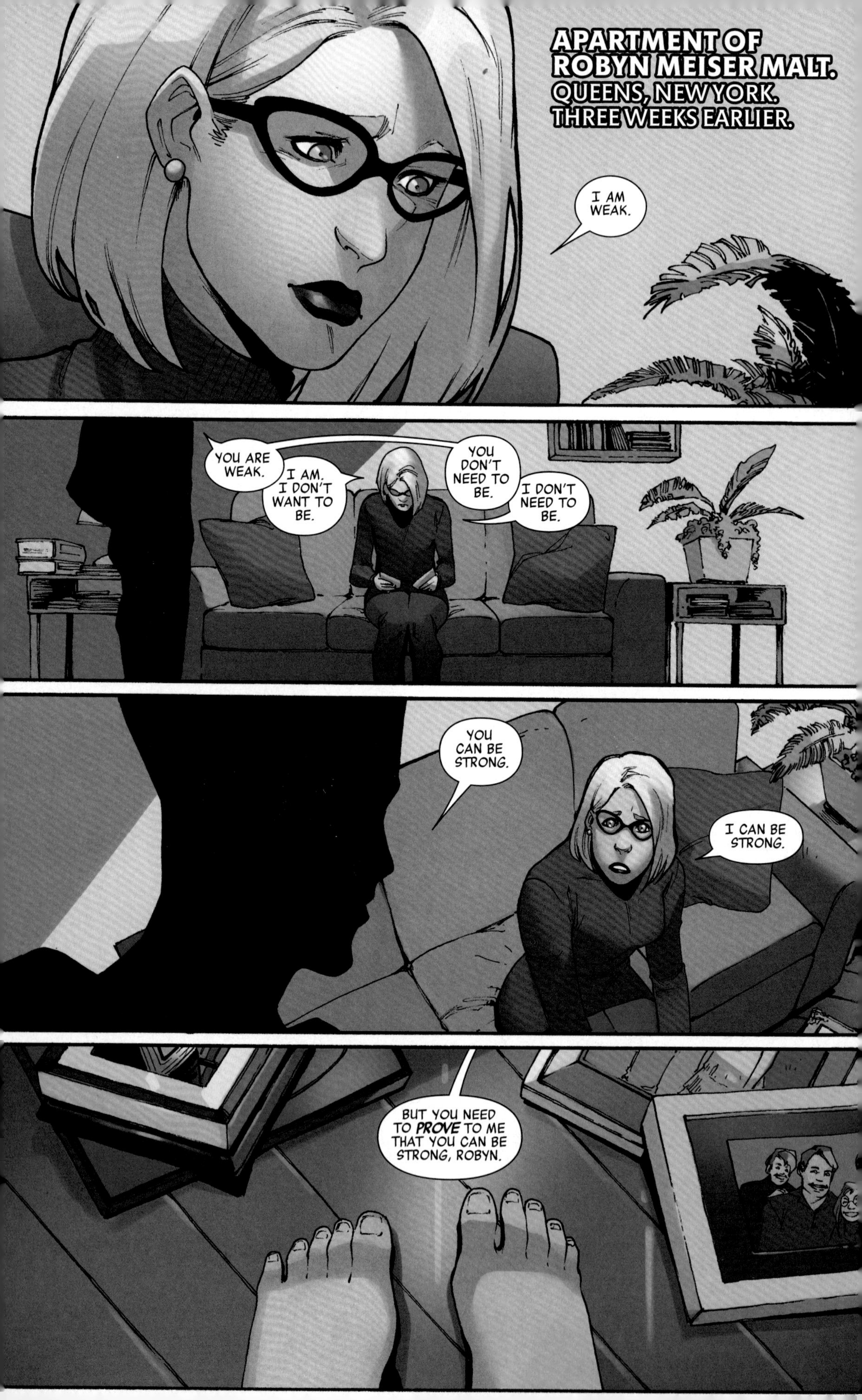
APARTMENT OF ROBYN MEISER MALT. QUEENS, NEW YORK. THREE WEEKS EARLIER.
I AM WEAK.
YOU ARE WEAK.
I AM. I DON'T WANT TO BE.
YOU DON'T NEED TO BE.
I DON'T NEED TO BE.
YOU CAN BE STRONG.
I CAN BE STRONG.
BUT YOU NEED TO *PROVE* TO ME THAT YOU CAN BE STRONG, ROBYN.

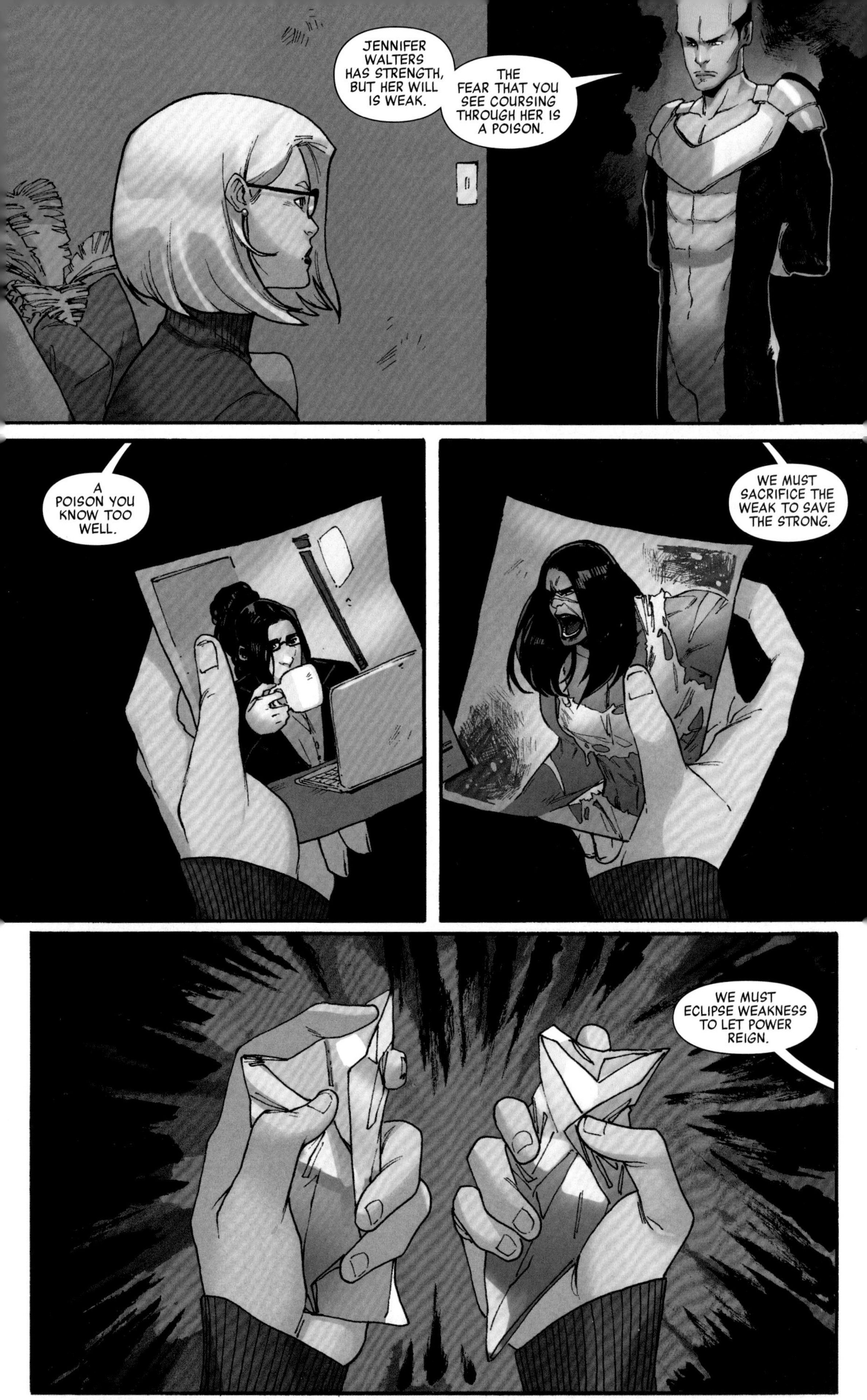
JENNIFER WALTERS HAS STRENGTH, BUT HER WILL IS WEAK.
THE FEAR THAT YOU SEE COURSING THROUGH HER IS A POISON.
A POISON YOU KNOW TOO WELL.
WE MUST SACRIFICE THE WEAK TO SAVE THE STRONG.
WE MUST ECLIPSE WEAKNESS TO LET POWER REIGN.

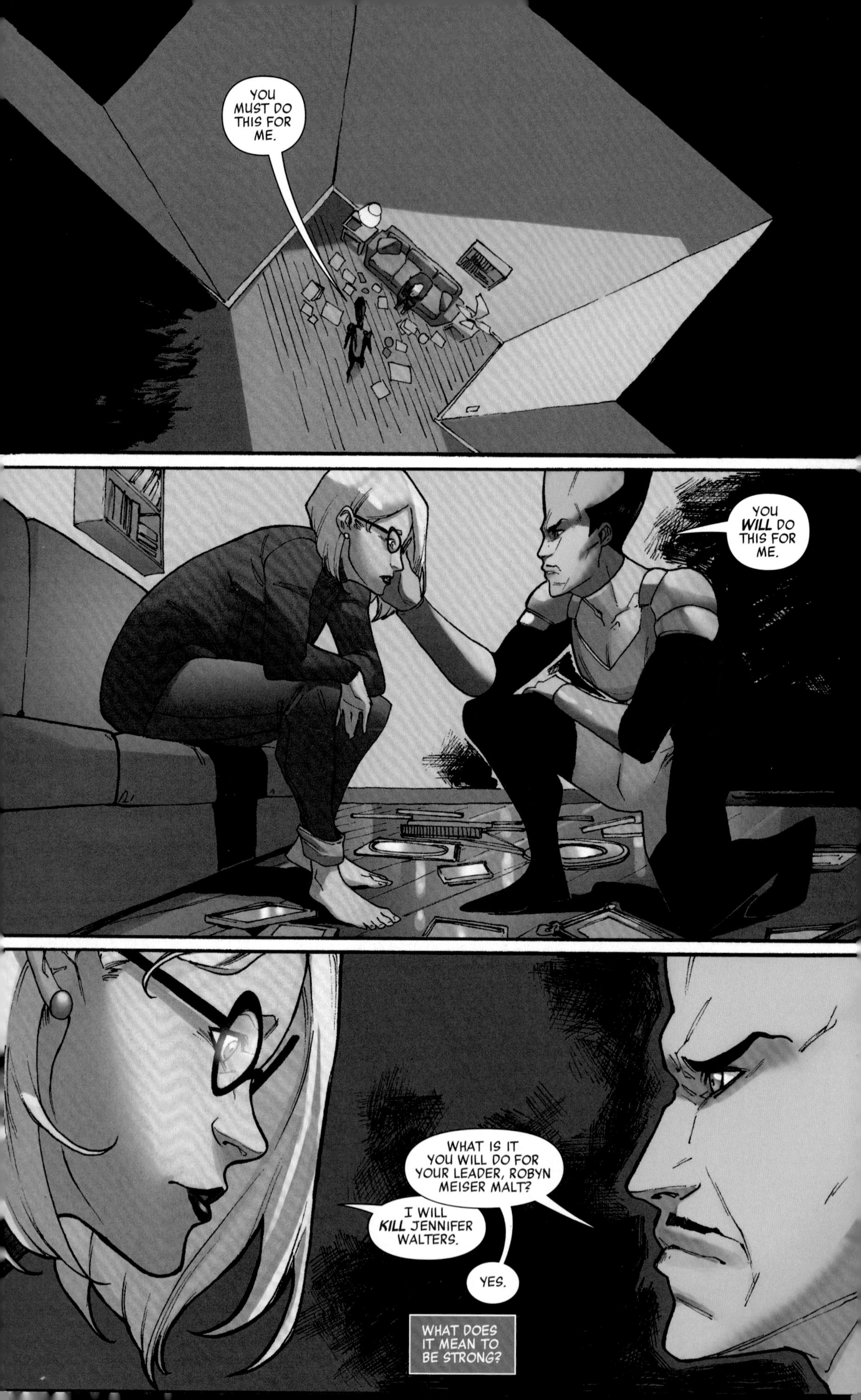
YOU MUST DO THIS FOR ME.
YOU WILL DO THIS FOR ME.
WHAT IS IT YOU WILL DO FOR YOUR LEADER, ROBYN MEISER MALT?
I WILL KILL JENNIFER WALTERS.
YES.
WHAT DOES IT MEAN TO BE STRONG?

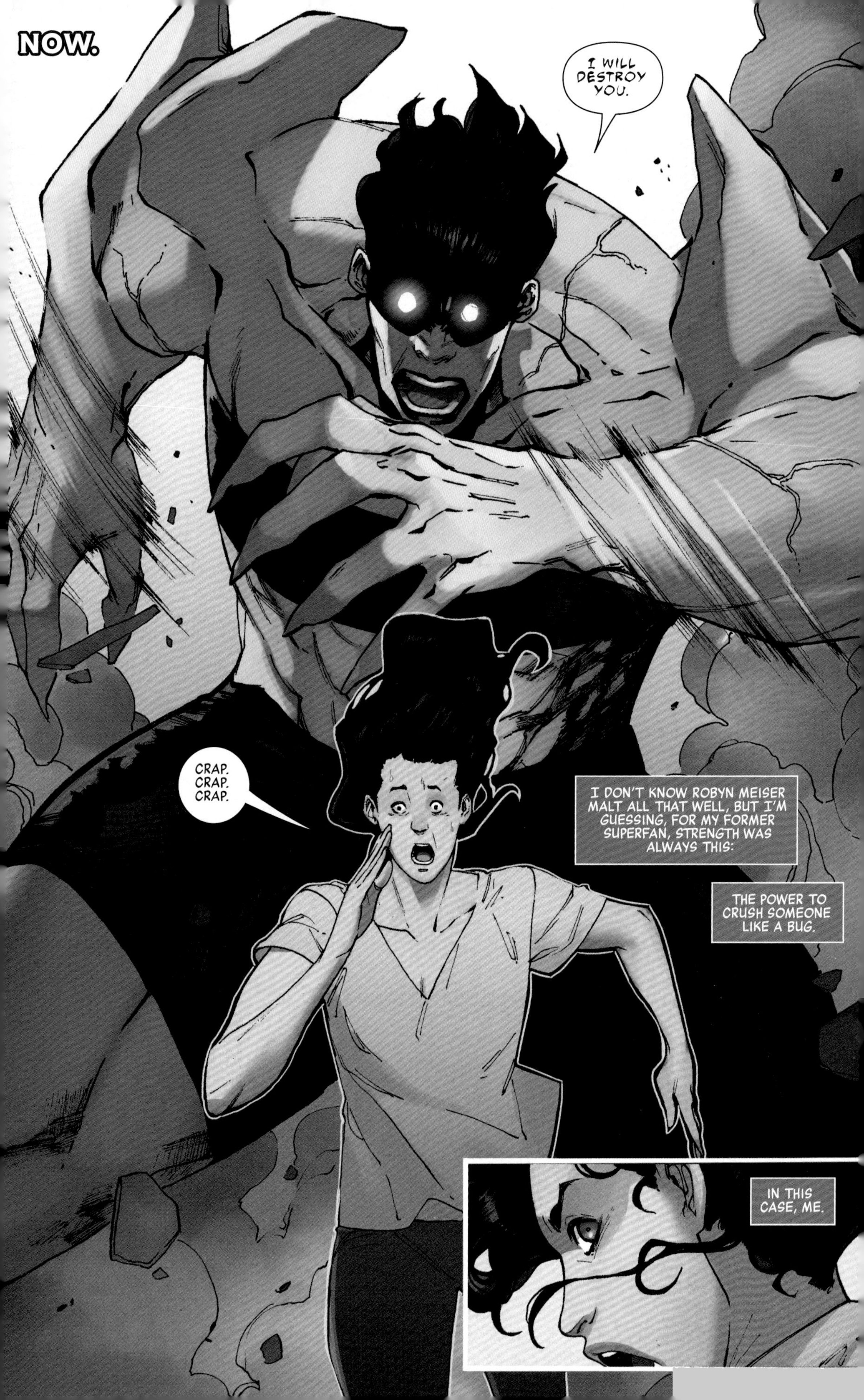
NOW.
I WILL DESTROY YOU.
CRAP. CRAP. CRAP.
I DON'T KNOW ROBYN MEISER MALT ALL THAT WELL, BUT I'M GUESSING, FOR MY FORMER SUPERFAN, STRENGTH WAS ALWAYS THIS:
THE POWER TO CRUSH SOMEONE LIKE A BUG.
IN THIS CASE, ME.

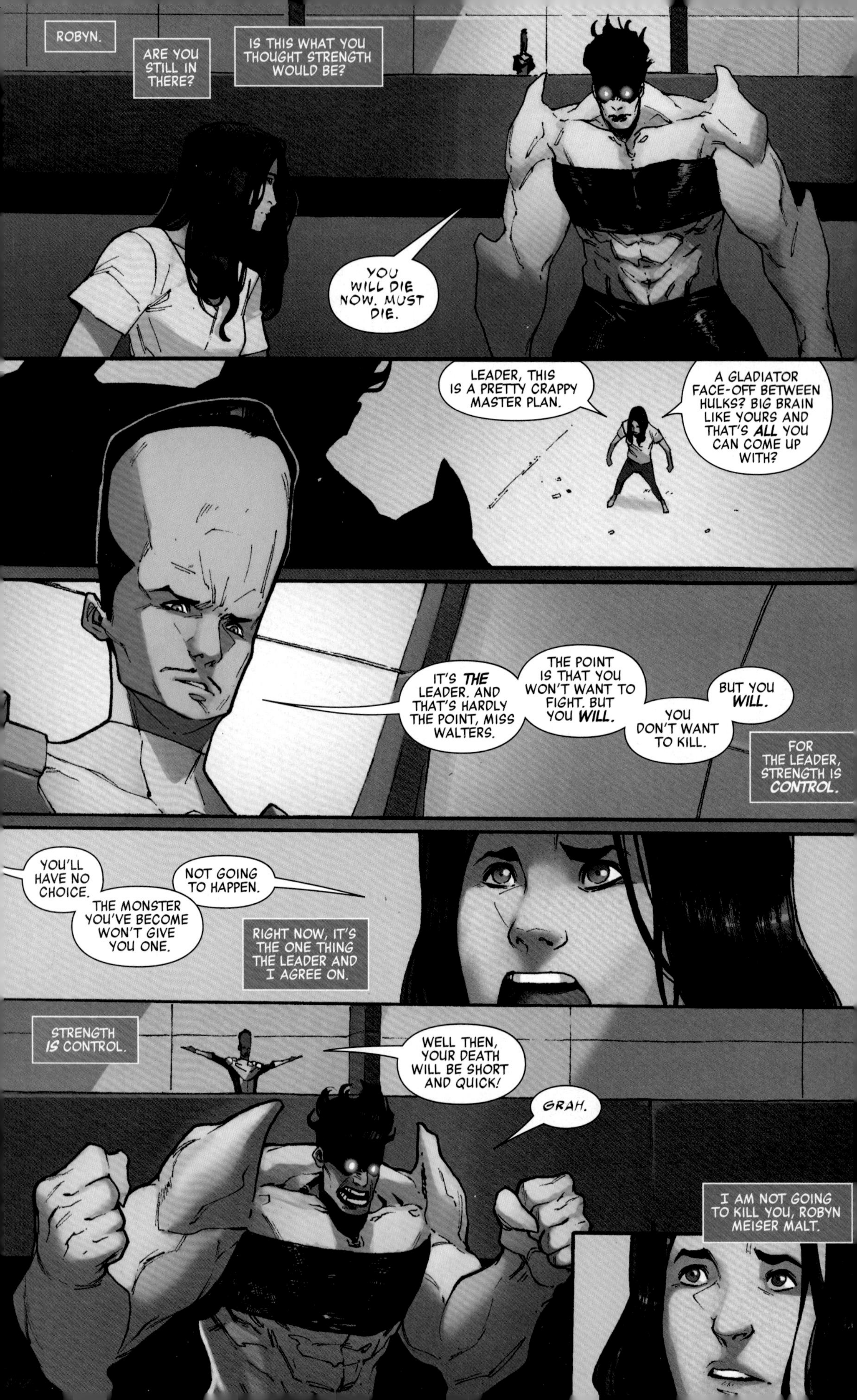
ROBYN.
ARE YOU STILL IN THERE?
IS THIS WHAT YOU THOUGHT STRENGTH WOULD BE?
YOU WILL DIE NOW. MUST DIE.
LEADER, THIS IS A PRETTY CRAPPY MASTER PLAN.
A GLADIATOR FACE-OFF BETWEEN HULKS? BIG BRAIN LIKE YOURS AND THAT'S ALL YOU CAN COME UP WITH?
IT'S THE LEADER. AND THAT'S HARDLY THE POINT, MISS WALTERS.
THE POINT IS THAT YOU WON'T WANT TO FIGHT. BUT YOU WILL.
YOU DON'T WANT TO KILL.
BUT YOU WILL.
FOR THE LEADER, STRENGTH IS CONTROL.
YOU'LL HAVE NO CHOICE.
THE MONSTER YOU'VE BECOME WON'T GIVE YOU ONE.
NOT GOING TO HAPPEN.
RIGHT NOW, IT'S THE ONE THING THE LEADER AND I AGREE ON.
STRENGTH IS CONTROL.
WELL THEN, YOUR DEATH WILL BE SHORT AND QUICK!
GRAH.
I AM NOT GOING TO KILL YOU, ROBYN MEISER MALT.

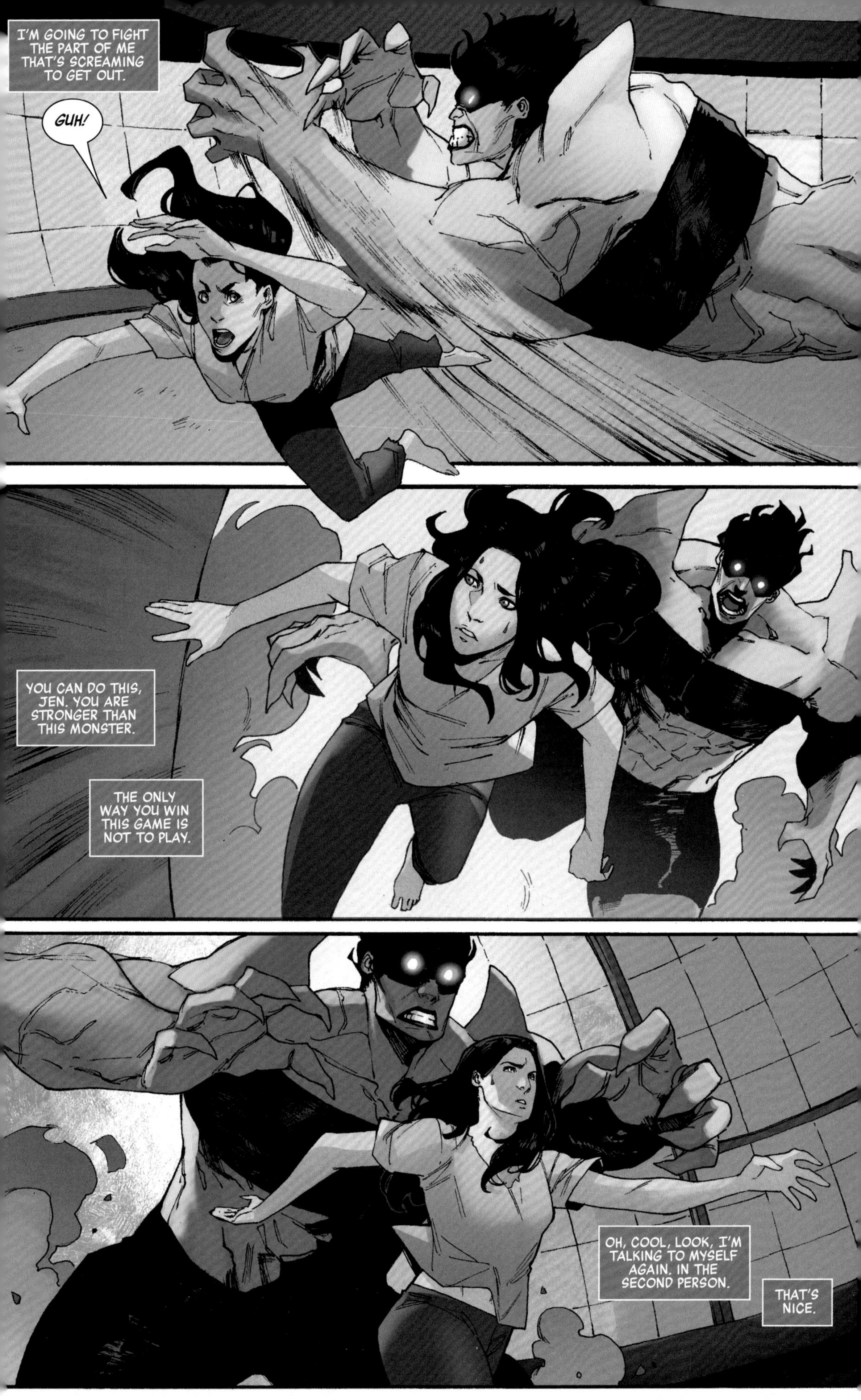
I'M GOING TO FIGHT THE PART OF ME THAT'S SCREAMING TO GET OUT.
GUH!
YOU CAN DO THIS, JEN. YOU ARE STRONGER THAN THIS MONSTER.
THE ONLY WAY YOU WIN THIS GAME IS NOT TO PLAY.
OH, COOL, LOOK, I'M TALKING TO MYSELF AGAIN. IN THE SECOND PERSON.
THAT'S NICE.

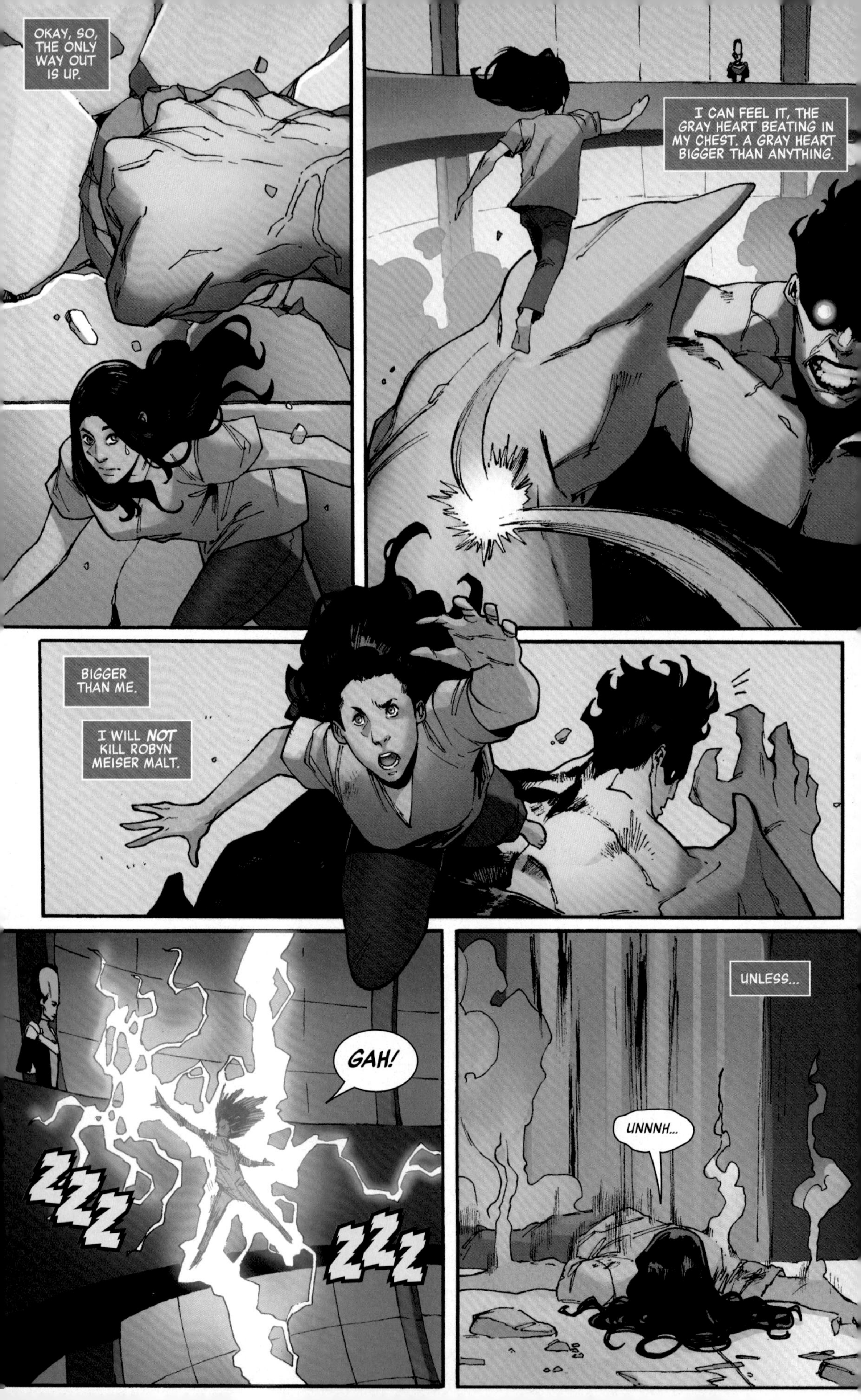
OKAY, SO, THE ONLY WAY OUT IS UP.
I CAN FEEL IT, THE GRAY HEART BEATING IN MY CHEST. A GRAY HEART BIGGER THAN ANYTHING.
BIGGER THAN ME.
I WILL NOT KILL ROBYN MEISER MALT.
GAH!
ZZZ
ZZZ
UNLESS...
UNNNH...

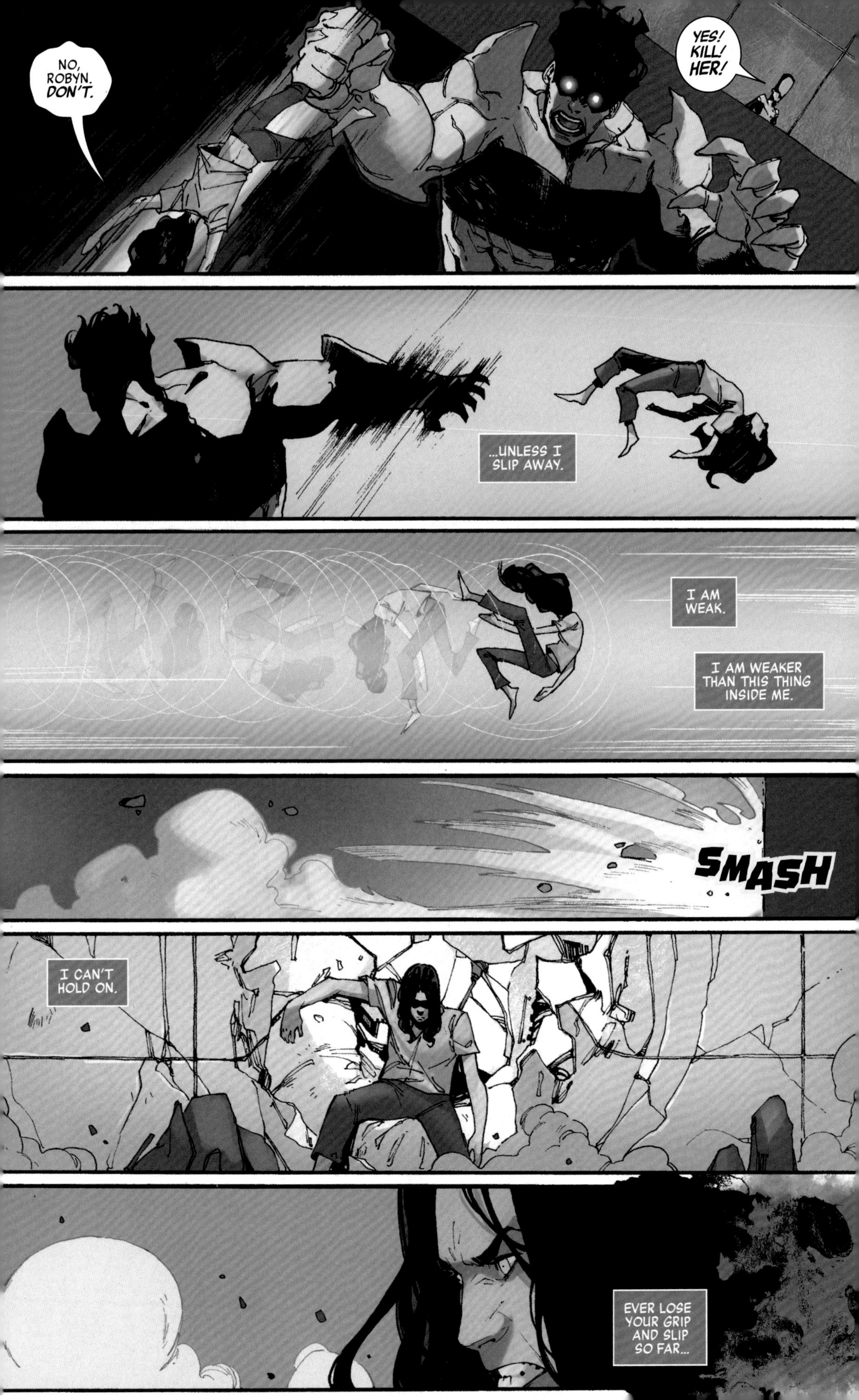

NO, ROBYN. DON'T.
YES! KILL! HER!
...UNLESS I SLIP AWAY.
I AM WEAK.
I AM WEAKER THAN THIS THING INSIDE ME.
SMASH
I CAN'T HOLD ON.
EVER LOSE YOUR GRIP AND SLIP SO FAR...

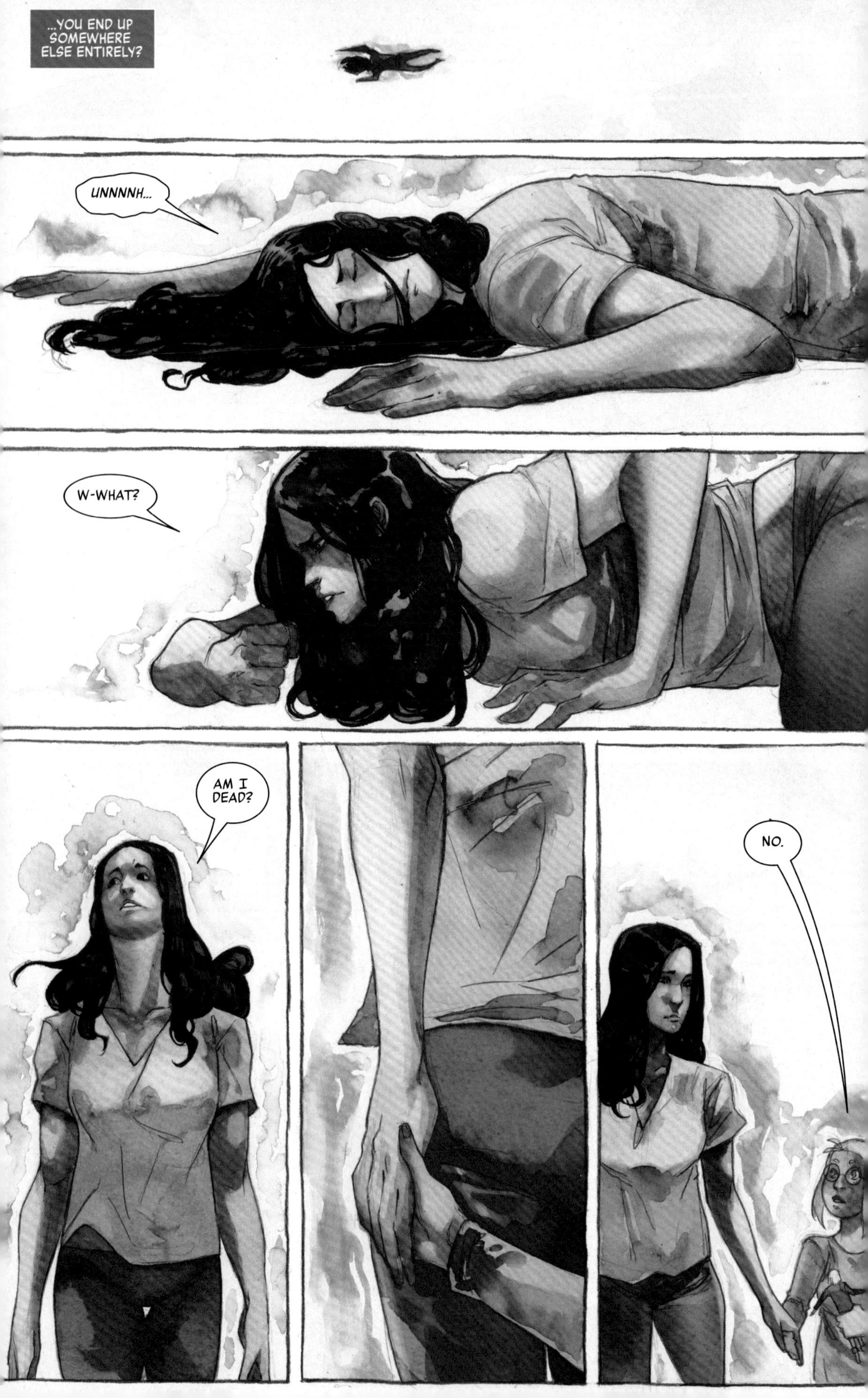
...YOU END UP SOMEWHERE ELSE ENTIRELY?
UNNNNH...
W-WHAT?
AM I DEAD?
NO.

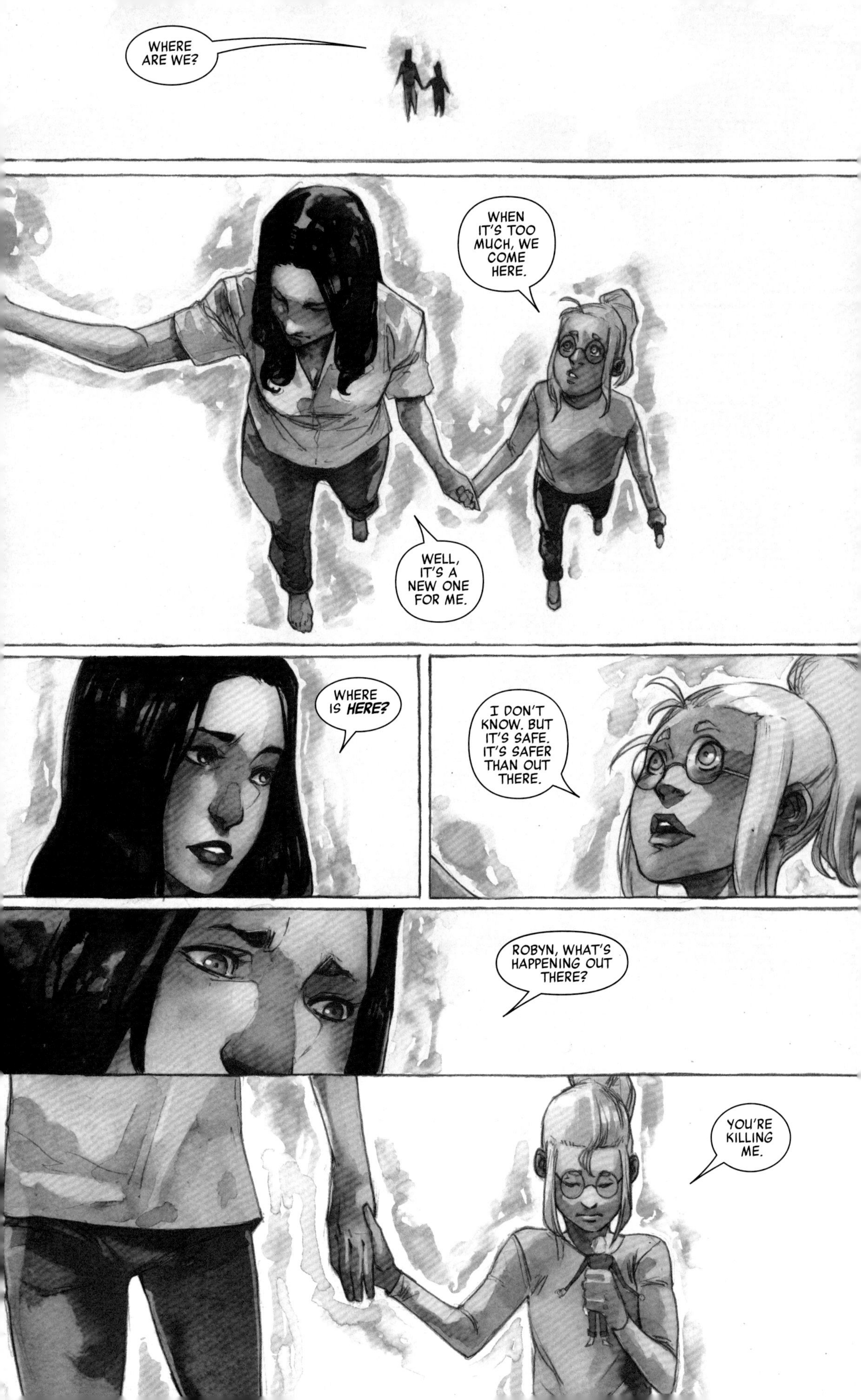
WHERE ARE WE?
WHEN IT'S TOO MUCH, WE COME HERE.
WELL, IT'S A NEW ONE FOR ME.
WHERE IS *HERE?*
I DON'T KNOW. BUT IT'S SAFE. IT'S SAFER THAN OUT THERE.
ROBYN, WHAT'S HAPPENING OUT THERE?
YOU'RE KILLING ME.

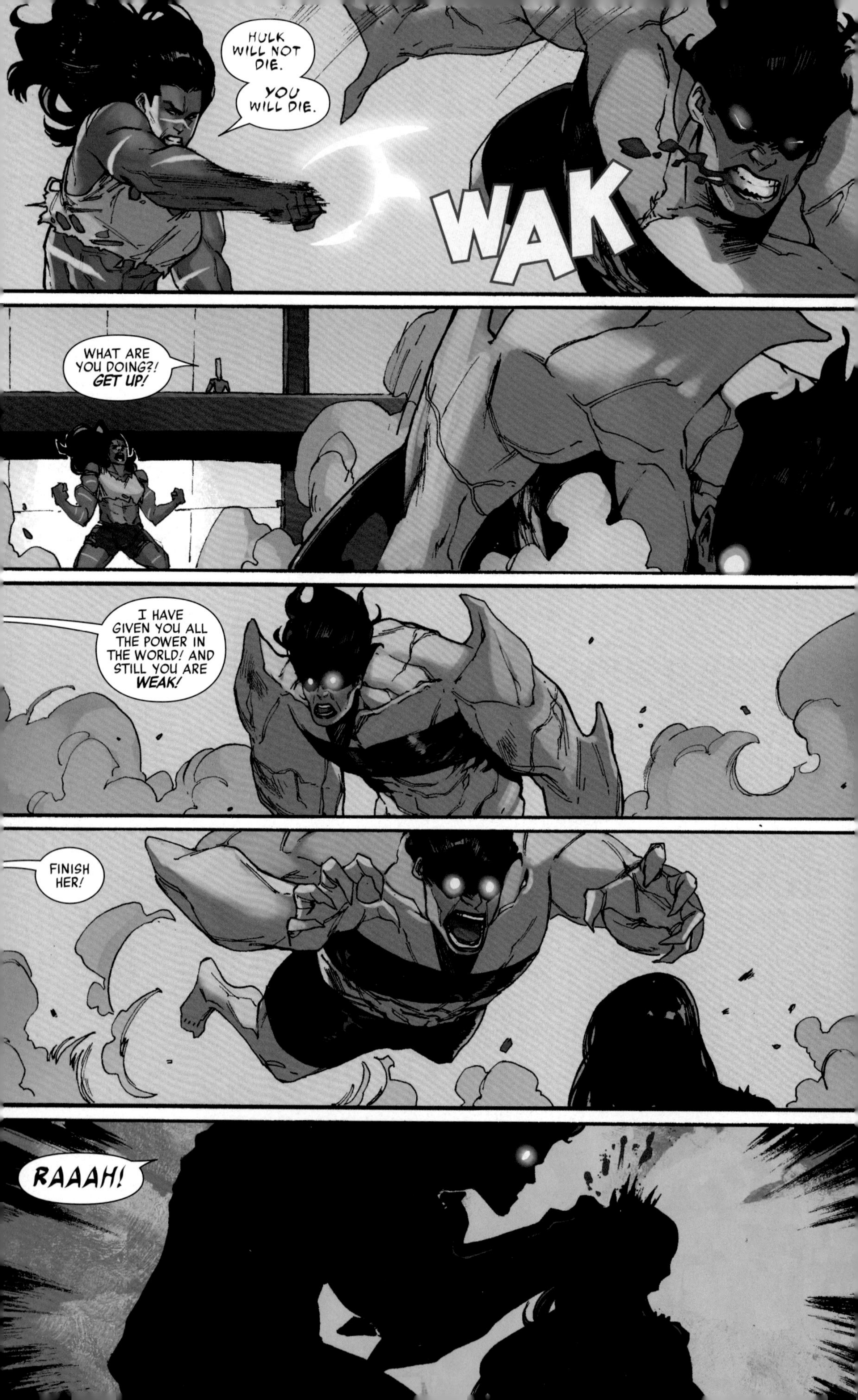
HULK WILL NOT DIE.
YOU WILL DIE.
WAK
WHAT ARE YOU DOING?! GET UP!
I HAVE GIVEN YOU ALL THE POWER IN THE WORLD! AND STILL YOU ARE WEAK!
FINISH HER!
RAAAH!

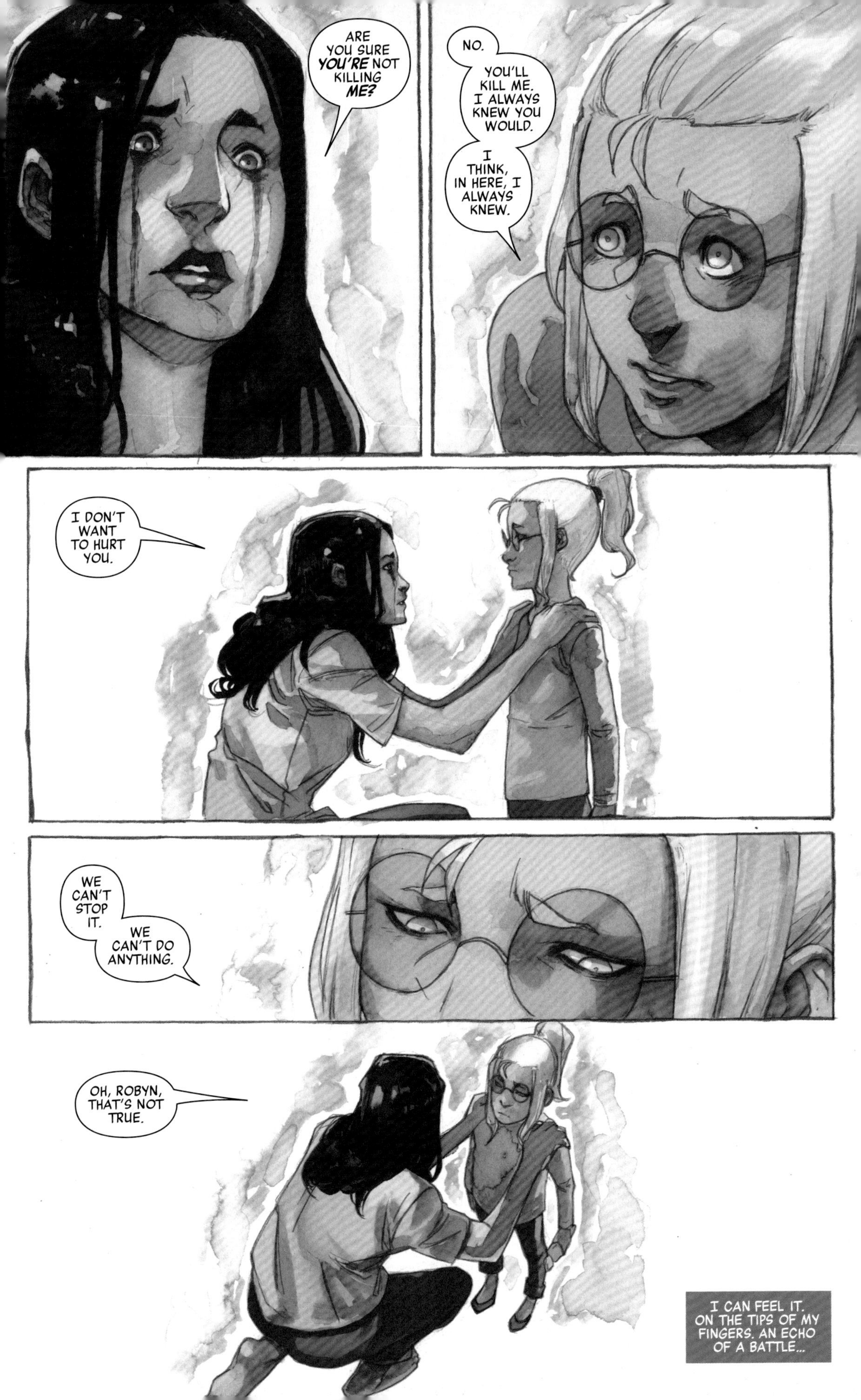
ARE YOU SURE *YOU'RE* NOT KILLING *ME?*
NO.
YOU'LL KILL ME. I ALWAYS KNEW YOU WOULD.
I THINK, IN HERE, I ALWAYS KNEW.
I DON'T WANT TO HURT YOU.
WE CAN'T STOP IT.
WE CAN'T DO ANYTHING.
OH, ROBYN, THAT'S NOT TRUE.
I CAN FEEL IT. ON THE TIPS OF MY FINGERS. AN ECHO OF A BATTLE...

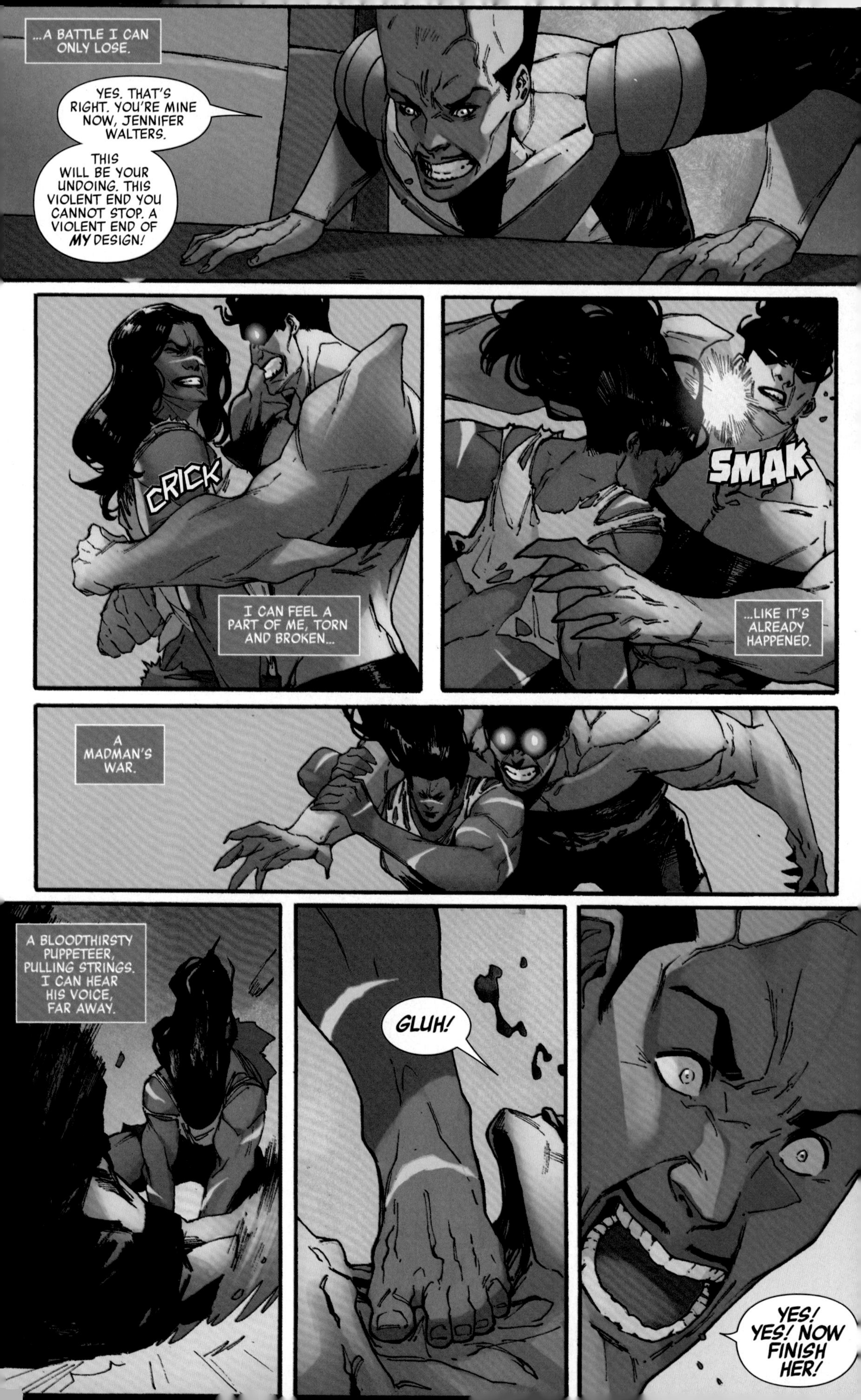

...A BATTLE I CAN ONLY LOSE.
YES. THAT'S RIGHT. YOU'RE MINE NOW, JENNIFER WALTERS.
THIS WILL BE YOUR UNDOING. THIS VIOLENT END YOU CANNOT STOP. A VIOLENT END OF MY DESIGN!
CRICK
I CAN FEEL A PART OF ME, TORN AND BROKEN...
SMAK
...LIKE IT'S ALREADY HAPPENED.
A MADMAN'S WAR.
A BLOODTHIRSTY PUPPETEER, PULLING STRINGS. I CAN HEAR HIS VOICE, FAR AWAY.
GLUH!
YES! YES! NOW FINISH HER!

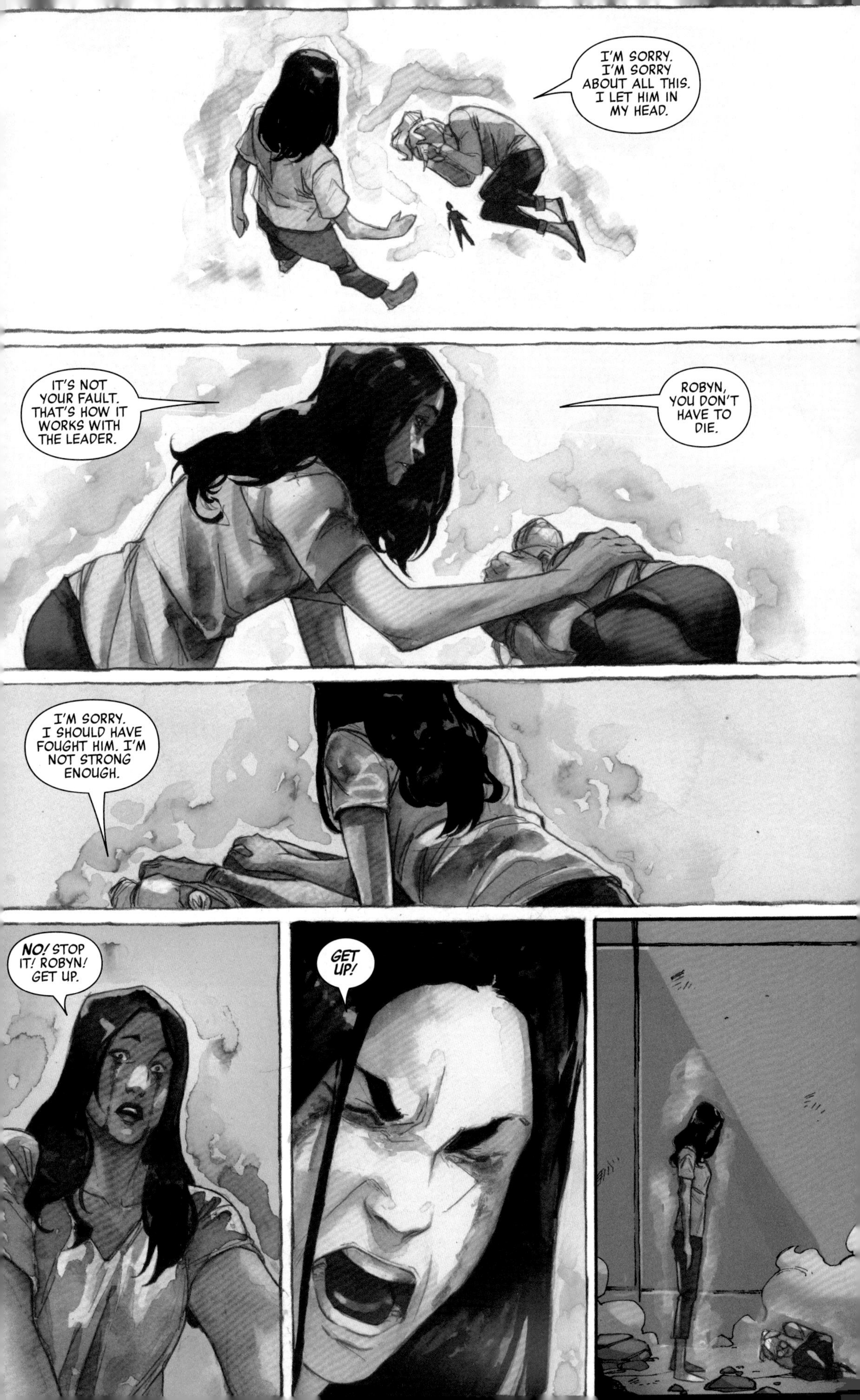
I'M SORRY. I'M SORRY ABOUT ALL THIS. I LET HIM IN MY HEAD.
IT'S NOT YOUR FAULT. THAT'S HOW IT WORKS WITH THE LEADER.
ROBYN, YOU DON'T HAVE TO DIE.
I'M SORRY. I SHOULD HAVE FOUGHT HIM. I'M NOT STRONG ENOUGH.
NO! STOP IT! ROBYN! GET UP.
GET UP!

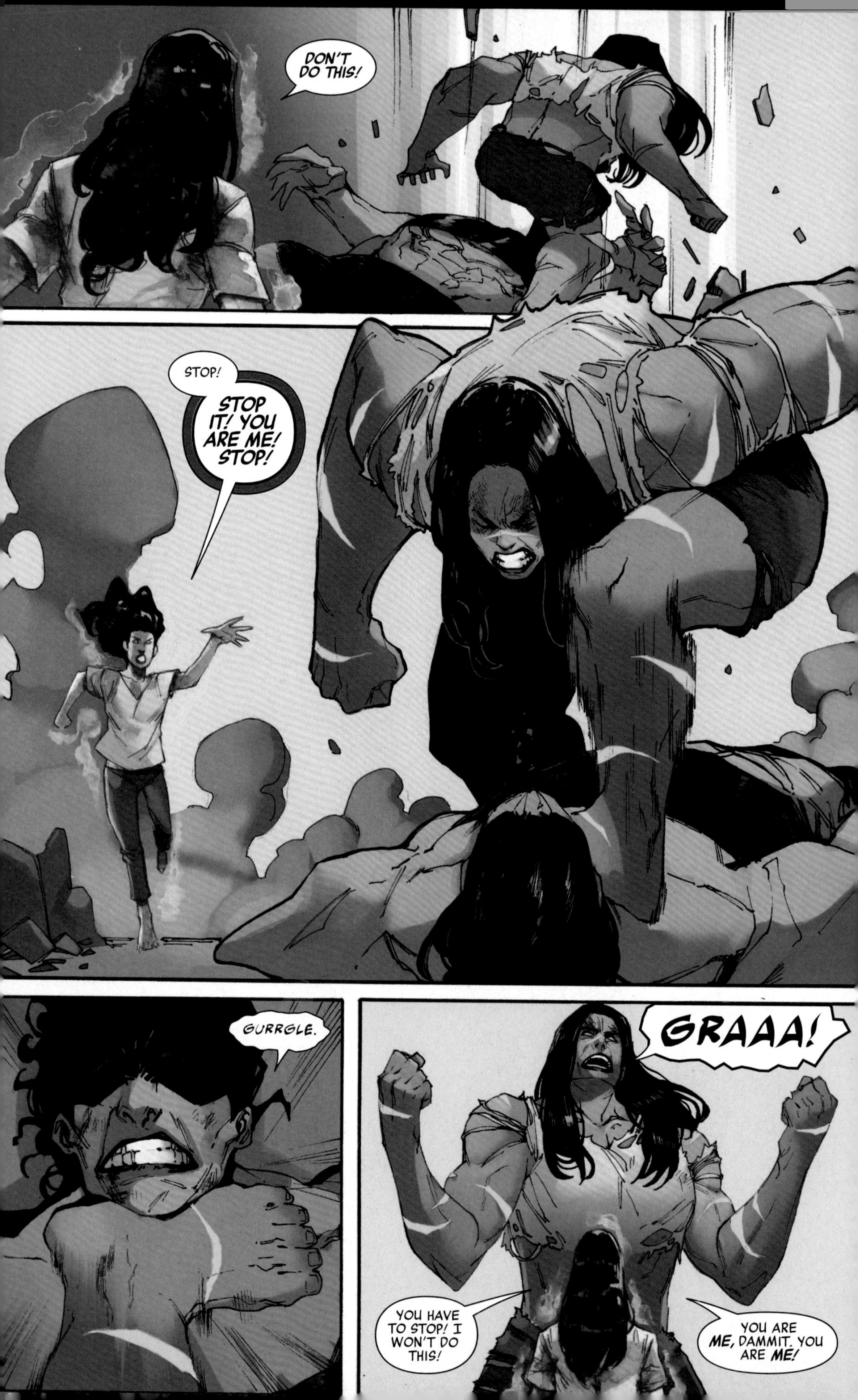
DON'T DO THIS!
STOP!
STOP IT! YOU ARE ME! STOP!
GURRGLE.
GRAAA!
YOU HAVE TO STOP! I WON'T DO THIS!
YOU ARE ME, DAMMIT. YOU ARE ME!

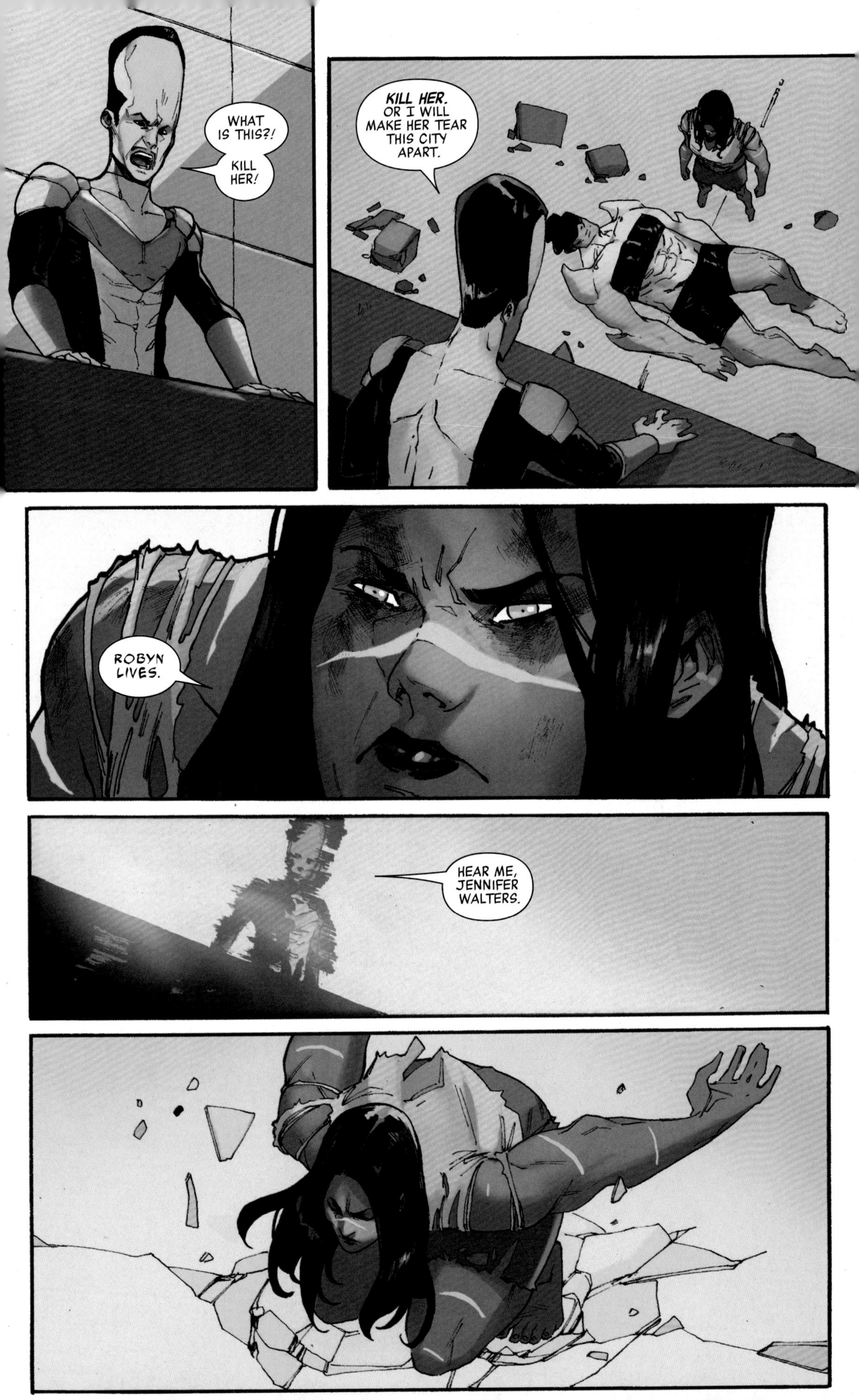
WHAT IS THIS?!
KILL HER!
KILL HER. OR I WILL MAKE HER TEAR THIS CITY APART.
ROBYN LIVES.
HEAR ME, JENNIFER WALTERS.

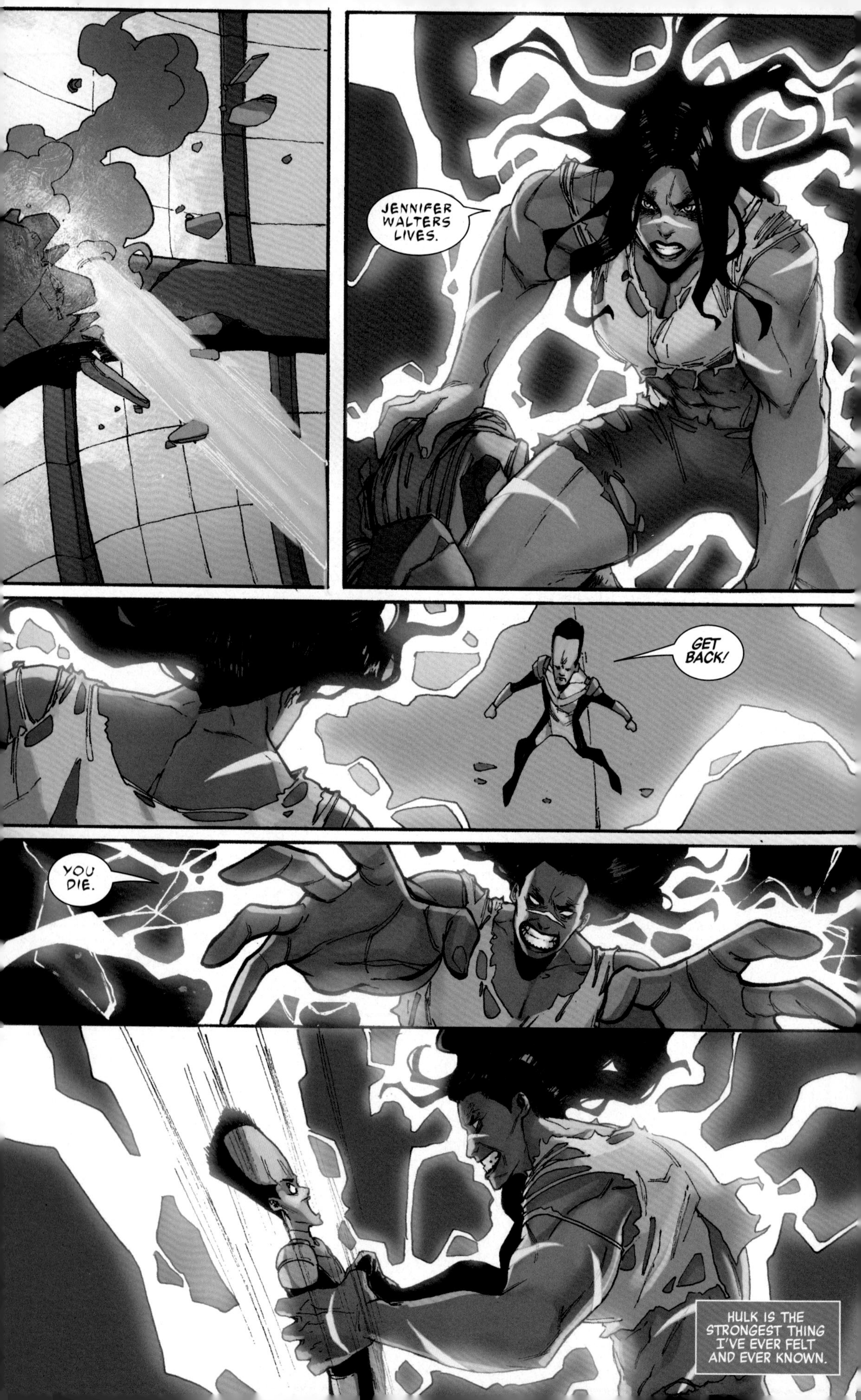
JENNIFER WALTERS LIVES.
GET BACK!
YOU DIE.
HULK IS THE STRONGEST THING I'VE EVER FELT AND EVER KNOWN.

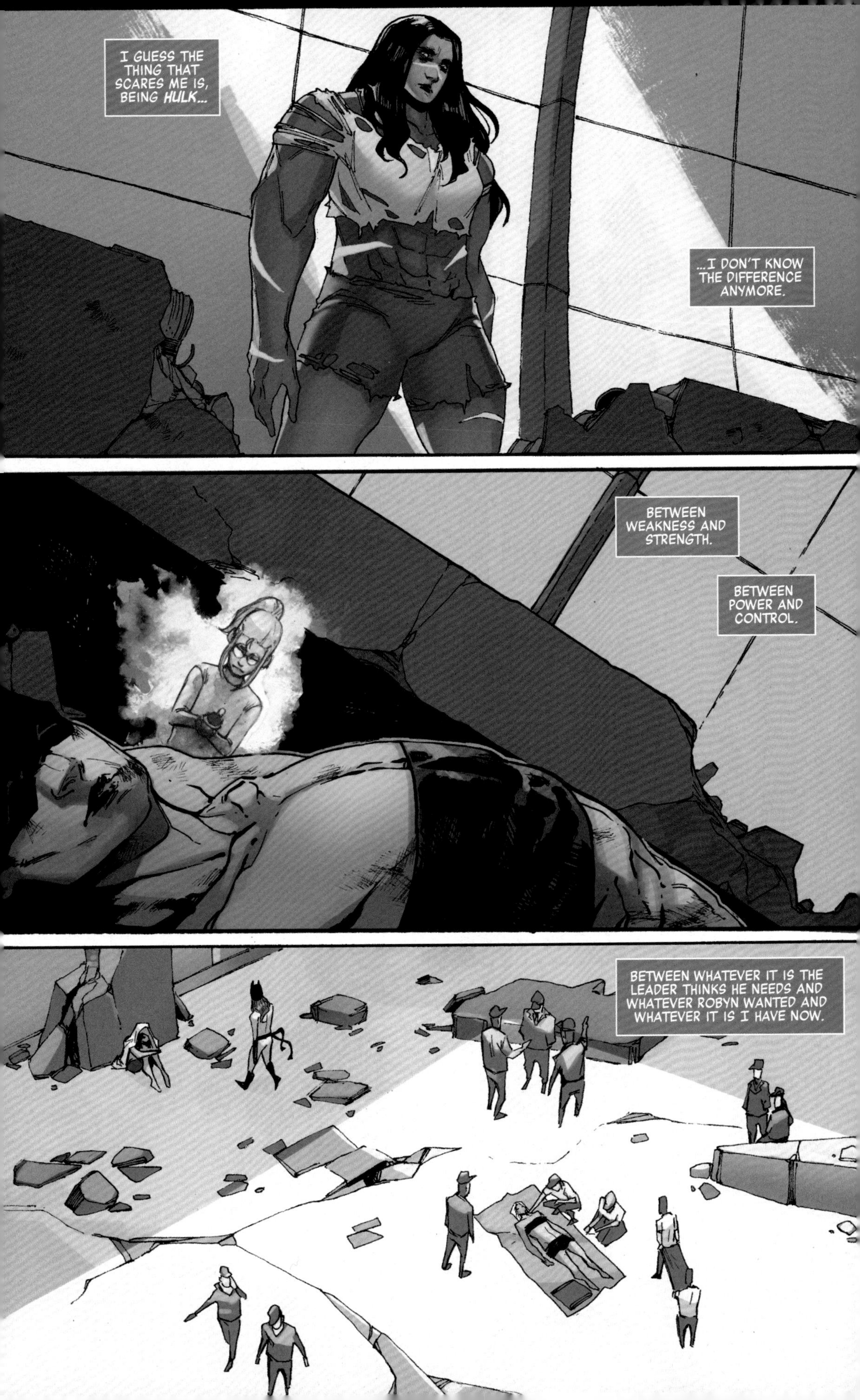
I GUESS THE THING THAT SCARES ME IS, BEING HULK...
...I DON'T KNOW THE DIFFERENCE ANYMORE.
BETWEEN WEAKNESS AND STRENGTH.
BETWEEN POWER AND CONTROL.
BETWEEN WHATEVER IT IS THE LEADER THINKS HE NEEDS AND WHATEVER ROBYN WANTED AND WHATEVER IT IS I HAVE NOW.

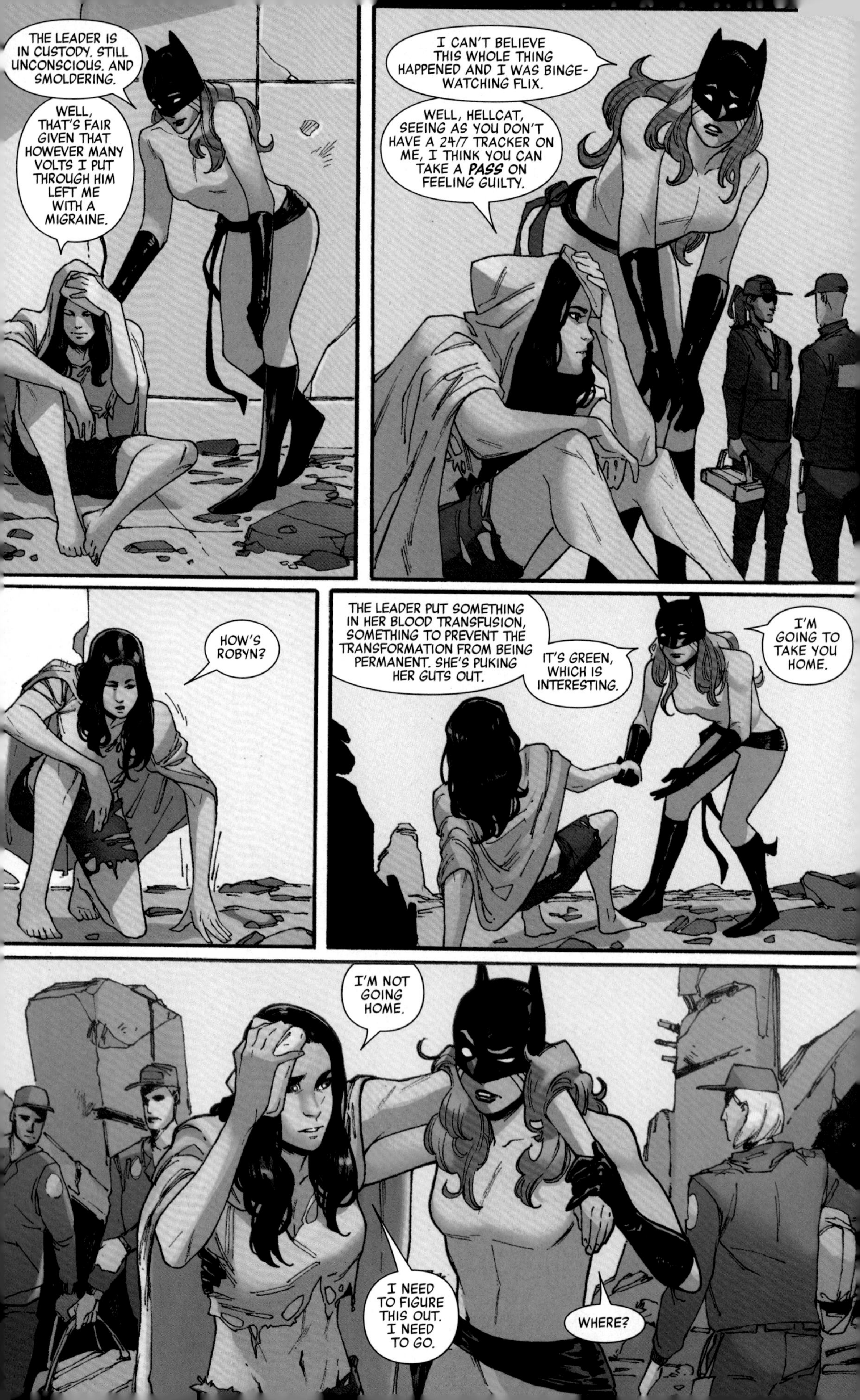
THE LEADER IS IN CUSTODY. STILL UNCONSCIOUS. AND SMOLDERING.
WELL, THAT'S FAIR GIVEN THAT HOWEVER MANY VOLTS I PUT THROUGH HIM LEFT ME WITH A MIGRAINE.
I CAN'T BELIEVE THIS WHOLE THING HAPPENED AND I WAS BINGE-WATCHING FLIX.
WELL, HELLCAT, SEEING AS YOU DON'T HAVE A 24/7 TRACKER ON ME, I THINK YOU CAN TAKE A PASS ON FEELING GUILTY.
HOW'S ROBYN?
THE LEADER PUT SOMETHING IN HER BLOOD TRANSFUSION, SOMETHING TO PREVENT THE TRANSFORMATION FROM BEING PERMANENT. SHE'S PUKING HER GUTS OUT.
IT'S GREEN, WHICH IS INTERESTING.
I'M GOING TO TAKE YOU HOME.
I'M NOT GOING HOME.
I NEED TO FIGURE THIS OUT. I NEED TO GO.
WHERE?

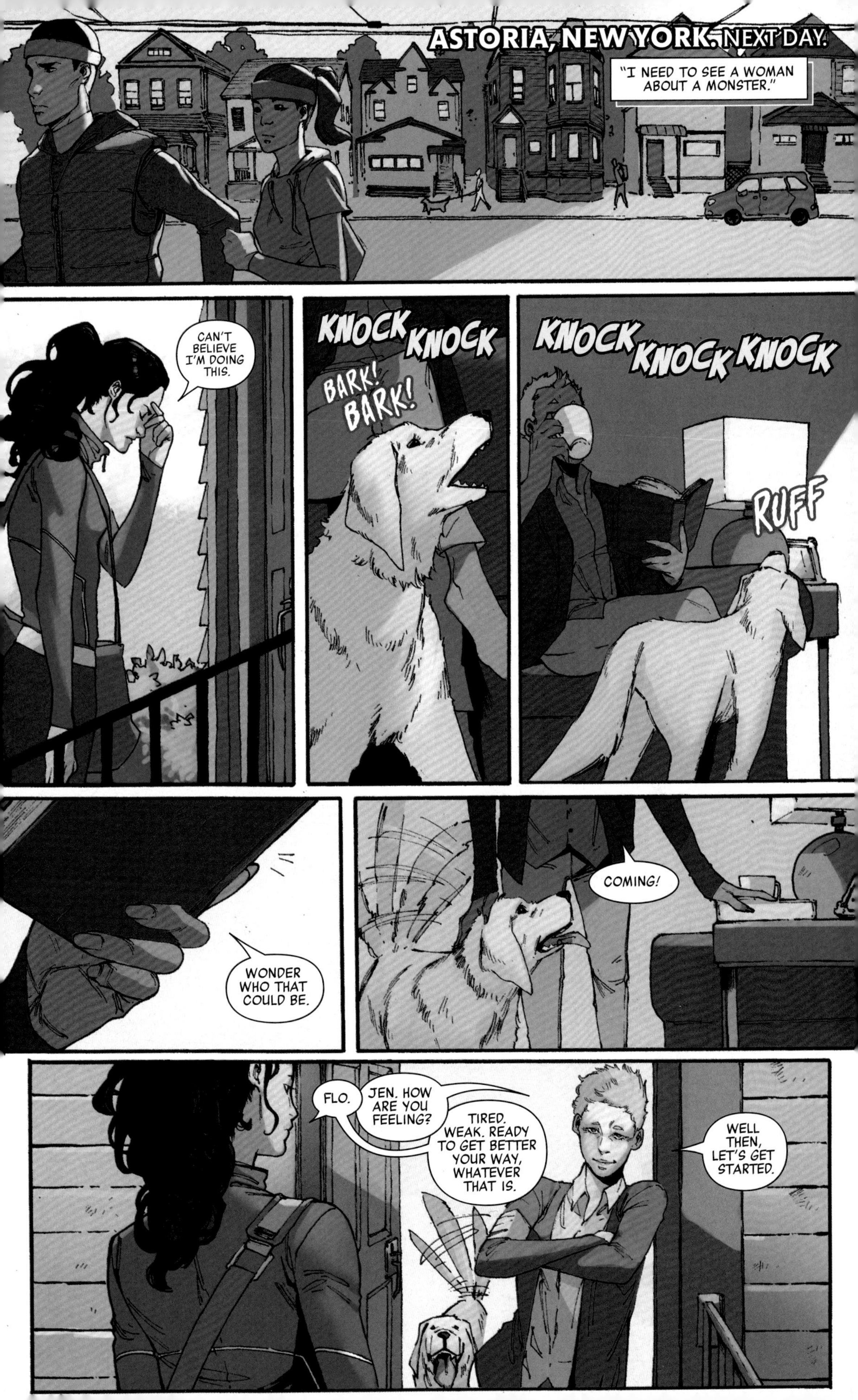
ASTORIA, NEW YORK. NEXT DAY.
"I NEED TO SEE A WOMAN ABOUT A MONSTER."
CAN'T BELIEVE I'M DOING THIS.
KNOCK KNOCK
BARK! BARK!
KNOCK KNOCK KNOCK
RUFF
WONDER WHO THAT COULD BE.
COMING!
FLO.
JEN. HOW ARE YOU FEELING?
TIRED. WEAK. READY TO GET BETTER YOUR WAY, WHATEVER THAT IS.
WELL THEN, LET'S GET STARTED.

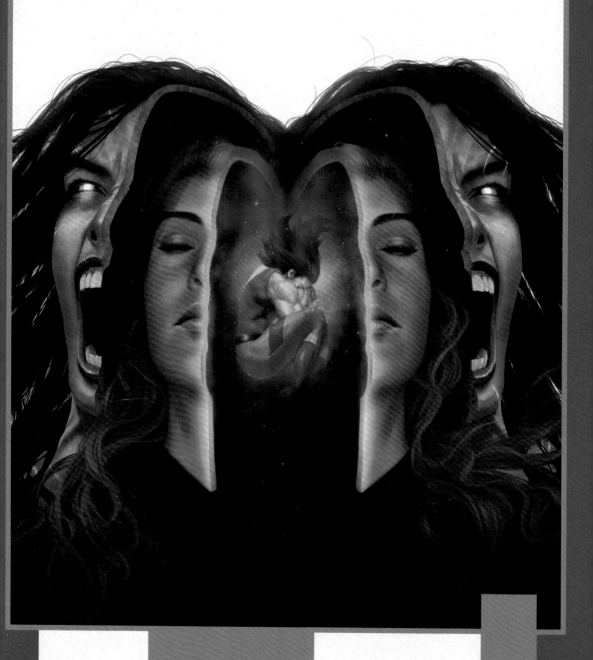

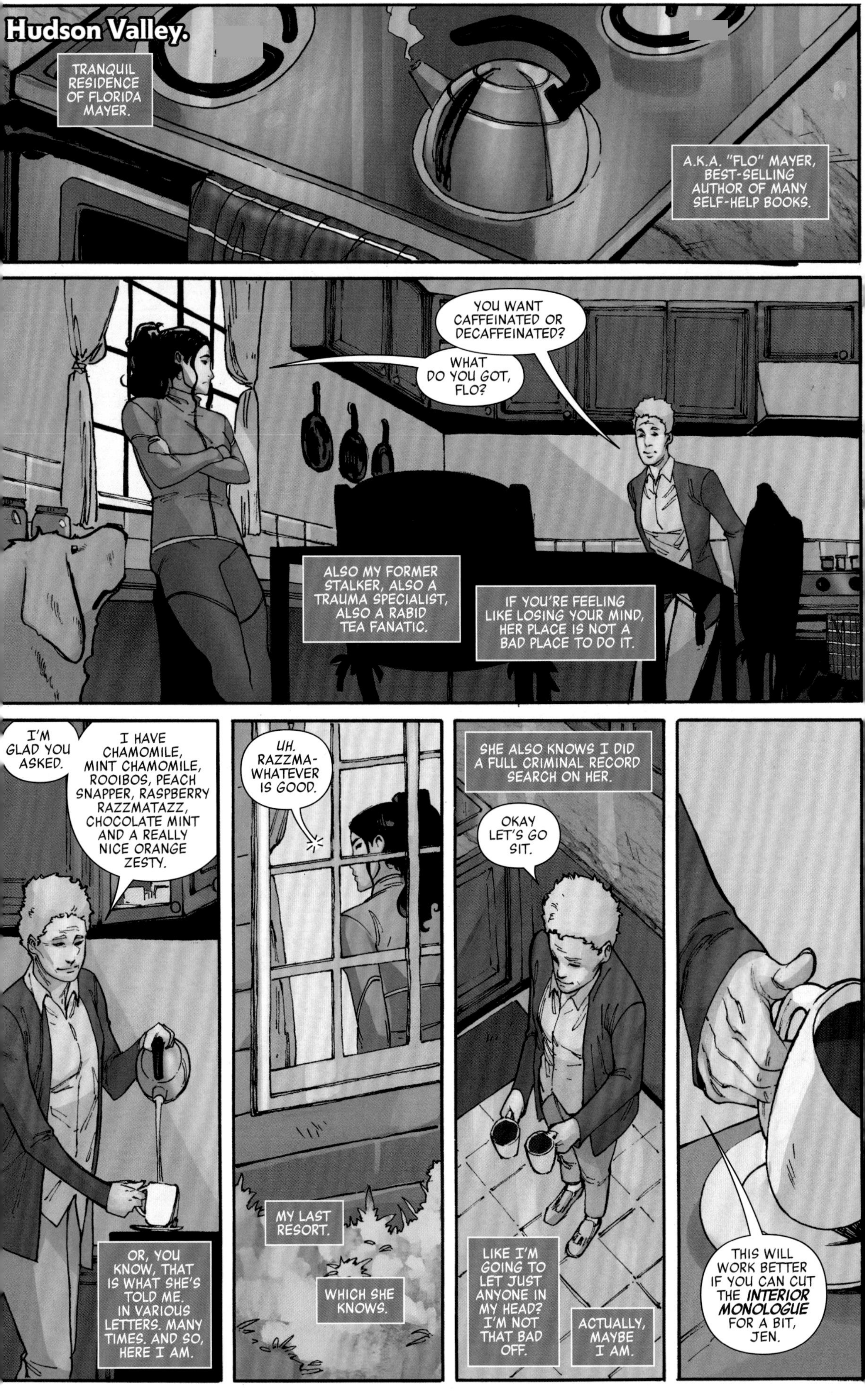

Hudson Valley.
TRANQUIL RESIDENCE OF FLORIDA MAYER.
A.K.A. "FLO" MAYER, BEST-SELLING AUTHOR OF MANY SELF-HELP BOOKS.
YOU WANT CAFFEINATED OR DECAFFEINATED?
WHAT DO YOU GOT, FLO?
ALSO MY FORMER STALKER, ALSO A TRAUMA SPECIALIST, ALSO A RABID TEA FANATIC.
IF YOU'RE FEELING LIKE LOSING YOUR MIND, HER PLACE IS NOT A BAD PLACE TO DO IT.
I'M GLAD YOU ASKED.
I HAVE CHAMOMILE, MINT CHAMOMILE, ROOIBOS, PEACH SNAPPER, RASPBERRY RAZZMATAZZ, CHOCOLATE MINT AND A REALLY NICE ORANGE ZESTY.
OR, YOU KNOW, THAT IS WHAT SHE'S TOLD ME. IN VARIOUS LETTERS. MANY TIMES. AND SO, HERE I AM.
UH. RAZZMA-WHATEVER IS GOOD.
MY LAST RESORT.
WHICH SHE KNOWS.
SHE ALSO KNOWS I DID A FULL CRIMINAL RECORD SEARCH ON HER.
OKAY LET'S GO SIT.
LIKE I'M GOING TO LET JUST ANYONE IN MY HEAD? I'M NOT THAT BAD OFF.
ACTUALLY, MAYBE I AM.
THIS WILL WORK BETTER IF YOU CAN CUT THE *INTERIOR MONOLOGUE* FOR A BIT, JEN.

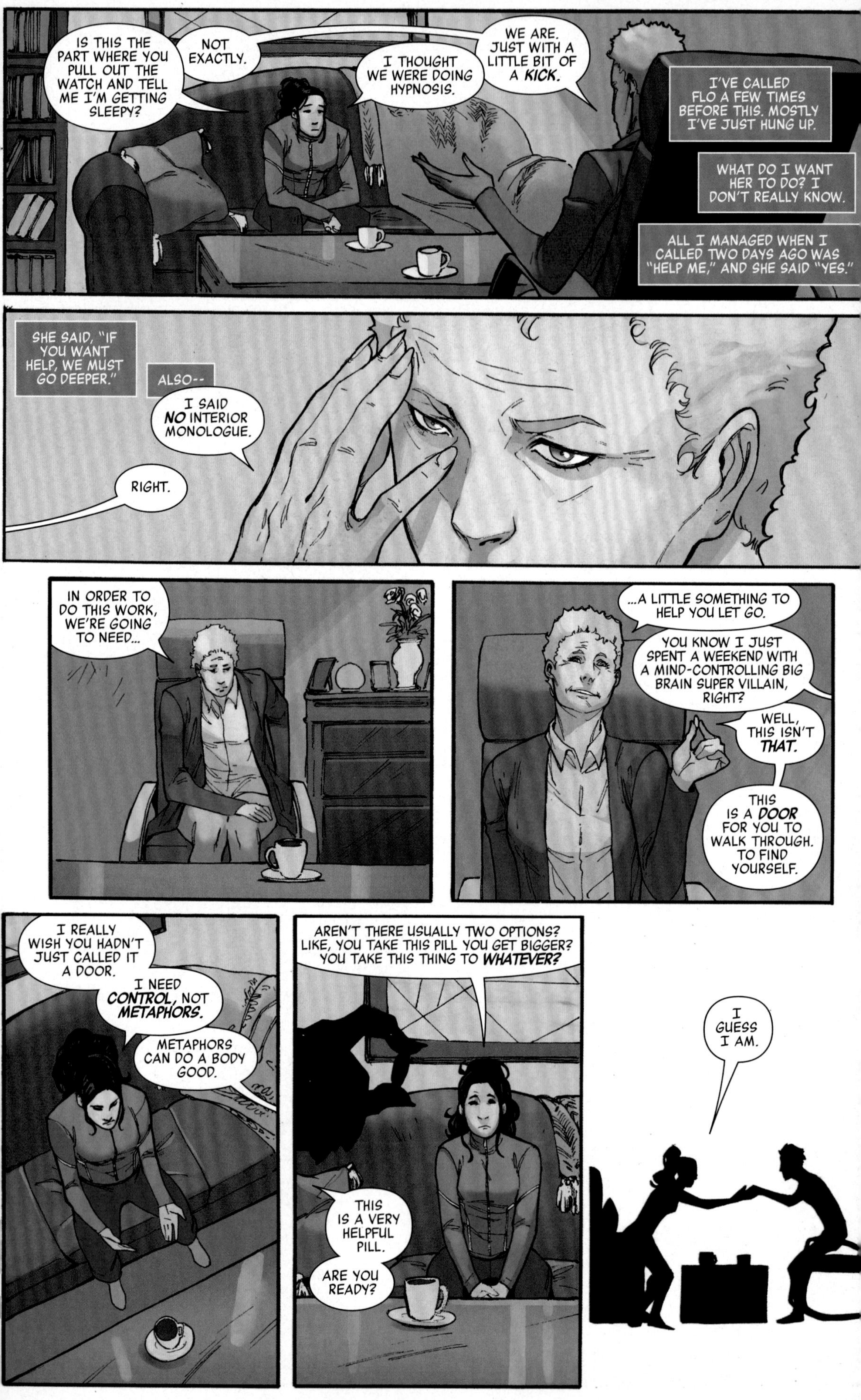
IS THIS THE PART WHERE YOU PULL OUT THE WATCH AND TELL ME I'M GETTING SLEEPY?
NOT EXACTLY.
I THOUGHT WE WERE DOING HYPNOSIS.
WE ARE. JUST WITH A LITTLE BIT OF A *KICK.*
I'VE CALLED FLO A FEW TIMES BEFORE THIS. MOSTLY I'VE JUST HUNG UP.
WHAT DO I WANT HER TO DO? I DON'T REALLY KNOW.
ALL I MANAGED WHEN I CALLED TWO DAYS AGO WAS "HELP ME," AND SHE SAID "YES."
SHE SAID, "IF YOU WANT HELP, WE MUST GO DEEPER."
ALSO--
I SAID *NO* INTERIOR MONOLOGUE.
RIGHT.
IN ORDER TO DO THIS WORK, WE'RE GOING TO NEED...
...A LITTLE SOMETHING TO HELP YOU LET GO.
YOU KNOW I JUST SPENT A WEEKEND WITH A MIND-CONTROLLING BIG BRAIN SUPER VILLAIN, RIGHT?
WELL, THIS ISN'T *THAT.*
THIS IS A *DOOR* FOR YOU TO WALK THROUGH. TO FIND YOURSELF.
I REALLY WISH YOU HADN'T JUST CALLED IT A DOOR.
I NEED *CONTROL,* NOT *METAPHORS.*
METAPHORS CAN DO A BODY GOOD.
AREN'T THERE USUALLY TWO OPTIONS? LIKE, YOU TAKE THIS PILL YOU GET BIGGER? YOU TAKE THIS THING TO *WHATEVER?*
THIS IS A VERY HELPFUL PILL.
ARE YOU READY?
I GUESS I AM.

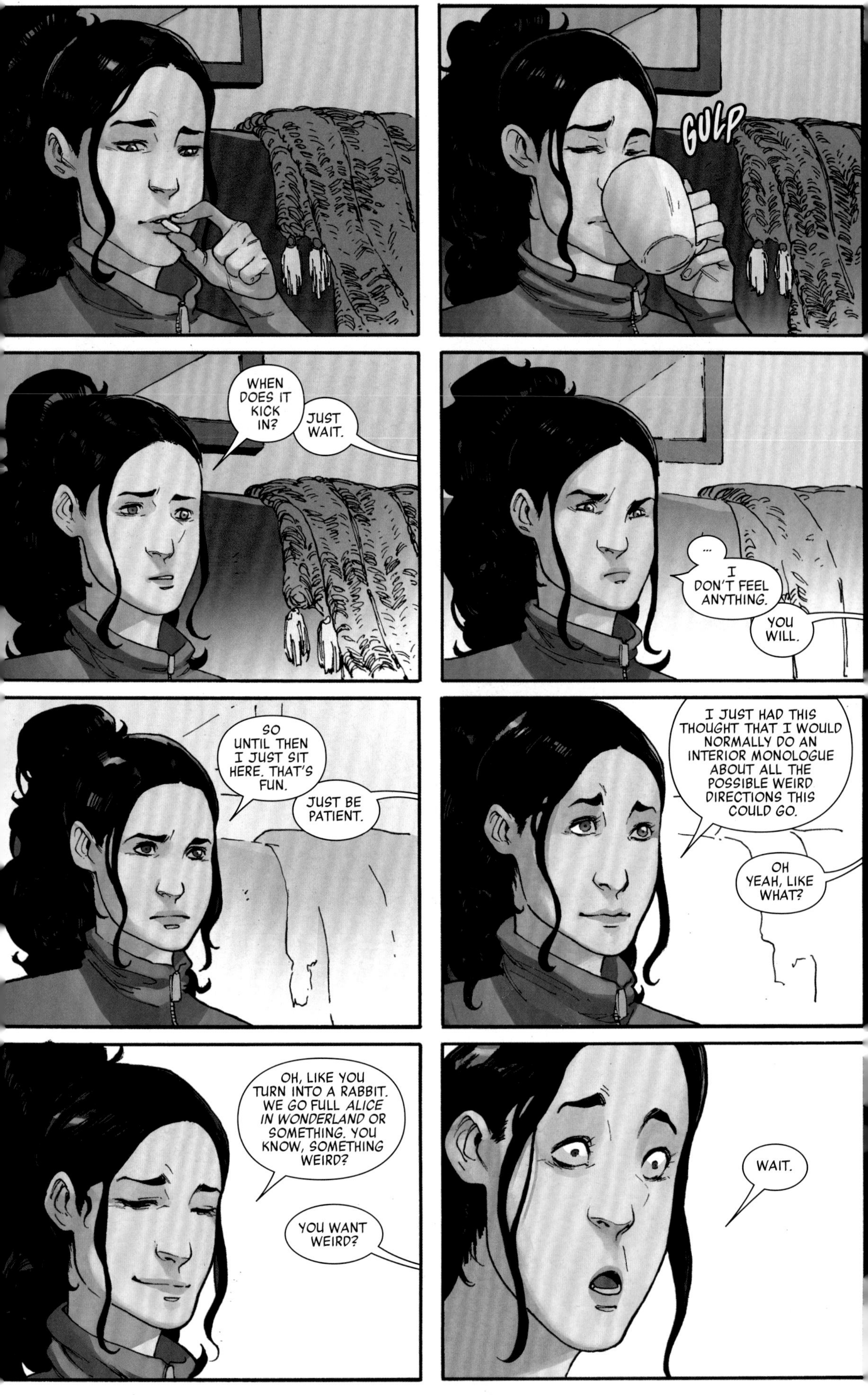
GULP
WHEN DOES IT KICK IN?
JUST WAIT.
...I DON'T FEEL ANYTHING.
YOU WILL.
SO UNTIL THEN I JUST SIT HERE. THAT'S FUN.
JUST BE PATIENT.
I JUST HAD THIS THOUGHT THAT I WOULD NORMALLY DO AN INTERIOR MONOLOGUE ABOUT ALL THE POSSIBLE WEIRD DIRECTIONS THIS COULD GO.
OH YEAH, LIKE WHAT?
OH, LIKE YOU TURN INTO A RABBIT. WE GO FULL *ALICE IN WONDERLAND* OR SOMETHING. YOU KNOW, SOMETHING WEIRD?
YOU WANT WEIRD?
WAIT.

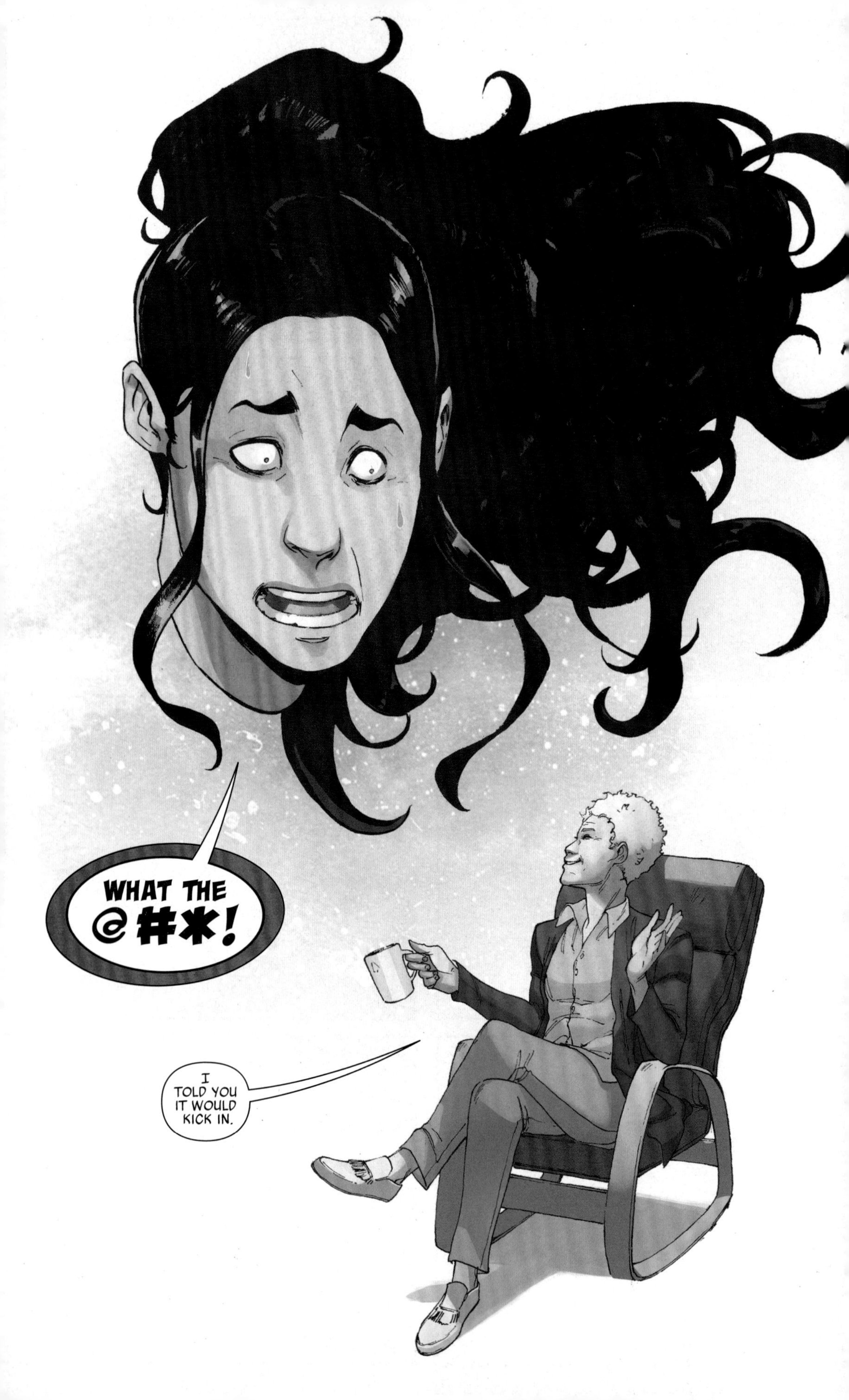
WHAT THE @#*!
I TOLD YOU IT WOULD KICK IN.

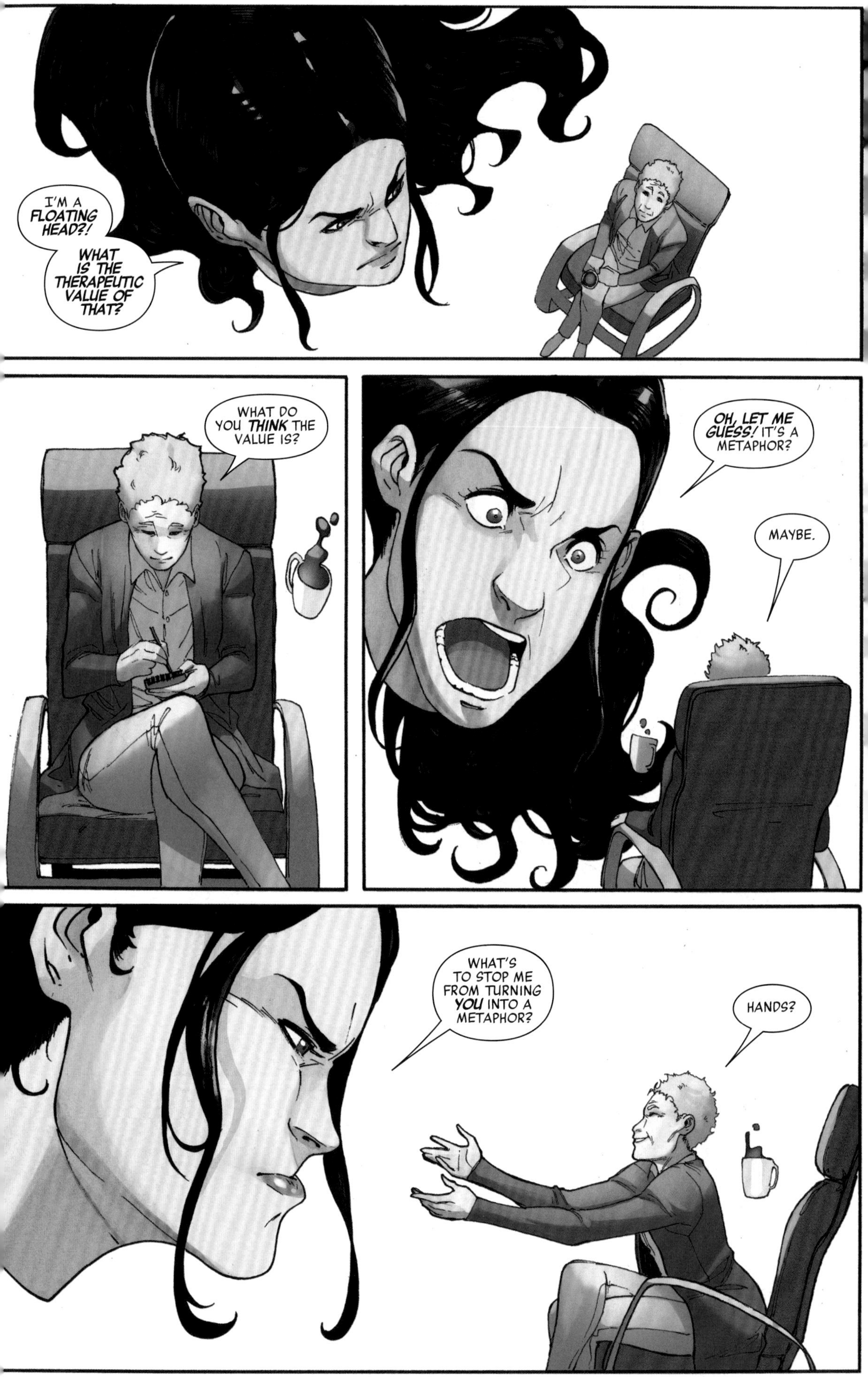
I'M A FLOATING HEAD?!
WHAT IS THE THERAPEUTIC VALUE OF THAT?
WHAT DO YOU THINK THE VALUE IS?
OH, LET ME GUESS! IT'S A METAPHOR?
MAYBE.
WHAT'S TO STOP ME FROM TURNING YOU INTO A METAPHOR?
HANDS?

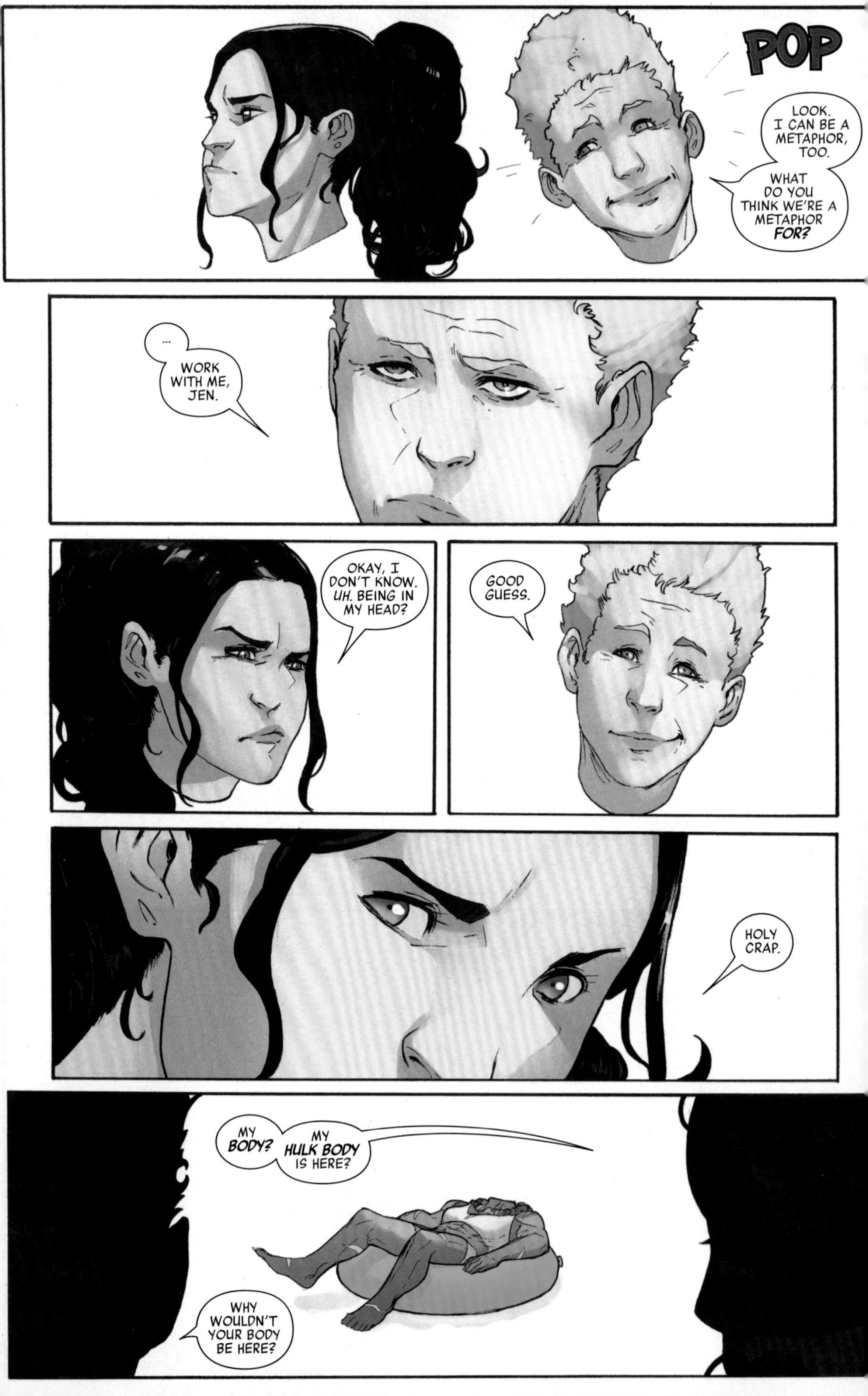
POP
LOOK. I CAN BE A METAPHOR, TOO.
WHAT DO YOU THINK WE'RE A METAPHOR FOR?
...
WORK WITH ME, JEN.
OKAY, I DON'T KNOW. UH. BEING IN MY HEAD?
GOOD GUESS.
HOLY CRAP.
MY BODY?
MY HULK BODY IS HERE?
WHY WOULDN'T YOUR BODY BE HERE?

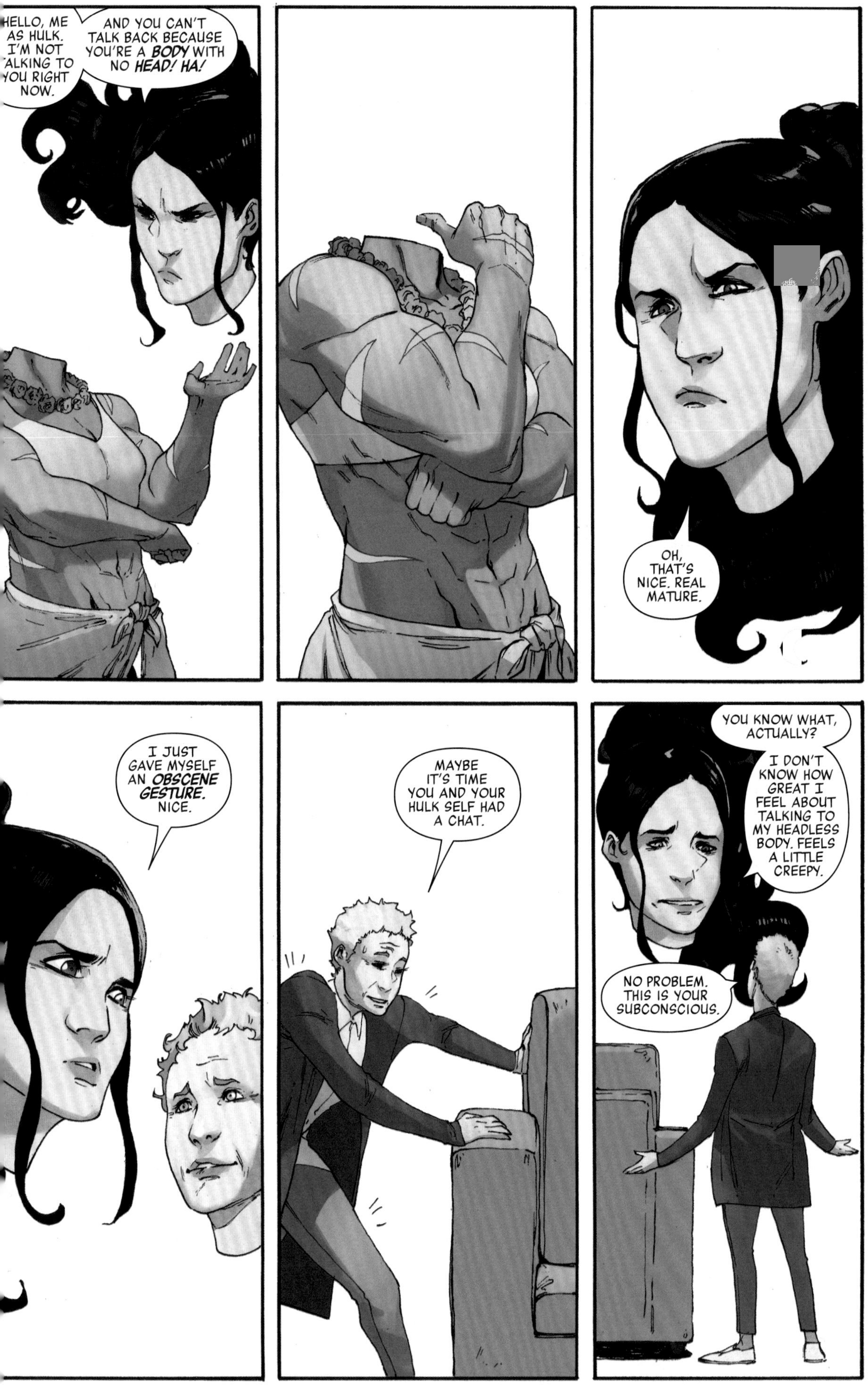
HELLO, ME AS HULK. I'M NOT TALKING TO YOU RIGHT NOW.
AND YOU CAN'T TALK BACK BECAUSE YOU'RE A *BODY* WITH NO *HEAD! HA!*
OH, THAT'S NICE. REAL MATURE.
I JUST GAVE MYSELF AN *OBSCENE GESTURE.* NICE.
MAYBE IT'S TIME YOU AND YOUR HULK SELF HAD A CHAT.
YOU KNOW WHAT, ACTUALLY?
I DON'T KNOW HOW GREAT I FEEL ABOUT TALKING TO MY HEADLESS BODY. FEELS A LITTLE CREEPY.
NO PROBLEM. THIS IS YOUR SUBCONSCIOUS.

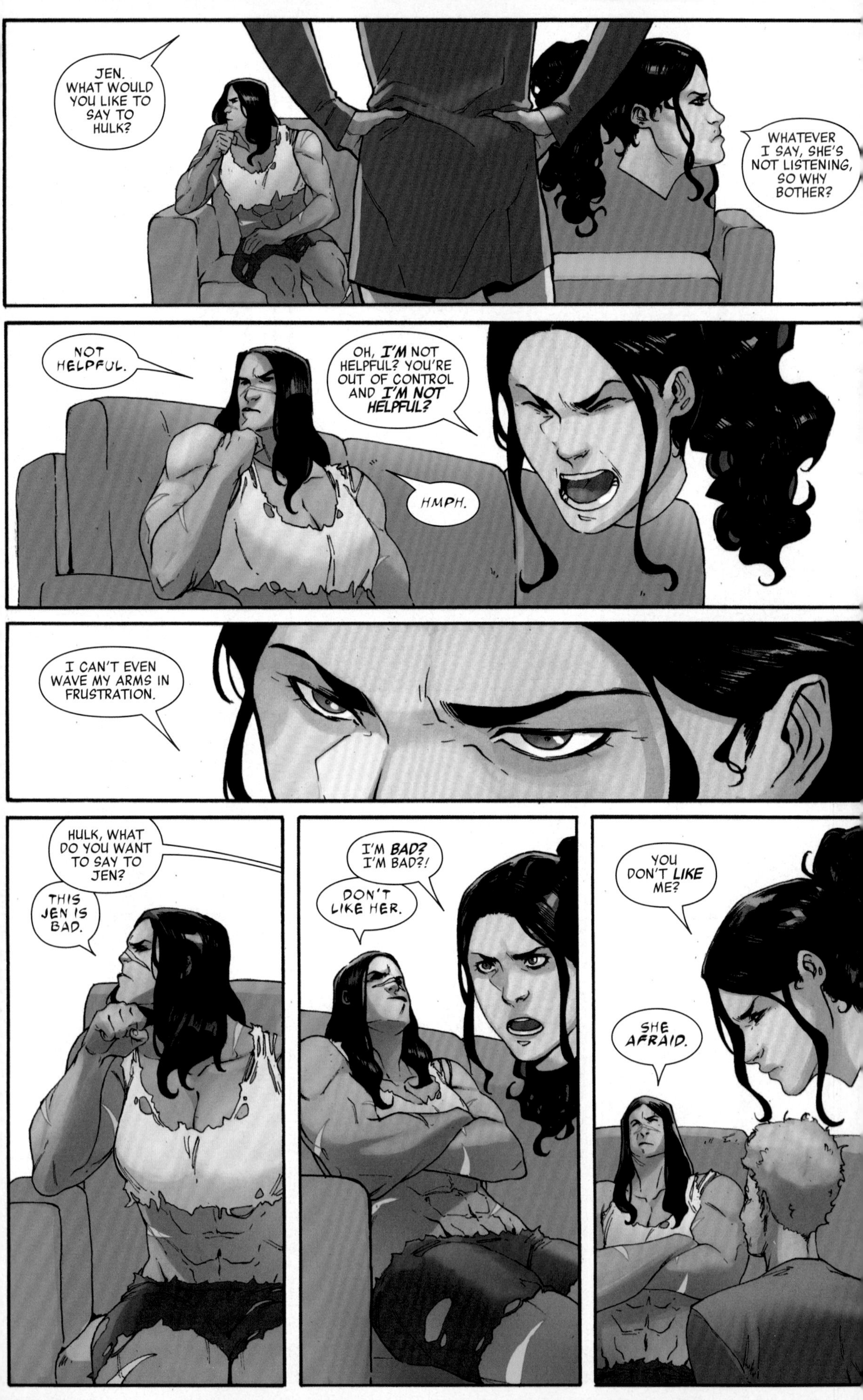
JEN. WHAT WOULD YOU LIKE TO SAY TO HULK?
WHATEVER I SAY, SHE'S NOT LISTENING, SO WHY BOTHER?
NOT HELPFUL.
OH, I'M NOT HELPFUL? YOU'RE OUT OF CONTROL AND I'M NOT HELPFUL?
HMPH.
I CAN'T EVEN WAVE MY ARMS IN FRUSTRATION.
HULK, WHAT DO YOU WANT TO SAY TO JEN?
THIS JEN IS BAD.
DON'T LIKE HER.
I'M BAD? I'M BAD?!
YOU DON'T LIKE ME?
SHE AFRAID.

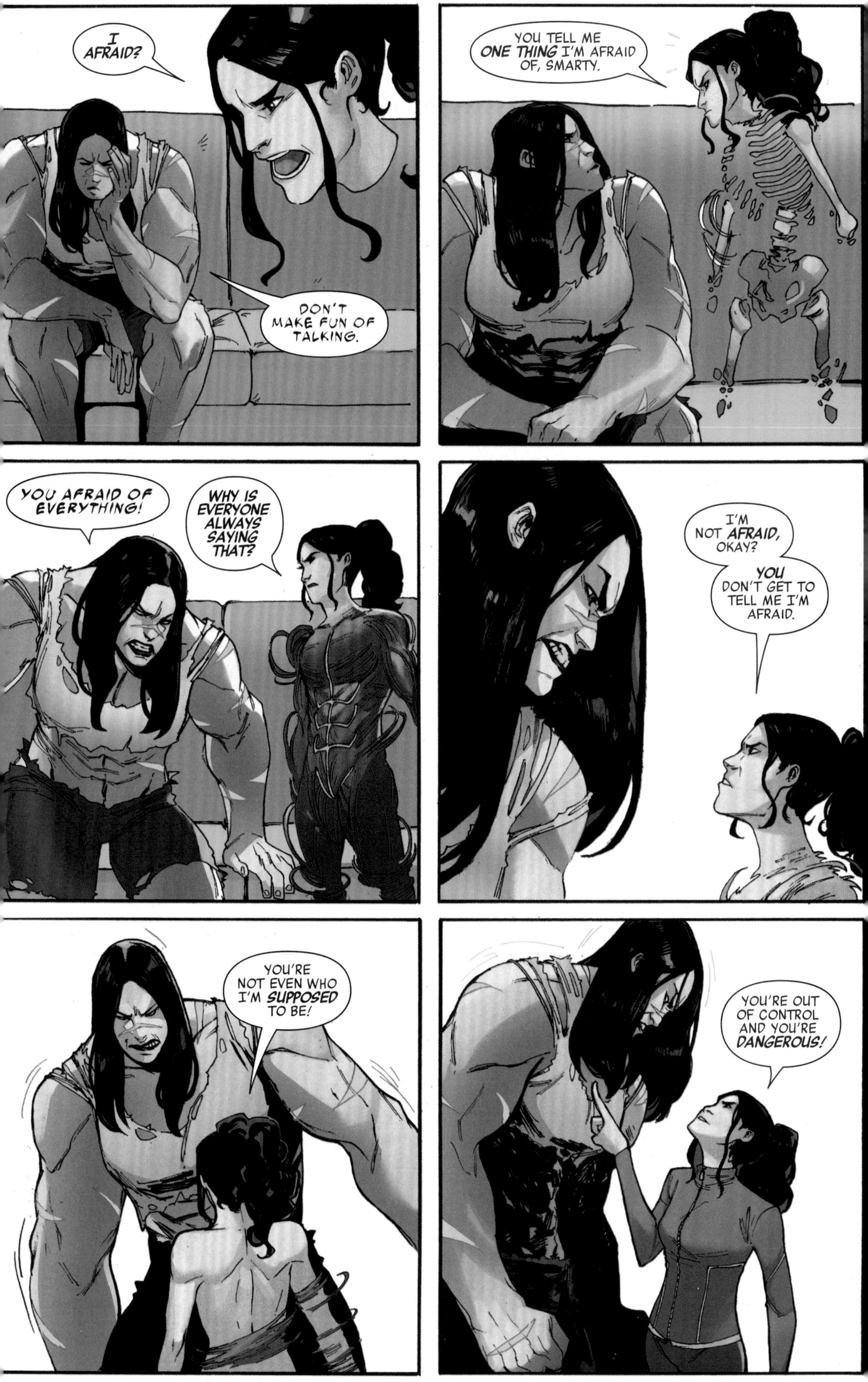
I AFRAID?
DON'T MAKE FUN OF TALKING.
YOU TELL ME ONE THING I'M AFRAID OF, SMARTY.
YOU AFRAID OF EVERYTHING!
WHY IS EVERYONE ALWAYS SAYING THAT?
I'M NOT AFRAID, OKAY?
YOU DON'T GET TO TELL ME I'M AFRAID.
YOU'RE NOT EVEN WHO I'M SUPPOSED TO BE!
YOU'RE OUT OF CONTROL AND YOU'RE DANGEROUS!

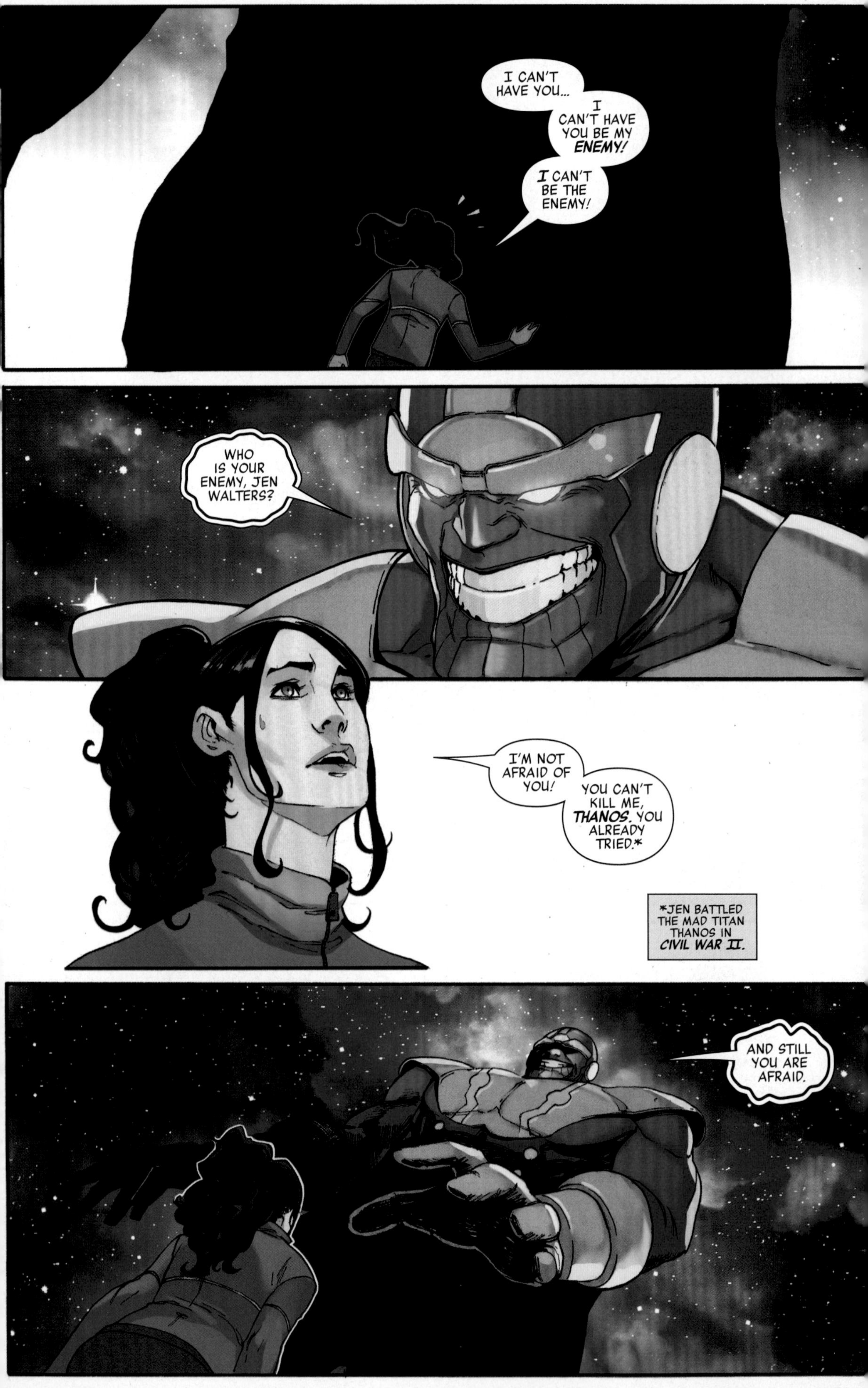
I CAN'T HAVE YOU...
I CAN'T HAVE YOU BE MY **ENEMY!**
I CAN'T BE THE ENEMY!
WHO IS YOUR ENEMY, JEN WALTERS?
I'M NOT AFRAID OF YOU!
YOU CAN'T KILL ME, ***THANOS.*** YOU ALREADY TRIED.*
*JEN BATTLED THE MAD TITAN THANOS IN ***CIVIL WAR II.***
AND STILL YOU ARE AFRAID.

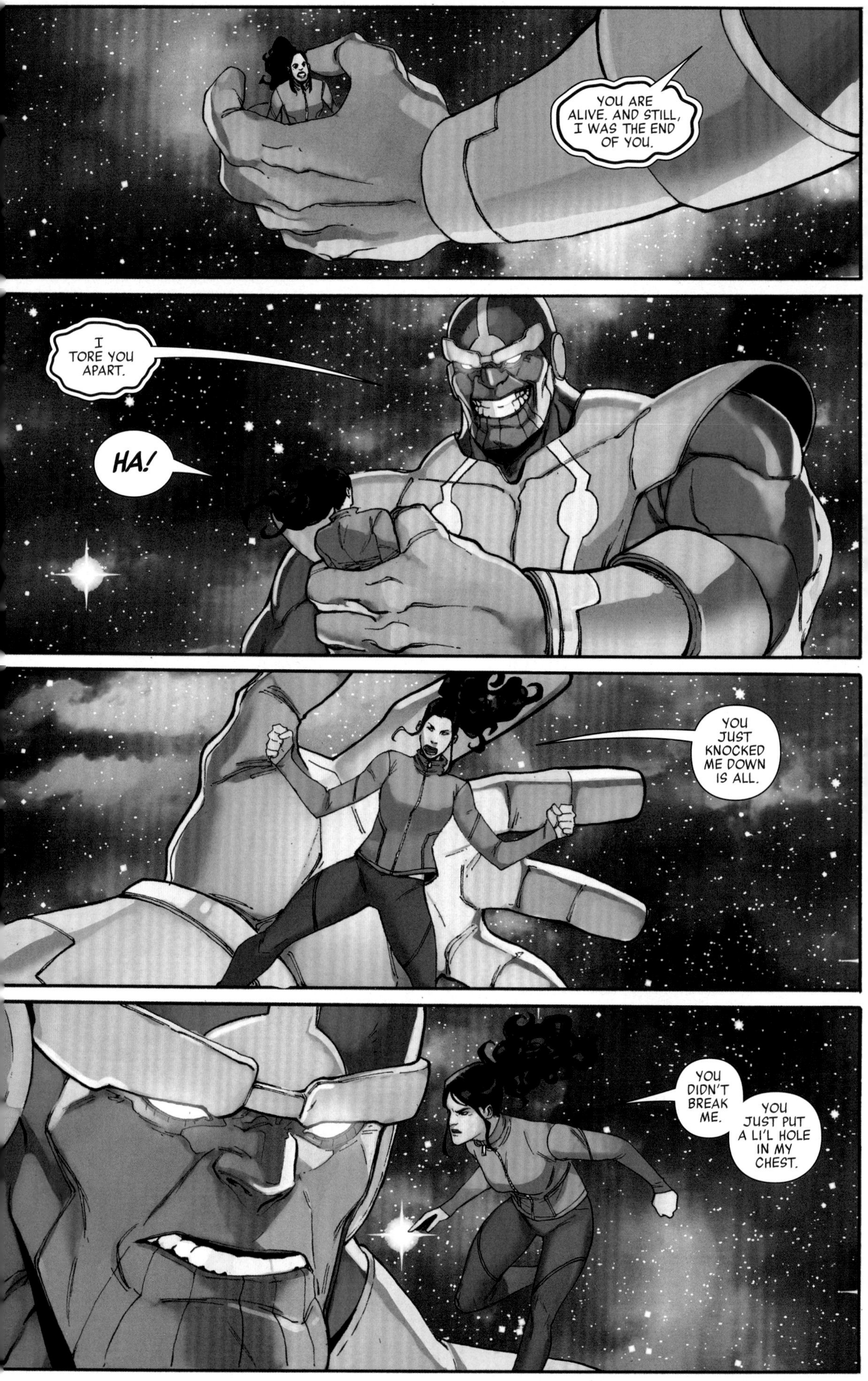
YOU ARE ALIVE. AND STILL, I WAS THE END OF YOU.
I TORE YOU APART.
HA!
YOU JUST KNOCKED ME DOWN IS ALL.
YOU DIDN'T BREAK ME.
YOU JUST PUT A LI'L HOLE IN MY CHEST.

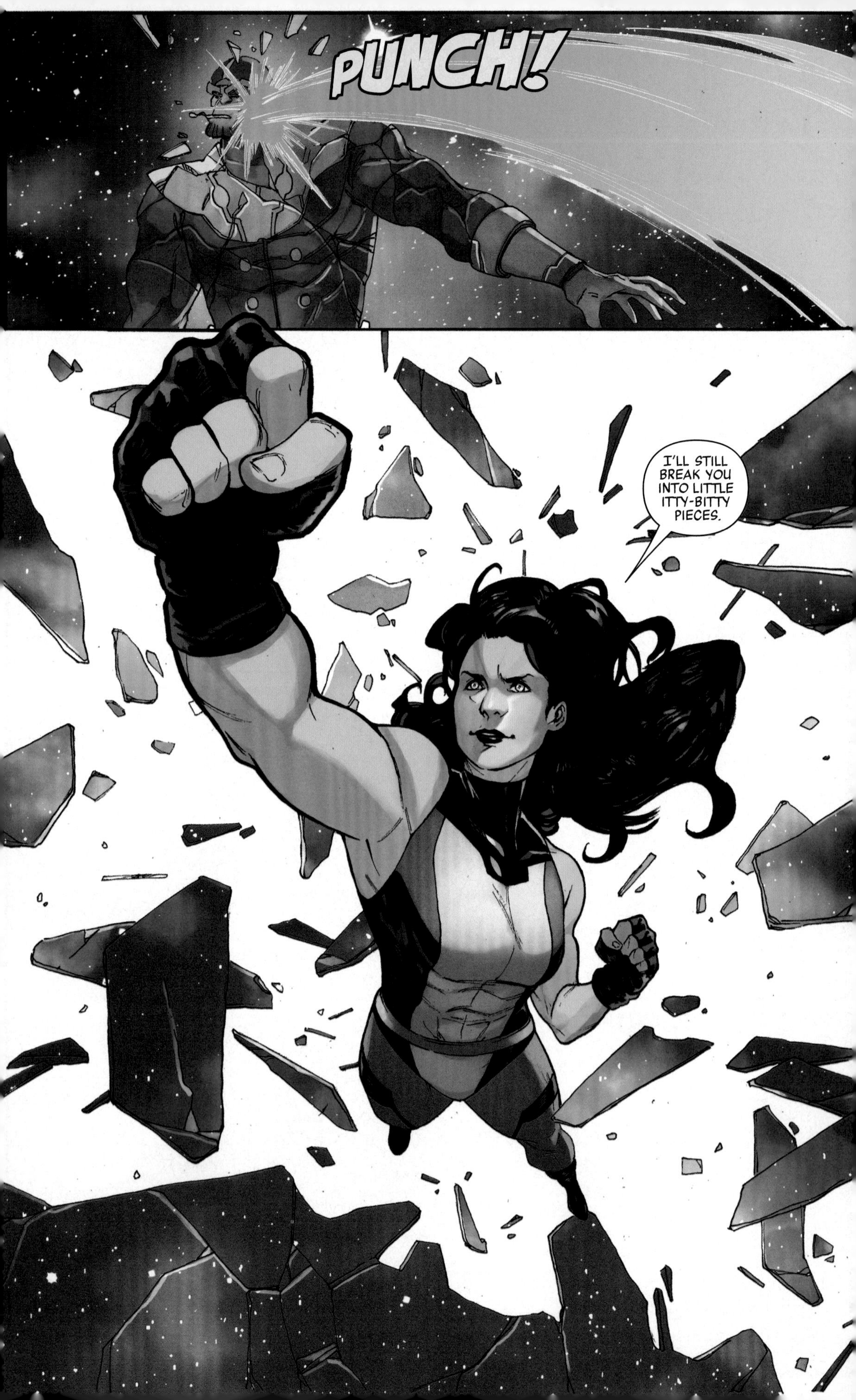
PUNCH!
I'LL STILL BREAK YOU INTO LITTLE ITTY-BITTY PIECES.

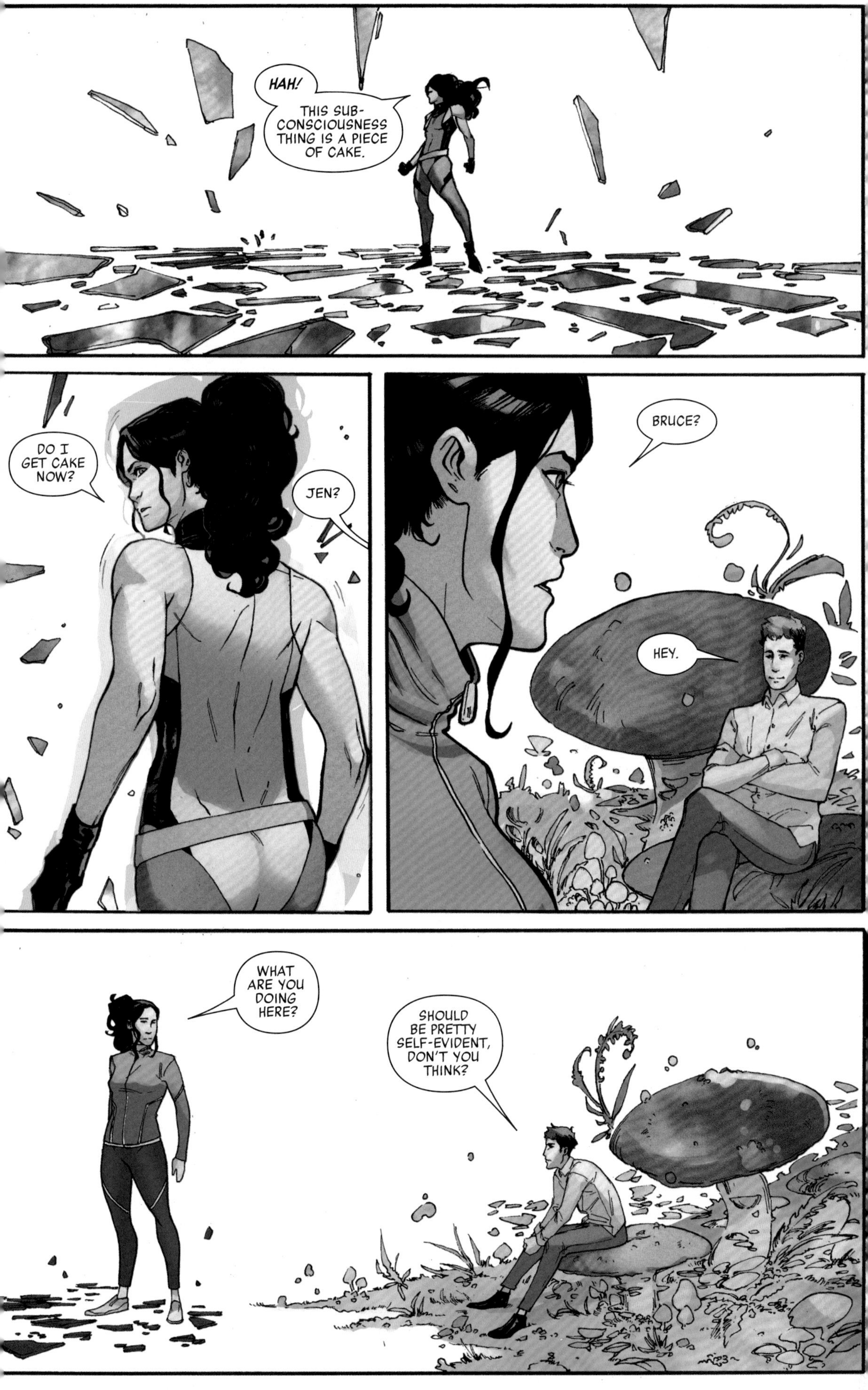
HAH!
THIS SUB-CONSCIOUSNESS THING IS A PIECE OF CAKE.
DO I GET CAKE NOW?
JEN?
BRUCE?
HEY.
WHAT ARE YOU DOING HERE?
SHOULD BE PRETTY SELF-EVIDENT, DON'T YOU THINK?

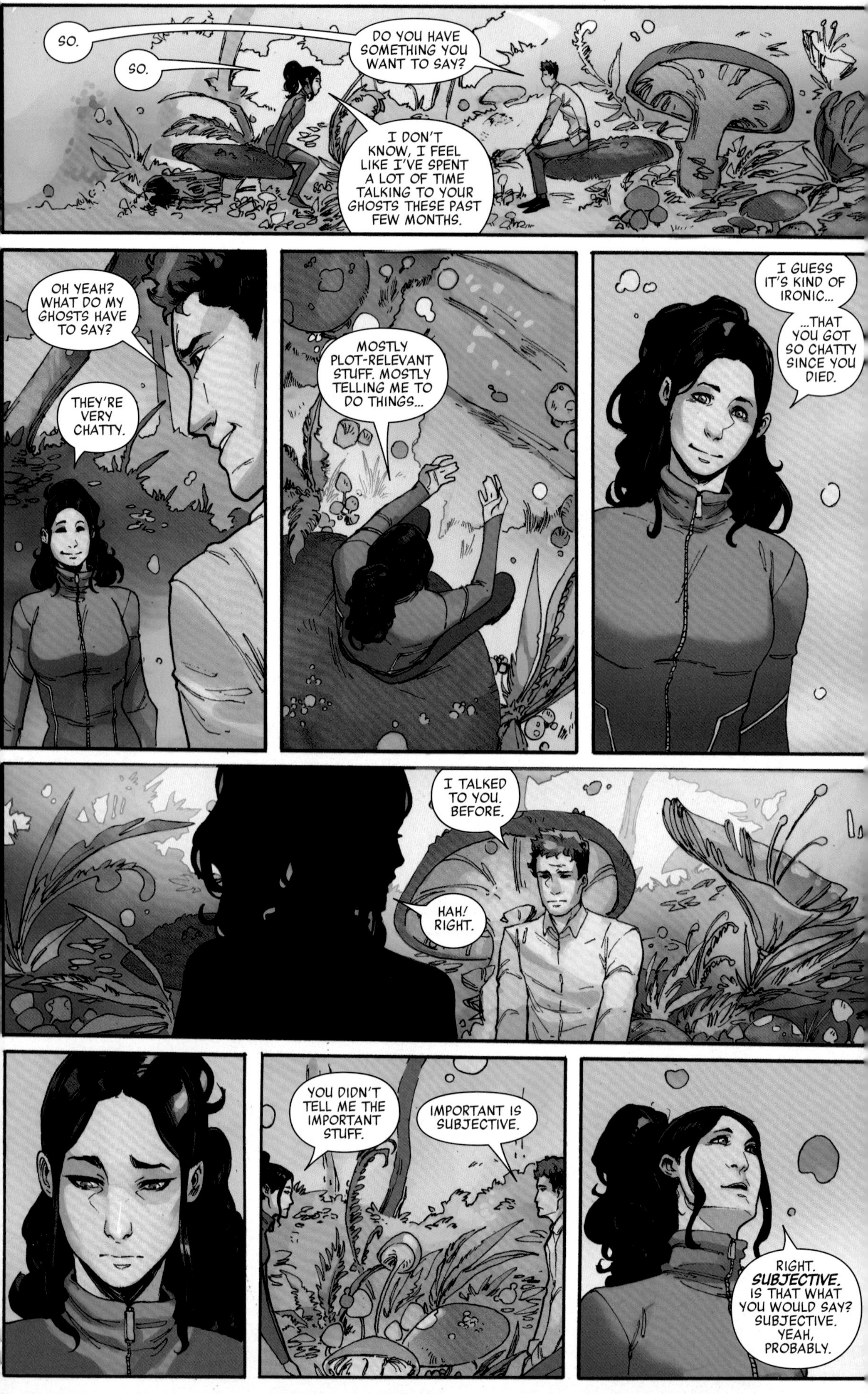
SO.
SO.
DO YOU HAVE SOMETHING YOU WANT TO SAY?
I DON'T KNOW, I FEEL LIKE I'VE SPENT A LOT OF TIME TALKING TO YOUR GHOSTS THESE PAST FEW MONTHS.
OH YEAH? WHAT DO MY GHOSTS HAVE TO SAY?
THEY'RE VERY CHATTY.
MOSTLY PLOT-RELEVANT STUFF. MOSTLY TELLING ME TO DO THINGS...
I GUESS IT'S KIND OF IRONIC...
...THAT YOU GOT SO CHATTY SINCE YOU DIED.
I TALKED TO YOU. BEFORE.
HAH! RIGHT.
YOU DIDN'T TELL ME THE IMPORTANT STUFF.
IMPORTANT IS SUBJECTIVE.
RIGHT. SUBJECTIVE. IS THAT WHAT YOU WOULD SAY? SUBJECTIVE. YEAH, PROBABLY.

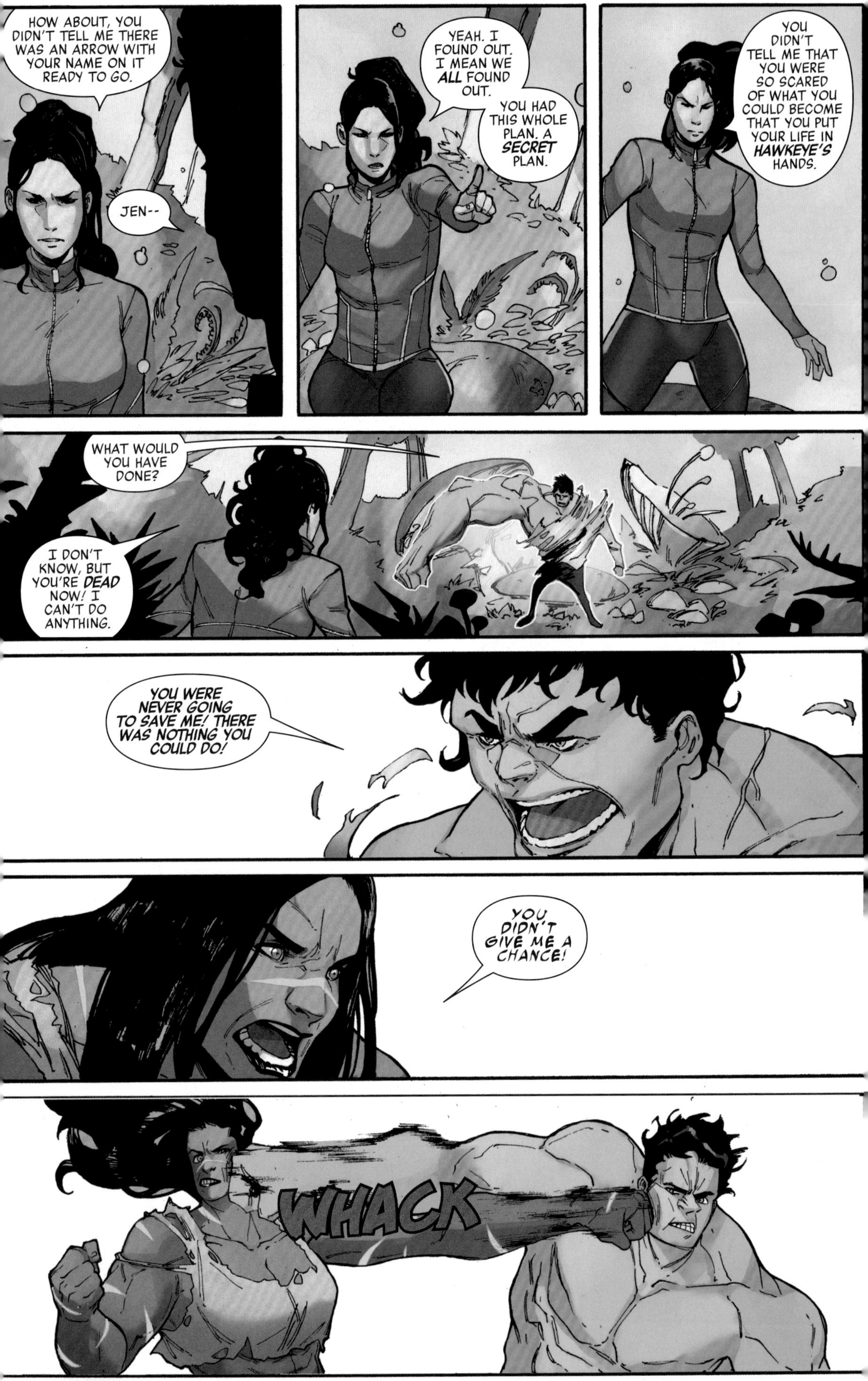
HOW ABOUT, YOU DIDN'T TELL ME THERE WAS AN ARROW WITH YOUR NAME ON IT READY TO GO.
JEN--
YEAH. I FOUND OUT. I MEAN WE ALL FOUND OUT.
YOU HAD THIS WHOLE PLAN. A SECRET PLAN.
YOU DIDN'T TELL ME THAT YOU WERE SO SCARED OF WHAT YOU COULD BECOME THAT YOU PUT YOUR LIFE IN HAWKEYE'S HANDS.
WHAT WOULD YOU HAVE DONE?
I DON'T KNOW, BUT YOU'RE DEAD NOW! I CAN'T DO ANYTHING.
YOU WERE NEVER GOING TO SAVE ME! THERE WAS NOTHING YOU COULD DO!
YOU DIDN'T GIVE ME A CHANCE!
WHACK

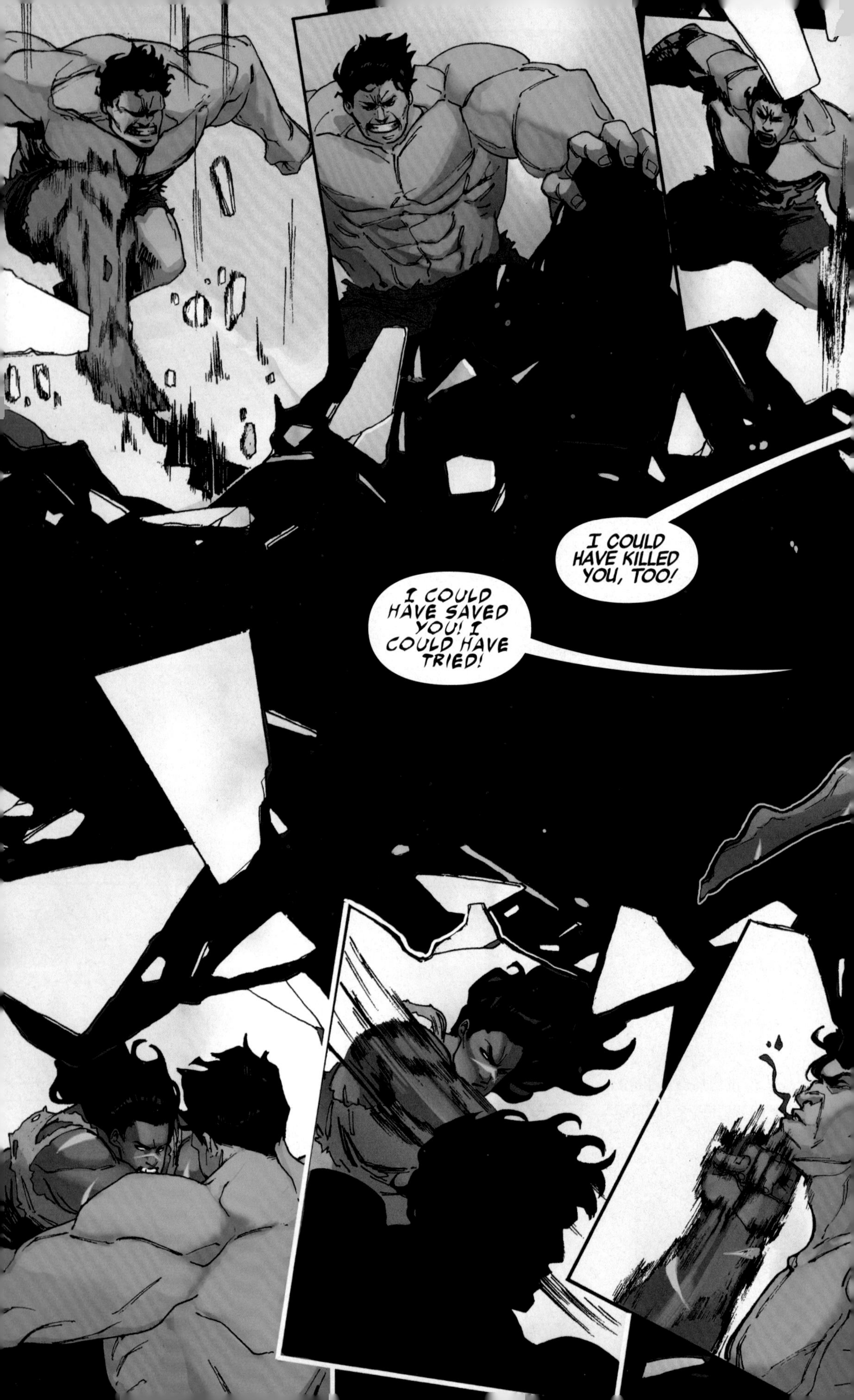
I COULD HAVE SAVED YOU! I COULD HAVE TRIED!
I COULD HAVE KILLED YOU, TOO!

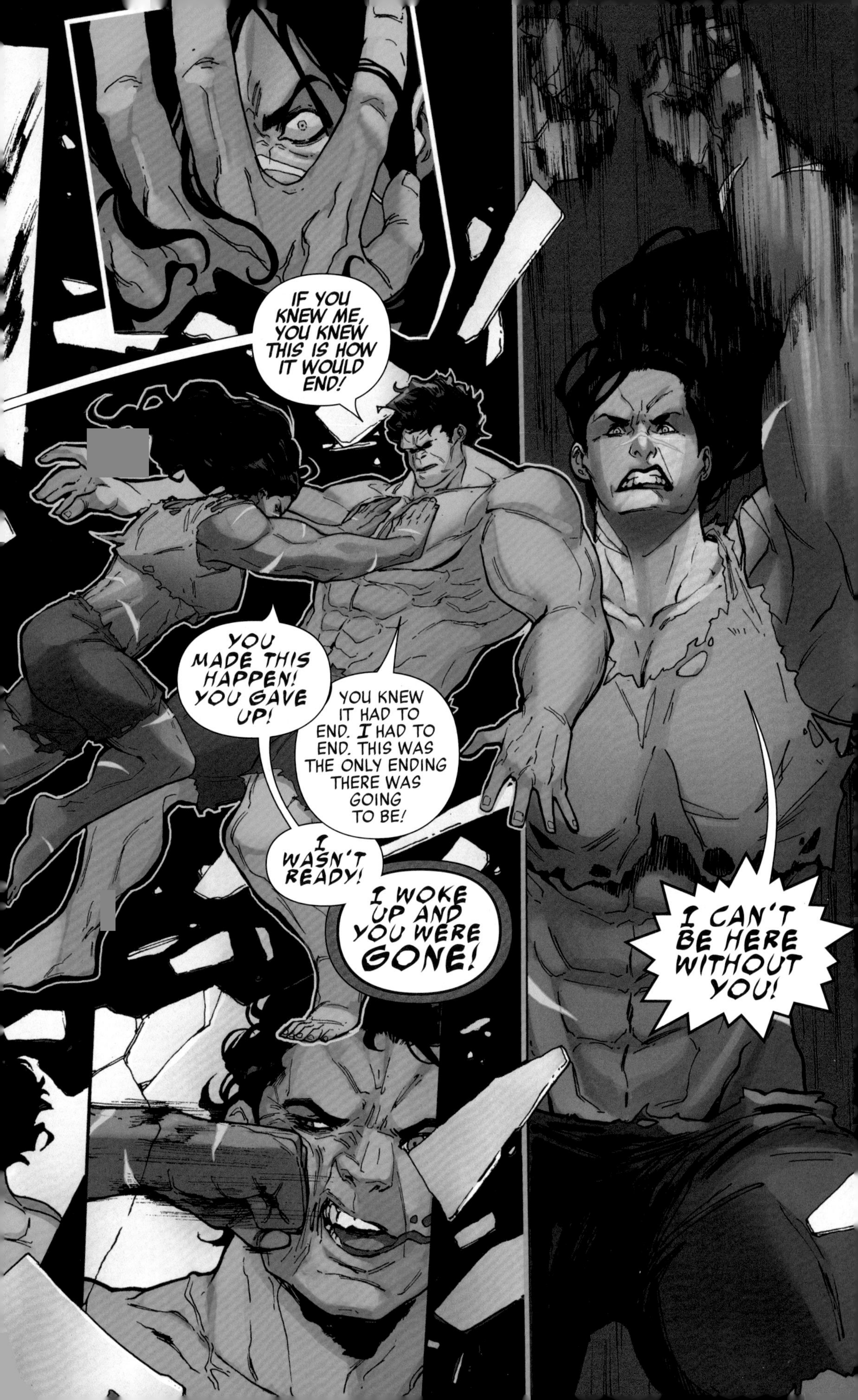
IF YOU KNEW ME, YOU KNEW THIS IS HOW IT WOULD END!
YOU MADE THIS HAPPEN! YOU GAVE UP!
YOU KNEW IT HAD TO END. I HAD TO END. THIS WAS THE ONLY ENDING THERE WAS GOING TO BE!
I WASN'T READY!
I WOKE UP AND YOU WERE GONE!
I CAN'T BE HERE WITHOUT YOU!

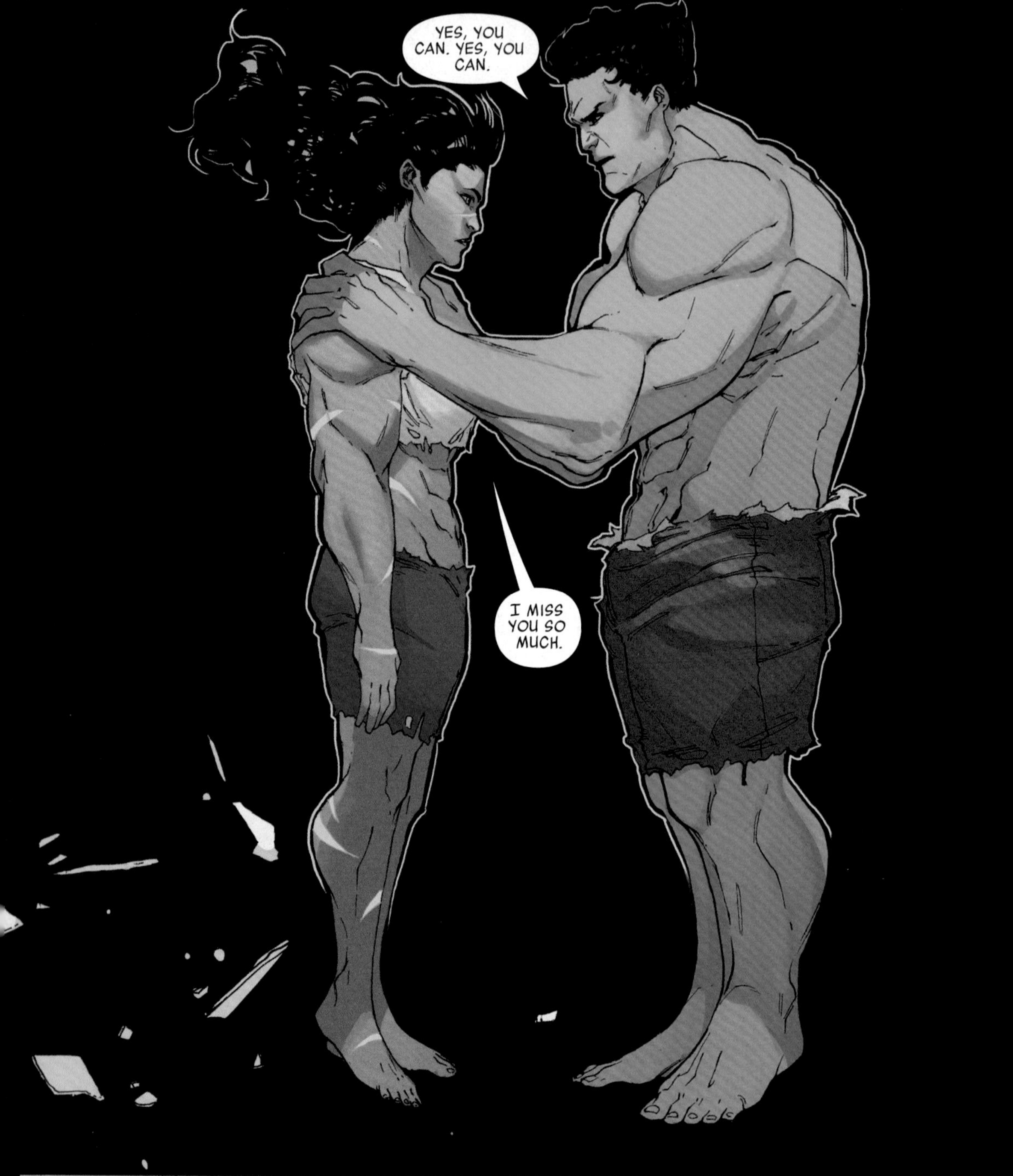
YES, YOU CAN. YES, YOU CAN.
I MISS YOU SO MUCH.

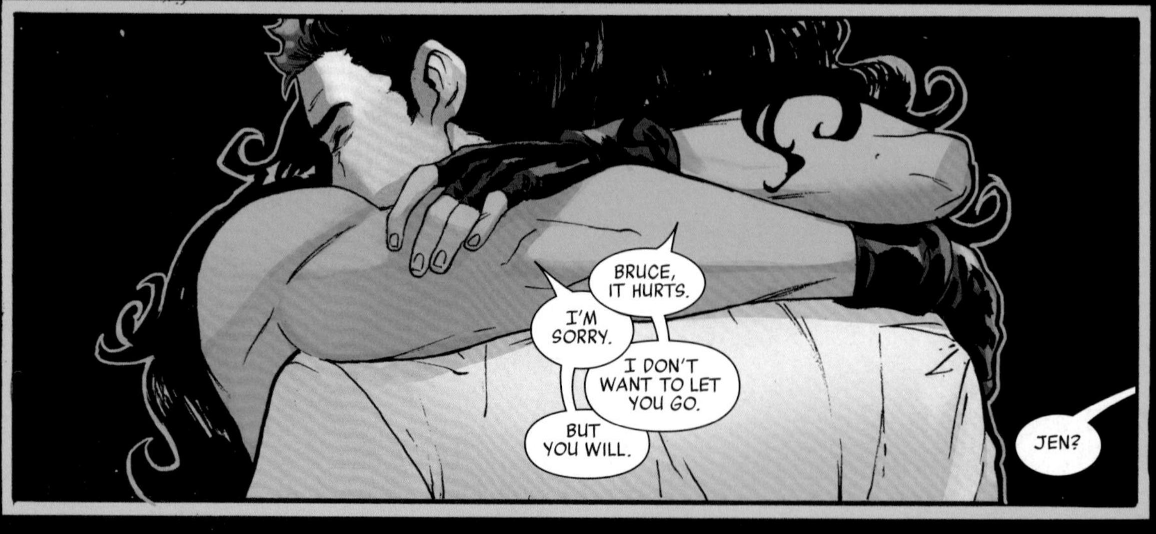
BRUCE, IT HURTS.
I'M SORRY.
I DON'T WANT TO LET YOU GO.
BUT YOU WILL.
JEN?

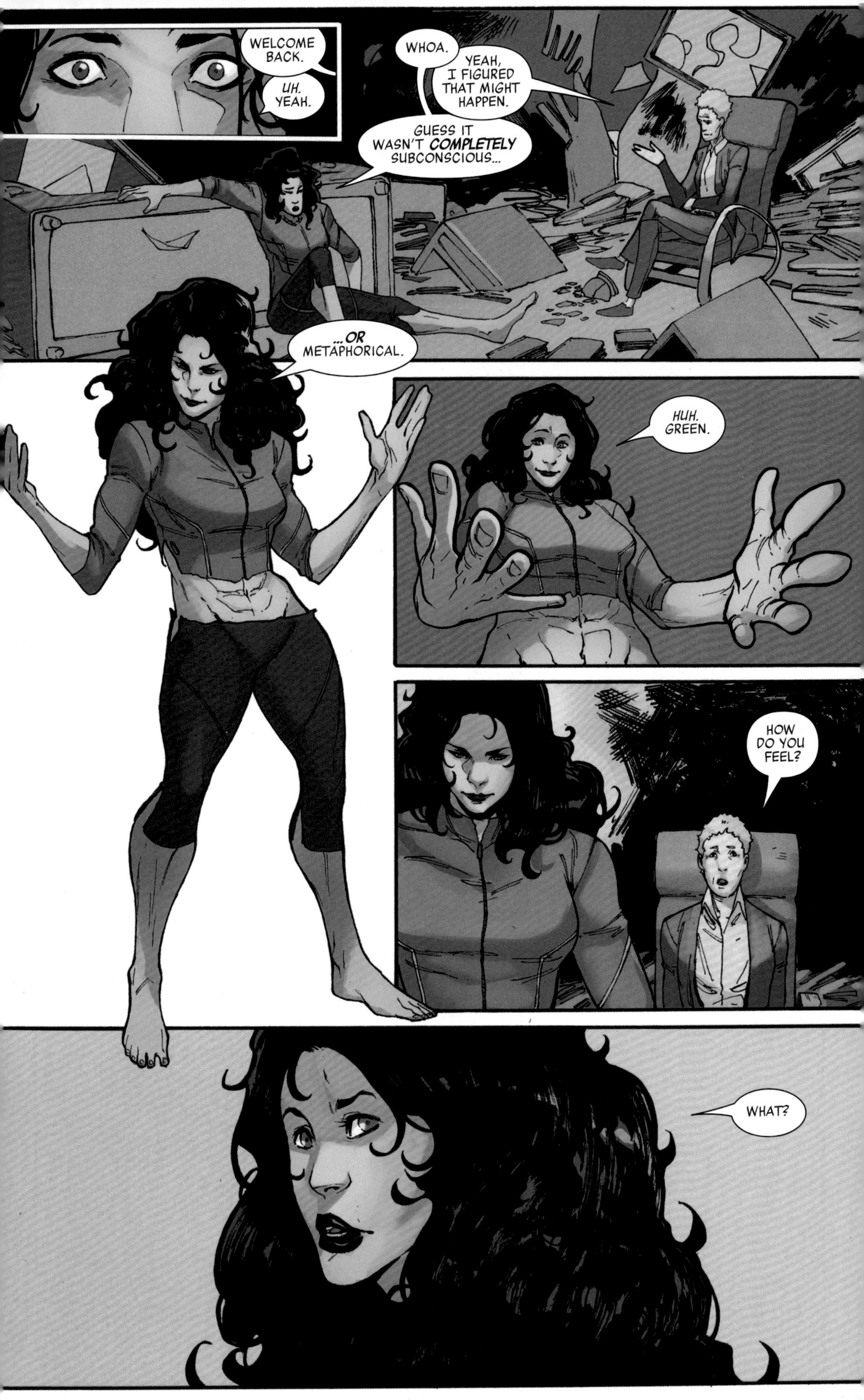
WELCOME BACK.
UH. YEAH.
WHOA.
YEAH, I FIGURED THAT MIGHT HAPPEN.
GUESS IT WASN'T **COMPLETELY** SUBCONSCIOUS...
...OR METAPHORICAL.
HUH. GREEN.
HOW DO YOU FEEL?
WHAT?

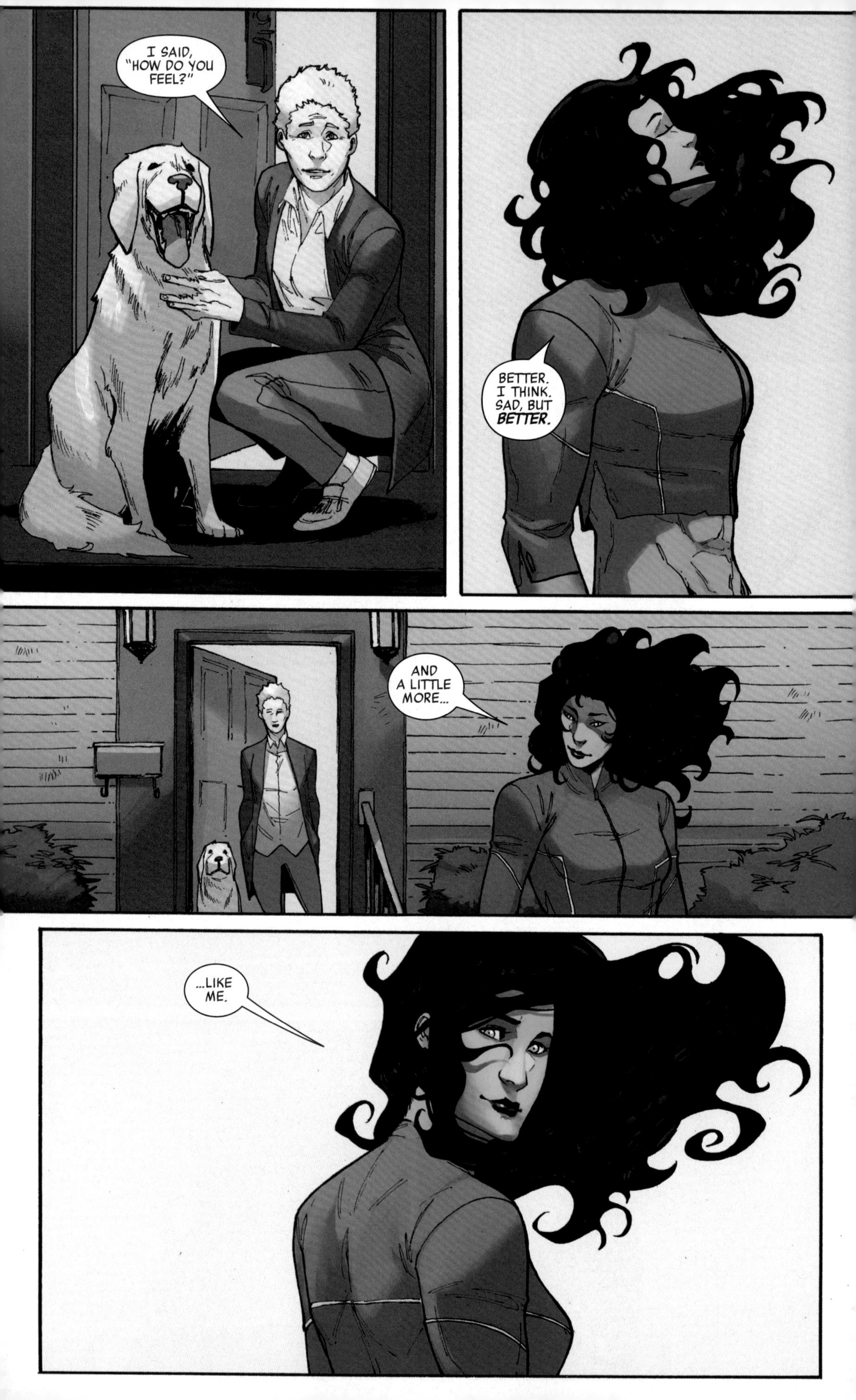
I SAID, "HOW DO YOU FEEL?"
BETTER. I THINK. SAD, BUT BETTER.
AND A LITTLE MORE...
...LIKE ME.

#159 VARIANT BY
BILQUIS EVELY
& **MAT LOPES**

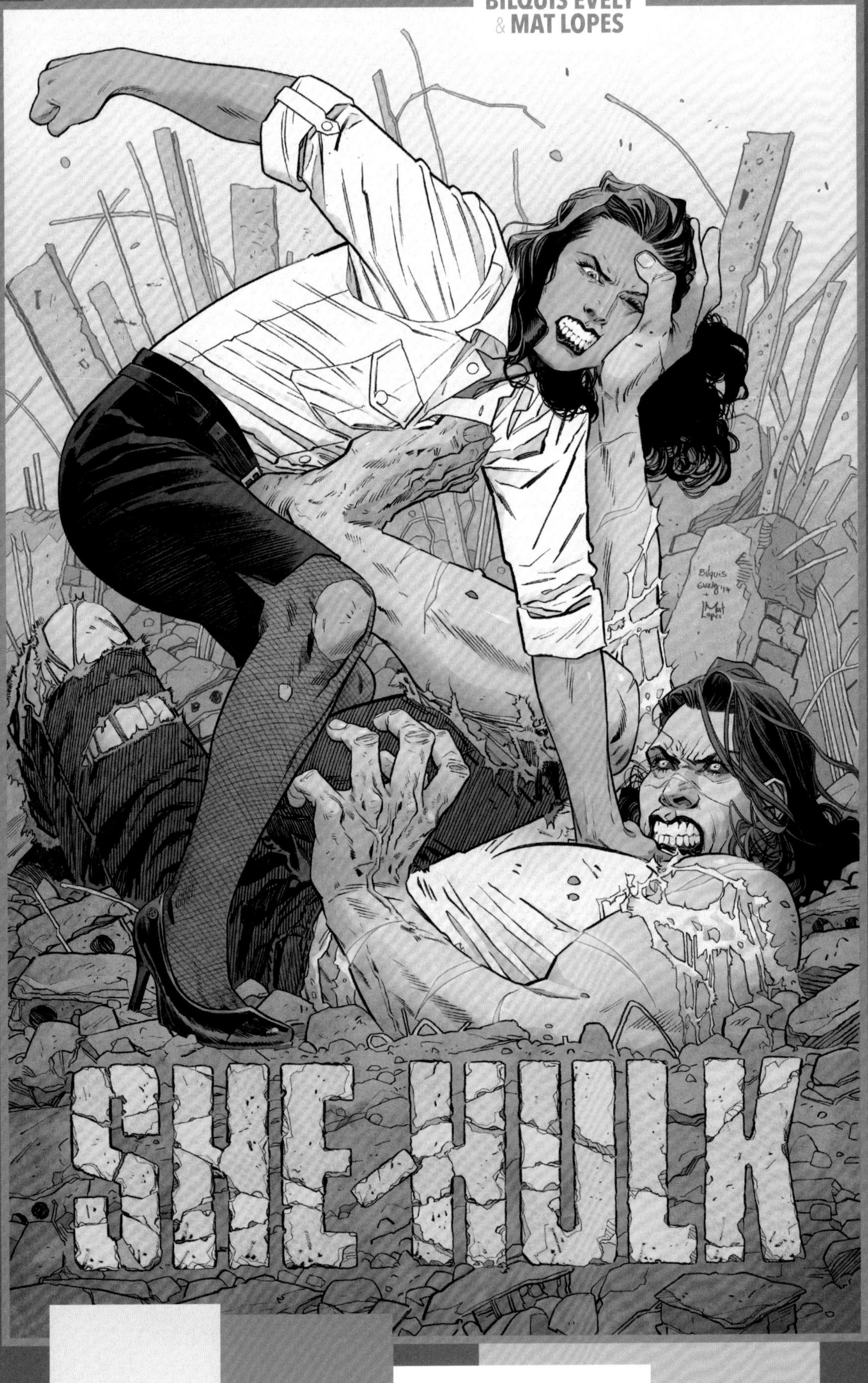
SHE-HULK

163

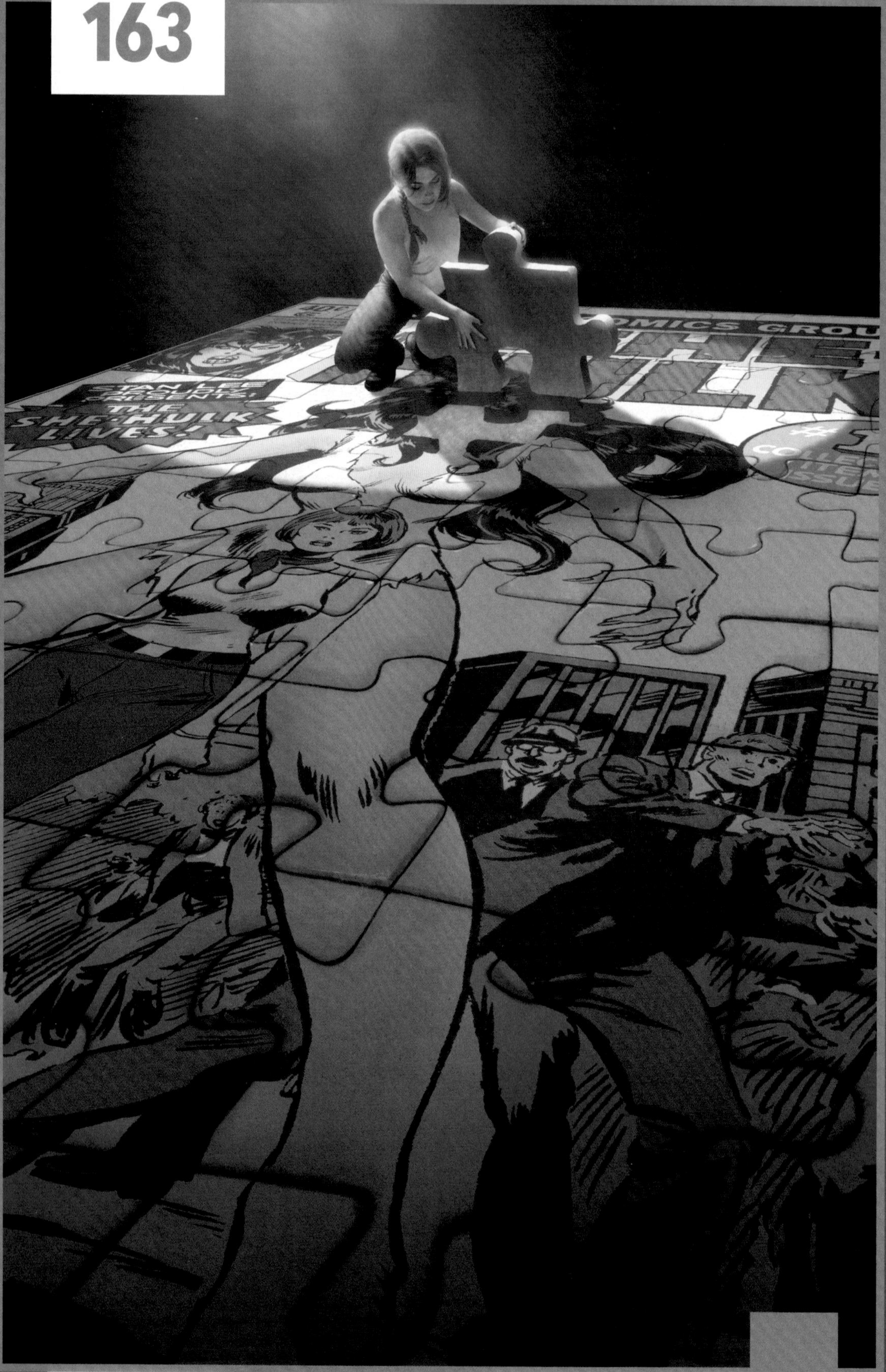
STAN LEE
PRESENTS:
THE SHE-HULK LIVES!

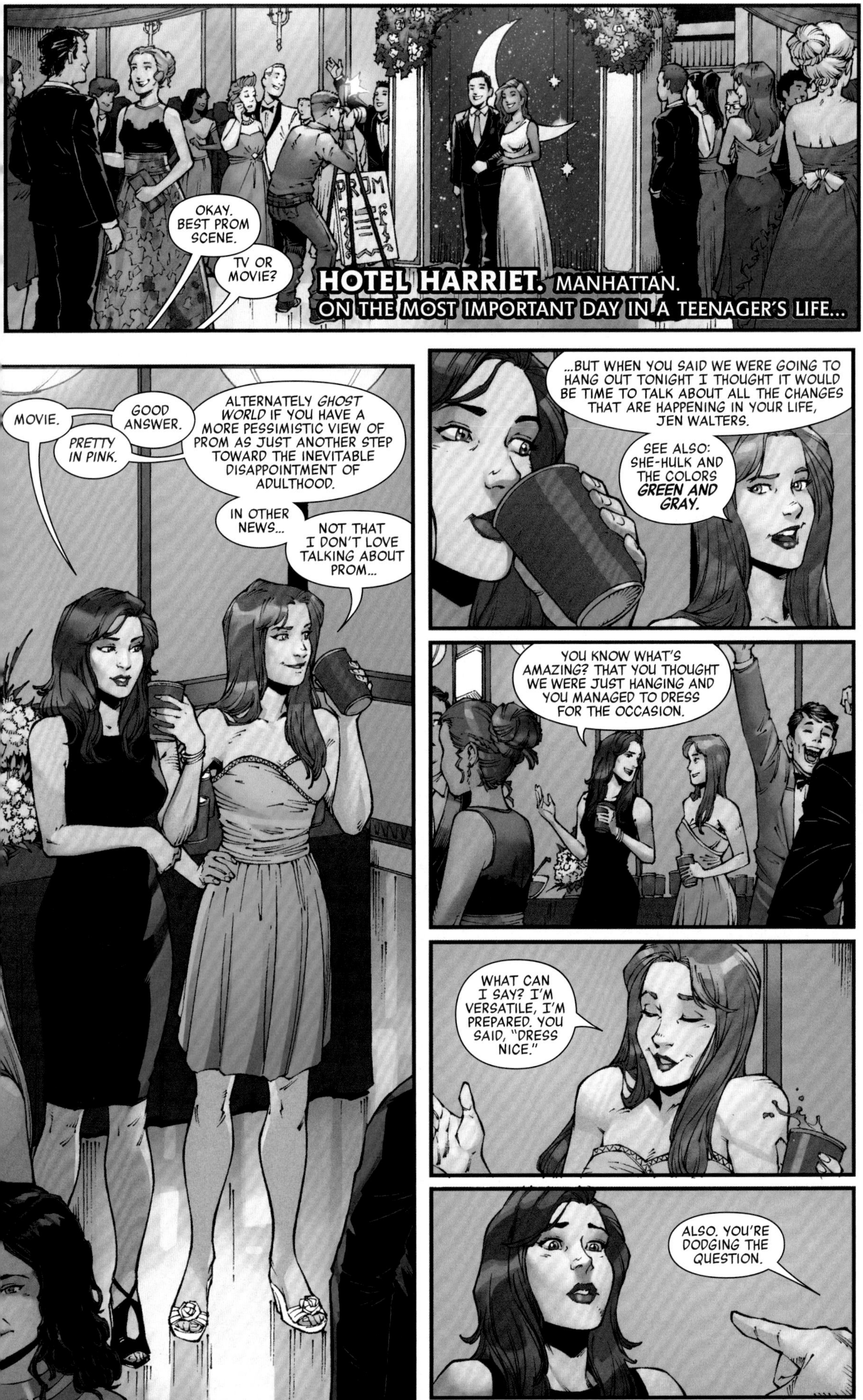
OKAY. BEST PROM SCENE.
TV OR MOVIE?
HOTEL HARRIET. MANHATTAN.
ON THE MOST IMPORTANT DAY IN A TEENAGER'S LIFE...
MOVIE.
GOOD ANSWER.
PRETTY IN PINK.
ALTERNATELY GHOST WORLD IF YOU HAVE A MORE PESSIMISTIC VIEW OF PROM AS JUST ANOTHER STEP TOWARD THE INEVITABLE DISAPPOINTMENT OF ADULTHOOD.
IN OTHER NEWS...
NOT THAT I DON'T LOVE TALKING ABOUT PROM...
...BUT WHEN YOU SAID WE WERE GOING TO HANG OUT TONIGHT I THOUGHT IT WOULD BE TIME TO TALK ABOUT ALL THE CHANGES THAT ARE HAPPENING IN YOUR LIFE, JEN WALTERS.
SEE ALSO: SHE-HULK AND THE COLORS GREEN AND GRAY.
YOU KNOW WHAT'S AMAZING? THAT YOU THOUGHT WE WERE JUST HANGING AND YOU MANAGED TO DRESS FOR THE OCCASION.
WHAT CAN I SAY? I'M VERSATILE, I'M PREPARED. YOU SAID, "DRESS NICE."
ALSO. YOU'RE DODGING THE QUESTION.

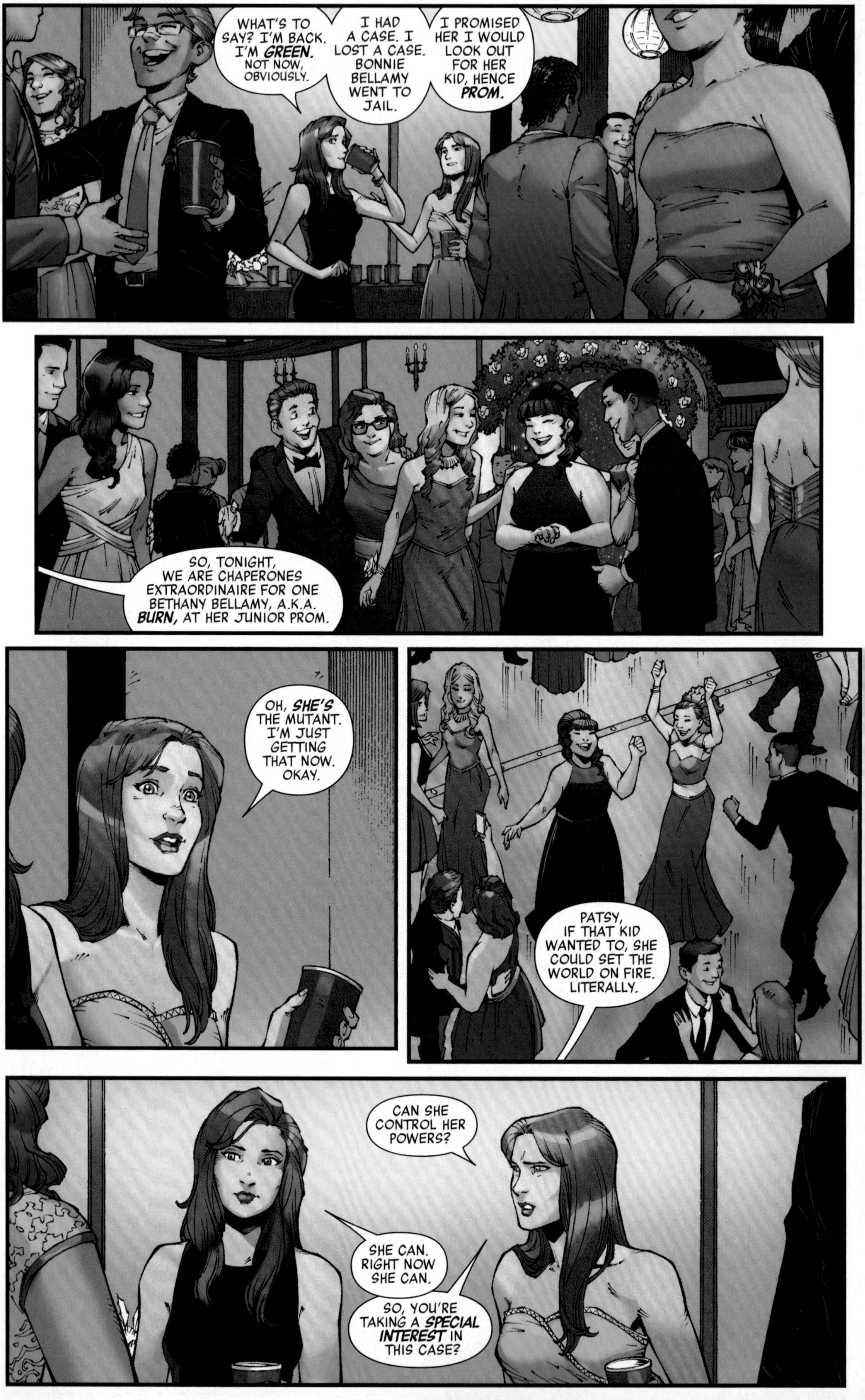

WHAT'S TO SAY? I'M BACK. I'M GREEN. NOT NOW, OBVIOUSLY.
I HAD A CASE. I LOST A CASE. BONNIE BELLAMY WENT TO JAIL.
I PROMISED HER I WOULD LOOK OUT FOR HER KID, HENCE PROM.
SO, TONIGHT, WE ARE CHAPERONES EXTRAORDINAIRE FOR ONE BETHANY BELLAMY, A.K.A. BURN, AT HER JUNIOR PROM.
OH, SHE'S THE MUTANT. I'M JUST GETTING THAT NOW. OKAY.
PATSY, IF THAT KID WANTED TO, SHE COULD SET THE WORLD ON FIRE. LITERALLY.
CAN SHE CONTROL HER POWERS?
SHE CAN. RIGHT NOW SHE CAN.
SO, YOU'RE TAKING A SPECIAL INTEREST IN THIS CASE?

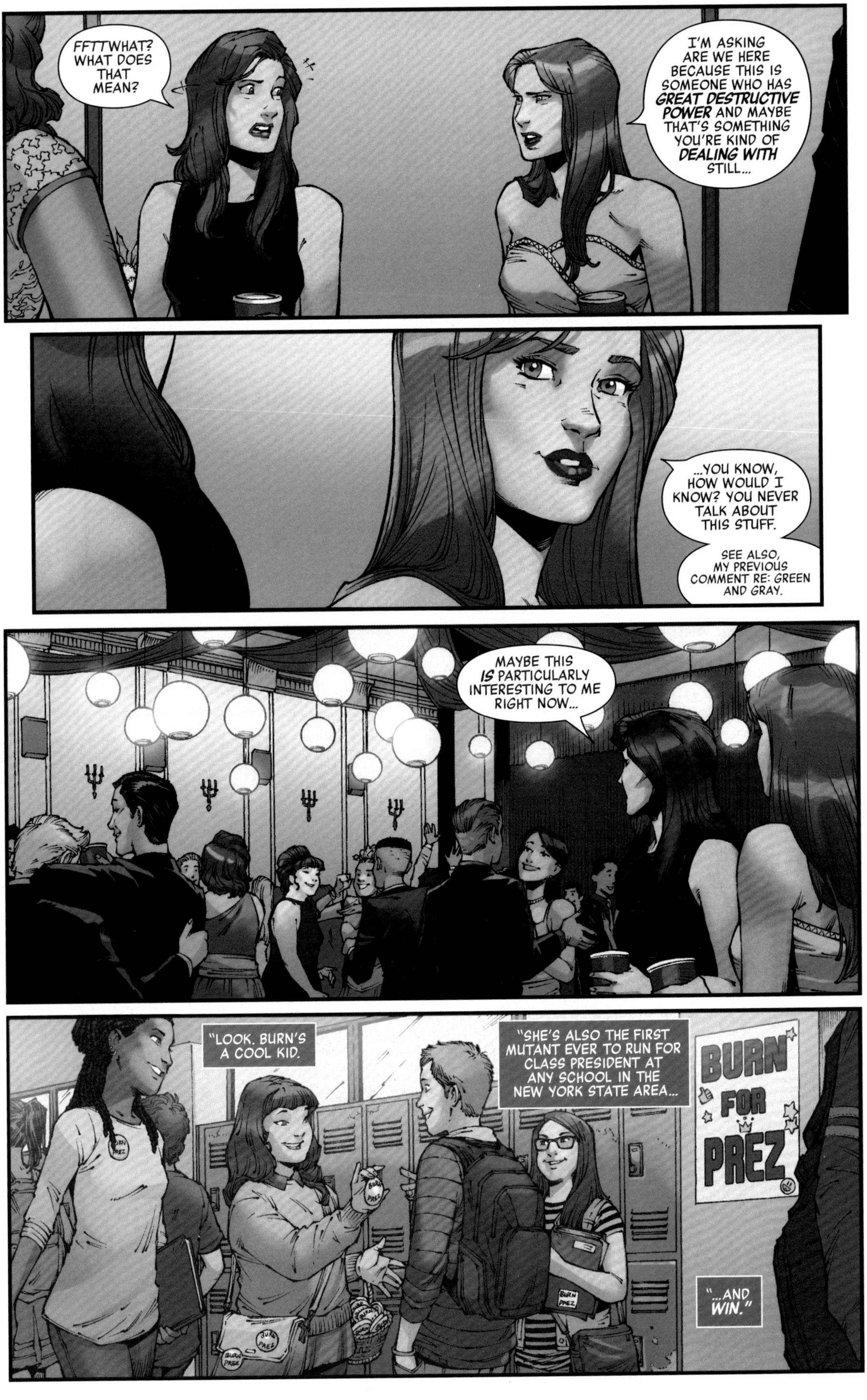
FFTTWHAT? WHAT DOES THAT MEAN?
I'M ASKING ARE WE HERE BECAUSE THIS IS SOMEONE WHO HAS **GREAT DESTRUCTIVE POWER** AND MAYBE THAT'S SOMETHING YOU'RE KIND OF **DEALING WITH** STILL...
...YOU KNOW, HOW WOULD I KNOW? YOU NEVER TALK ABOUT THIS STUFF.
SEE ALSO, MY PREVIOUS COMMENT RE: GREEN AND GRAY.
MAYBE THIS ***IS*** PARTICULARLY INTERESTING TO ME RIGHT NOW...
"LOOK. BURN'S A COOL KID.
"SHE'S ALSO THE FIRST MUTANT EVER TO RUN FOR CLASS PRESIDENT AT ANY SCHOOL IN THE NEW YORK STATE AREA...
BURN FOR PREZ
"...AND ***WIN.***"

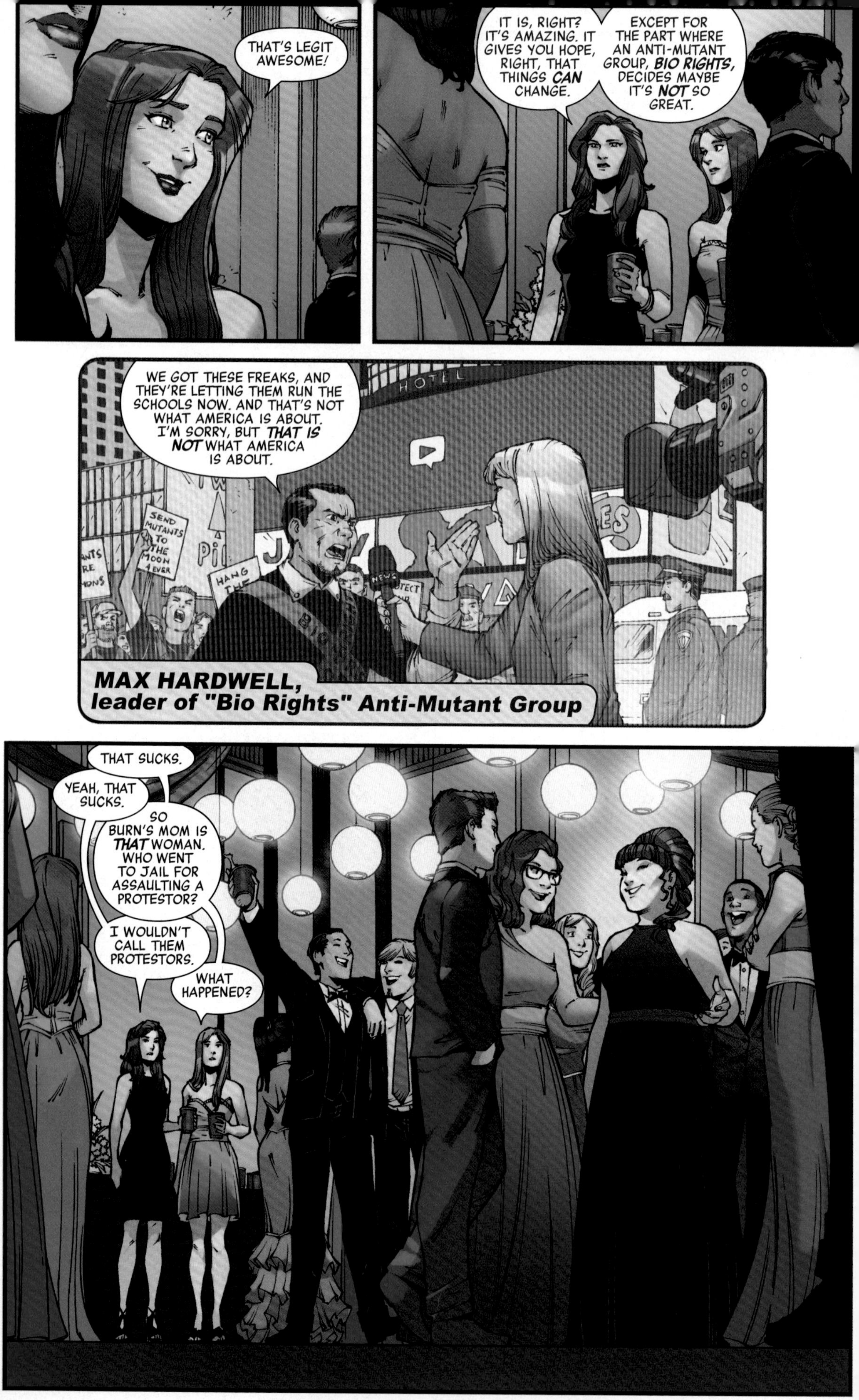
THAT'S LEGIT AWESOME!
IT IS, RIGHT? IT'S AMAZING. IT GIVES YOU HOPE, RIGHT, THAT THINGS CAN CHANGE.
EXCEPT FOR THE PART WHERE AN ANTI-MUTANT GROUP, BIO RIGHTS, DECIDES MAYBE IT'S NOT SO GREAT.
WE GOT THESE FREAKS, AND THEY'RE LETTING THEM RUN THE SCHOOLS NOW. AND THAT'S NOT WHAT AMERICA IS ABOUT. I'M SORRY, BUT THAT IS NOT WHAT AMERICA IS ABOUT.
HOTEL
SEND MUTANTS TO THE MOON 4 EVER
HANG THE
NEWS
MAX HARDWELL, leader of "Bio Rights" Anti-Mutant Group
THAT SUCKS.
YEAH, THAT SUCKS.
SO BURN'S MOM IS THAT WOMAN. WHO WENT TO JAIL FOR ASSAULTING A PROTESTOR?
I WOULDN'T CALL THEM PROTESTORS.
WHAT HAPPENED?

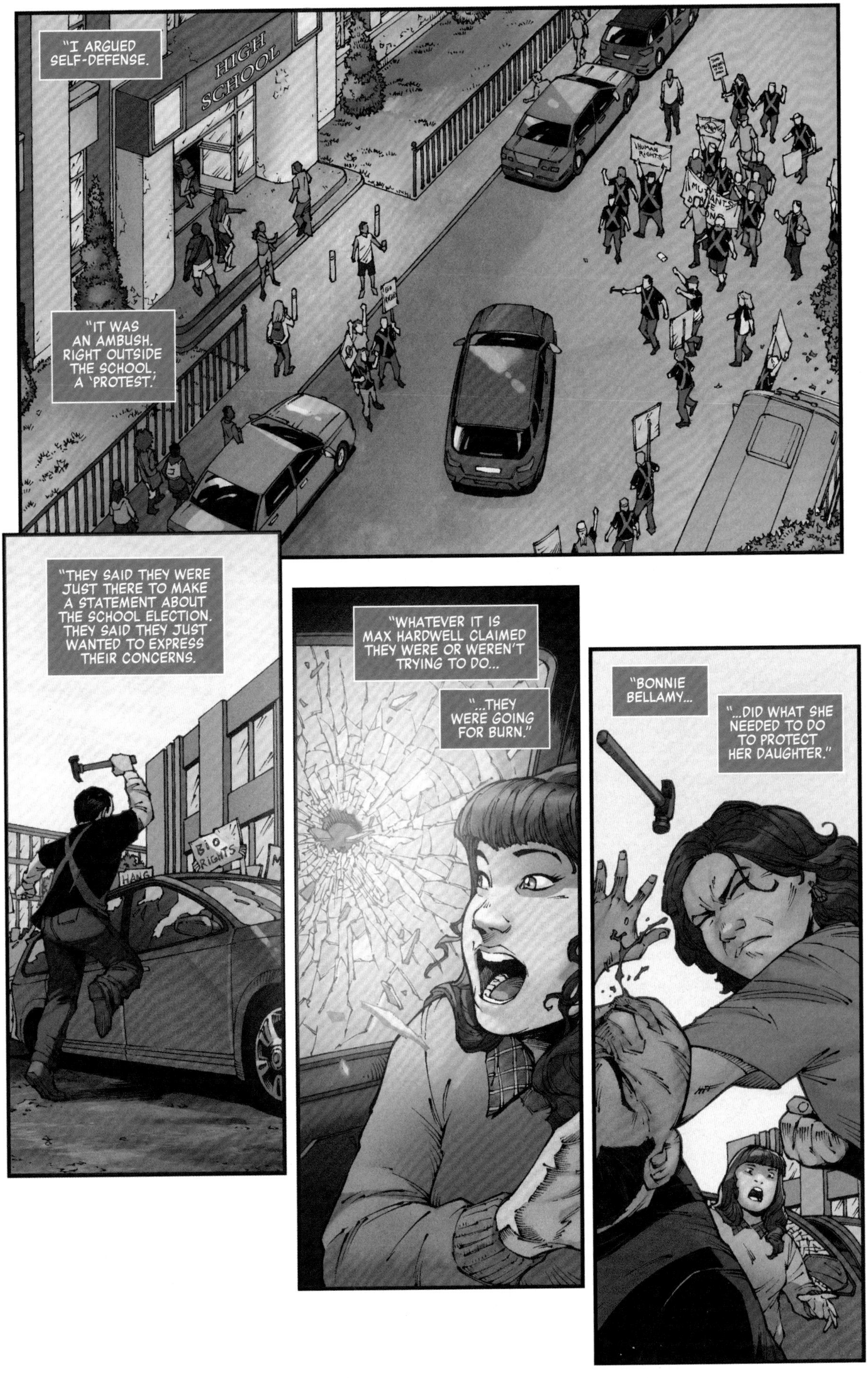
HIGH SCHOOL
"I ARGUED SELF-DEFENSE.
"IT WAS AN AMBUSH. RIGHT OUTSIDE THE SCHOOL. A 'PROTEST.'
HUMAN RIGHTS
"THEY SAID THEY WERE JUST THERE TO MAKE A STATEMENT ABOUT THE SCHOOL ELECTION. THEY SAID THEY JUST WANTED TO EXPRESS THEIR CONCERNS.
BIO RIGHTS
HANG
"WHATEVER IT IS MAX HARDWELL CLAIMED THEY WERE OR WEREN'T TRYING TO DO...
"...THEY WERE GOING FOR BURN."
"BONNIE BELLAMY...
"...DID WHAT SHE NEEDED TO DO TO PROTECT HER DAUGHTER."

WHAT DID SHE GET?

FIVE YEARS.

IS THAT A LOT?

I THOUGHT SO.

YOU KNOW WHAT'S WEIRD?

ALWAYS.

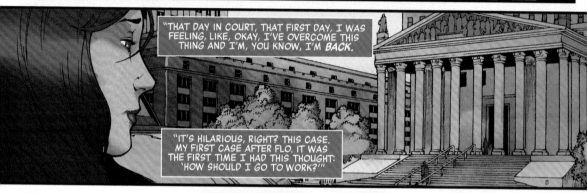

"THAT DAY IN COURT, THAT FIRST DAY, I WAS FEELING, LIKE, OKAY, I'VE OVERCOME THIS THING AND I'M, YOU KNOW, I'M *BACK*.

"IT'S HILARIOUS, RIGHT? THIS CASE. MY FIRST CASE AFTER FLO. IT WAS THE FIRST TIME I HAD THIS THOUGHT: 'HOW SHOULD I GO TO WORK?'"

I DON'T KNOW, DID I LOSE BONNIE'S CASE BECAUSE PEOPLE STILL HATE MUTANTS? EVEN THOUGH IT'S *BURN FOR PREZ*, THAT'S STILL TRUE?

DID I LOSE BECAUSE I'M IN THIS VOID WHERE I'M STILL NOT SURE WHO I AM SOME OF THE TIME AND MAYBE IF I WERE GREEN--

JEN.

IT'S NOT A SWEATER. IT'S YOUR *BODY*.

IT'S A FRICKING STRESSFUL THING TO FIGURE OUT AND I'M SO PROUD OF YOU FOR COMING THROUGH THIS AND I'M SO GLAD YOU CAN EVEN *START* TO TALK ABOUT IT.

AND THE MOST IMPORTANT THING IS...WE'RE STILL FIGHTING THE GOOD FIGHT.

YOU KNOW WHAT'S MAKING IT ALL SO MUCH MORE DIFFICULT?

MY FIRM ARE JERKS.

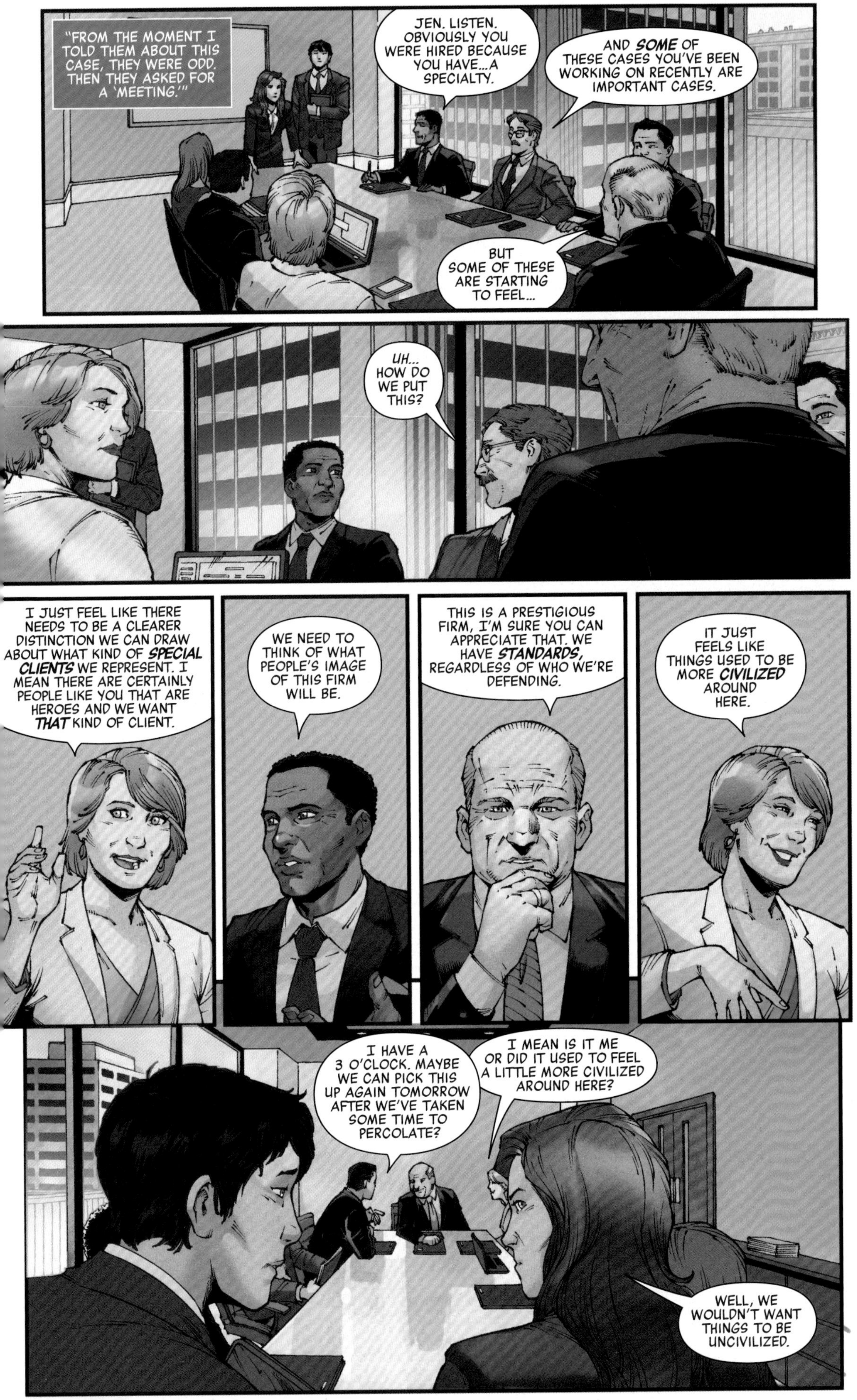
"FROM THE MOMENT I TOLD THEM ABOUT THIS CASE, THEY WERE ODD. THEN THEY ASKED FOR A 'MEETING.'"
JEN. LISTEN. OBVIOUSLY YOU WERE HIRED BECAUSE YOU HAVE...A SPECIALTY.
AND SOME OF THESE CASES YOU'VE BEEN WORKING ON RECENTLY ARE IMPORTANT CASES.
BUT SOME OF THESE ARE STARTING TO FEEL...
UH... HOW DO WE PUT THIS?
I JUST FEEL LIKE THERE NEEDS TO BE A CLEARER DISTINCTION WE CAN DRAW ABOUT WHAT KIND OF SPECIAL CLIENTS WE REPRESENT. I MEAN THERE ARE CERTAINLY PEOPLE LIKE YOU THAT ARE HEROES AND WE WANT THAT KIND OF CLIENT.
WE NEED TO THINK OF WHAT PEOPLE'S IMAGE OF THIS FIRM WILL BE.
THIS IS A PRESTIGIOUS FIRM, I'M SURE YOU CAN APPRECIATE THAT. WE HAVE STANDARDS, REGARDLESS OF WHO WE'RE DEFENDING.
IT JUST FEELS LIKE THINGS USED TO BE MORE CIVILIZED AROUND HERE.
I HAVE A 3 O'CLOCK. MAYBE WE CAN PICK THIS UP AGAIN TOMORROW AFTER WE'VE TAKEN SOME TIME TO PERCOLATE?
I MEAN IS IT ME OR DID IT USED TO FEEL A LITTLE MORE CIVILIZED AROUND HERE?
WELL, WE WOULDN'T WANT THINGS TO BE UNCIVILIZED.

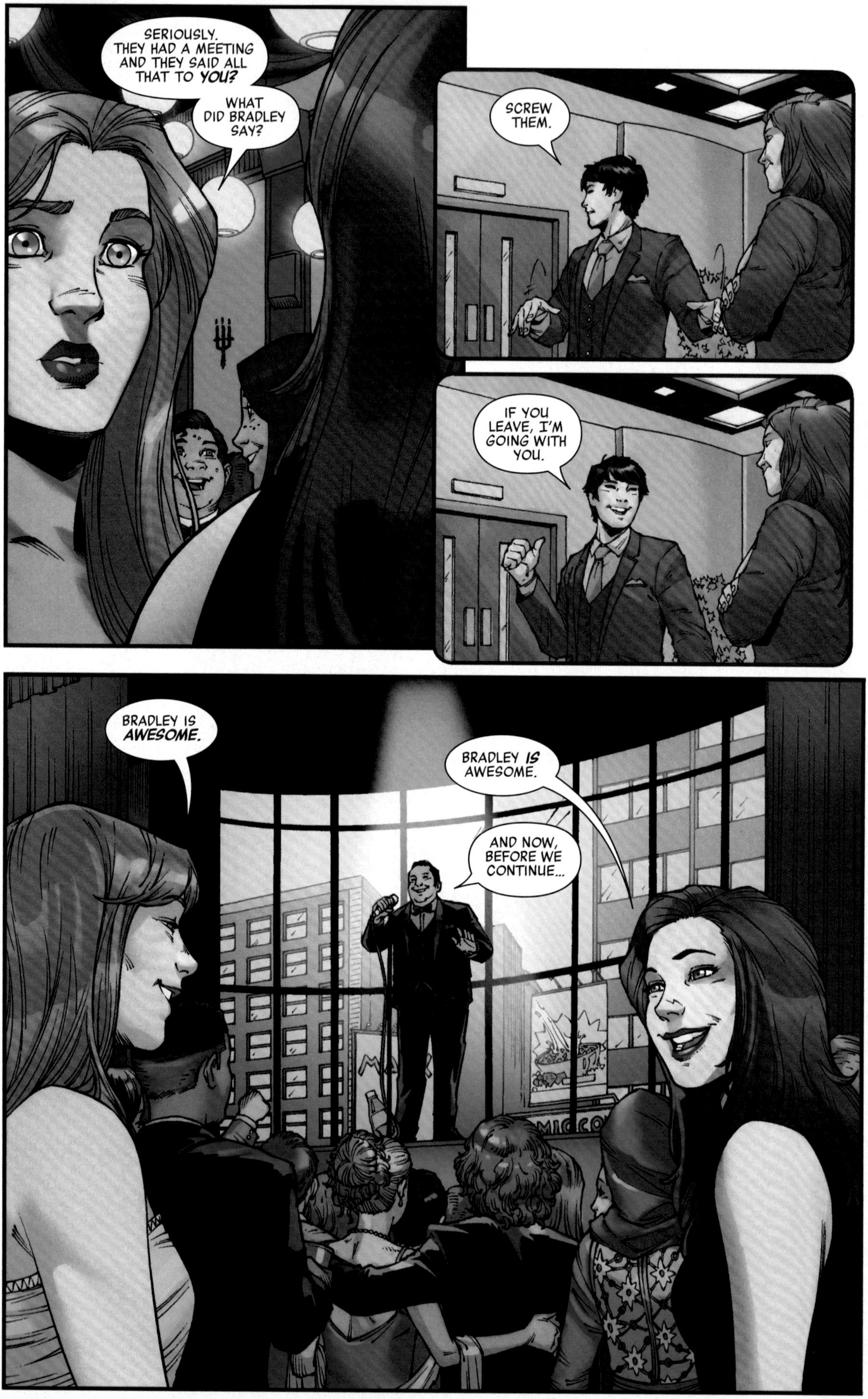
SERIOUSLY. THEY HAD A MEETING AND THEY SAID ALL THAT TO *YOU?*
WHAT DID BRADLEY SAY?
SCREW THEM.
IF YOU LEAVE, I'M GOING WITH YOU.
BRADLEY IS *AWESOME.*
BRADLEY *IS* AWESOME.
AND NOW, BEFORE WE CONTINUE...

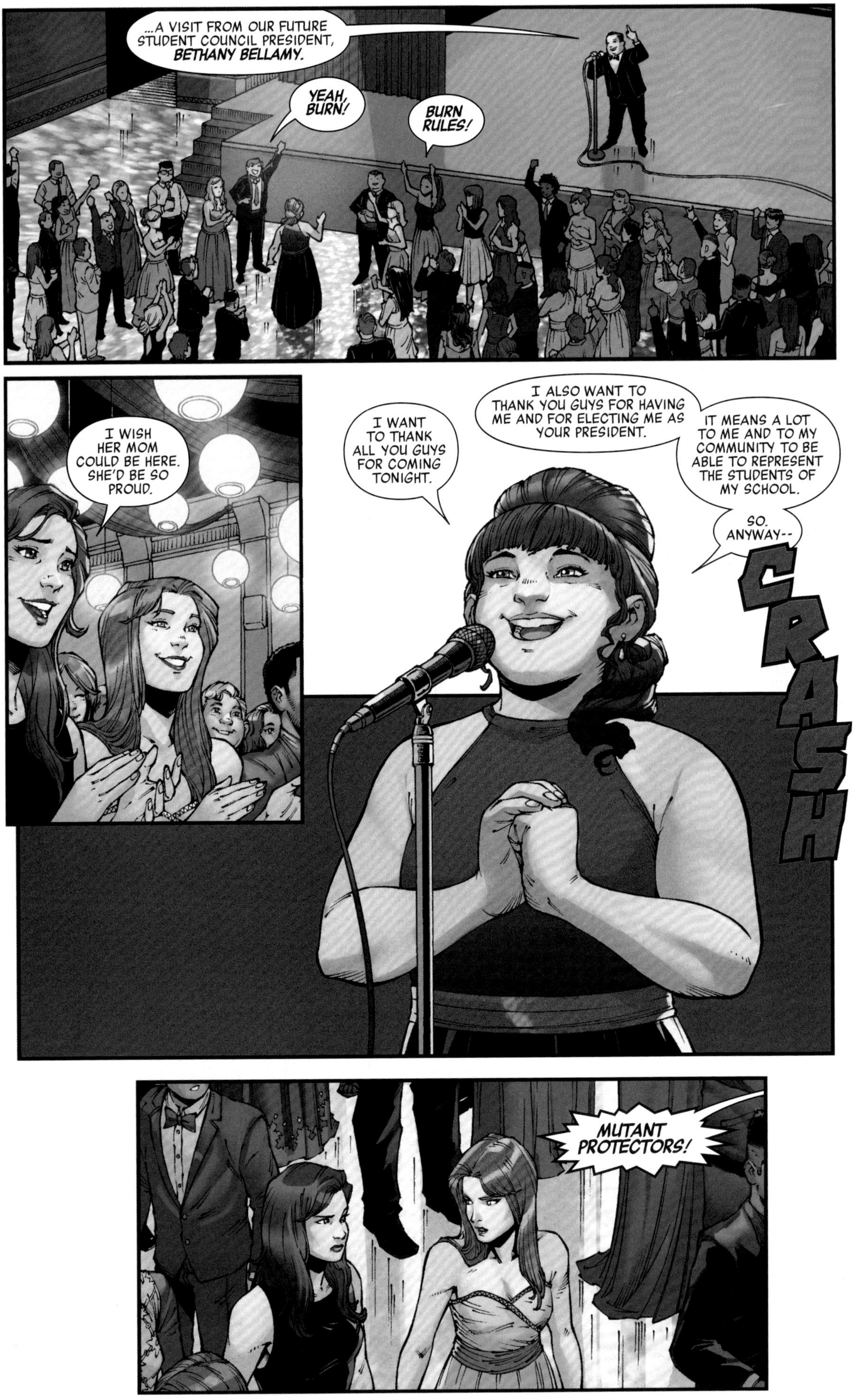
...A VISIT FROM OUR FUTURE STUDENT COUNCIL PRESIDENT, BETHANY BELLAMY.
YEAH, BURN!
BURN RULES!
I WISH HER MOM COULD BE HERE. SHE'D BE SO PROUD.
I WANT TO THANK ALL YOU GUYS FOR COMING TONIGHT.
I ALSO WANT TO THANK YOU GUYS FOR HAVING ME AND FOR ELECTING ME AS YOUR PRESIDENT.
IT MEANS A LOT TO ME AND TO MY COMMUNITY TO BE ABLE TO REPRESENT THE STUDENTS OF MY SCHOOL.
SO. ANYWAY--
CRASH
MUTANT PROTECTORS!

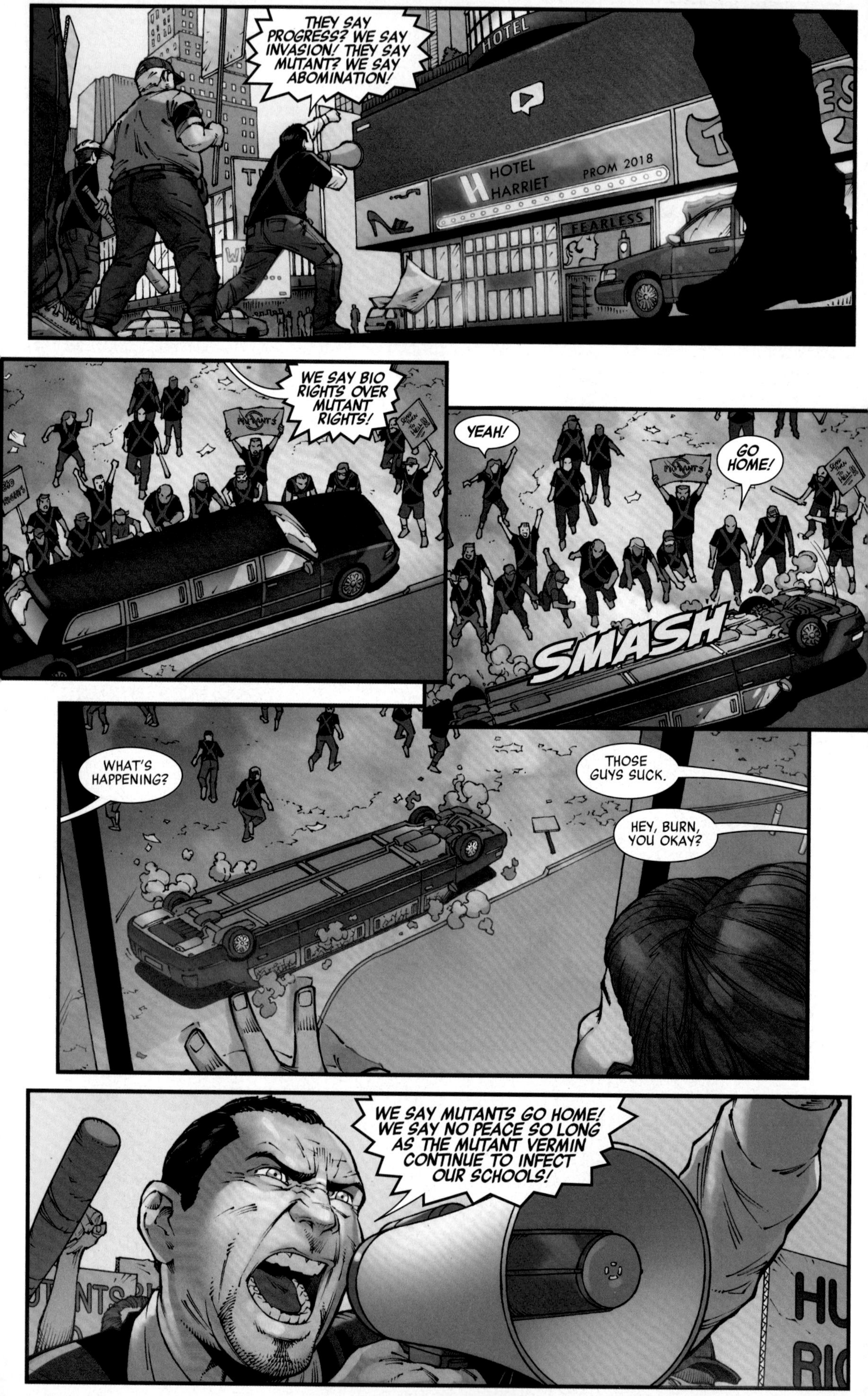
THEY SAY PROGRESS? WE SAY INVASION! THEY SAY MUTANT? WE SAY ABOMINATION!
HOTEL
HOTEL HARRIET
PROM 2018
FEARLESS
WE SAY BIO RIGHTS OVER MUTANT RIGHTS!
YEAH!
GO HOME!
SMASH
WHAT'S HAPPENING?
THOSE GUYS SUCK.
HEY, BURN, YOU OKAY?
WE SAY MUTANTS GO HOME! WE SAY NO PEACE SO LONG AS THE MUTANT VERMIN CONTINUE TO INFECT OUR SCHOOLS!

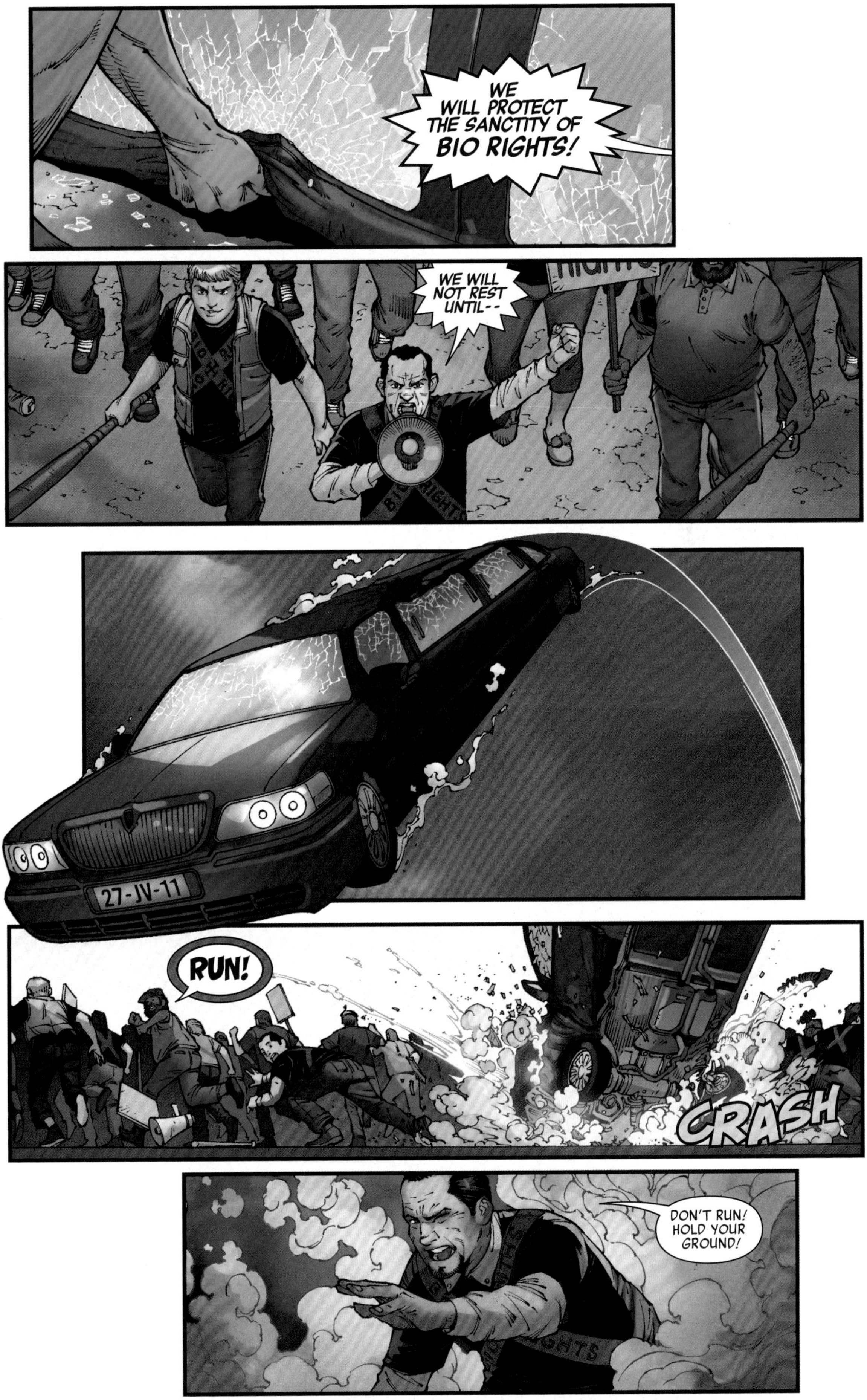
WE WILL PROTECT THE SANCTITY OF BIO RIGHTS!
WE WILL NOT REST UNTIL--
27-JV-11
RUN!
CRASH
DON'T RUN! HOLD YOUR GROUND!

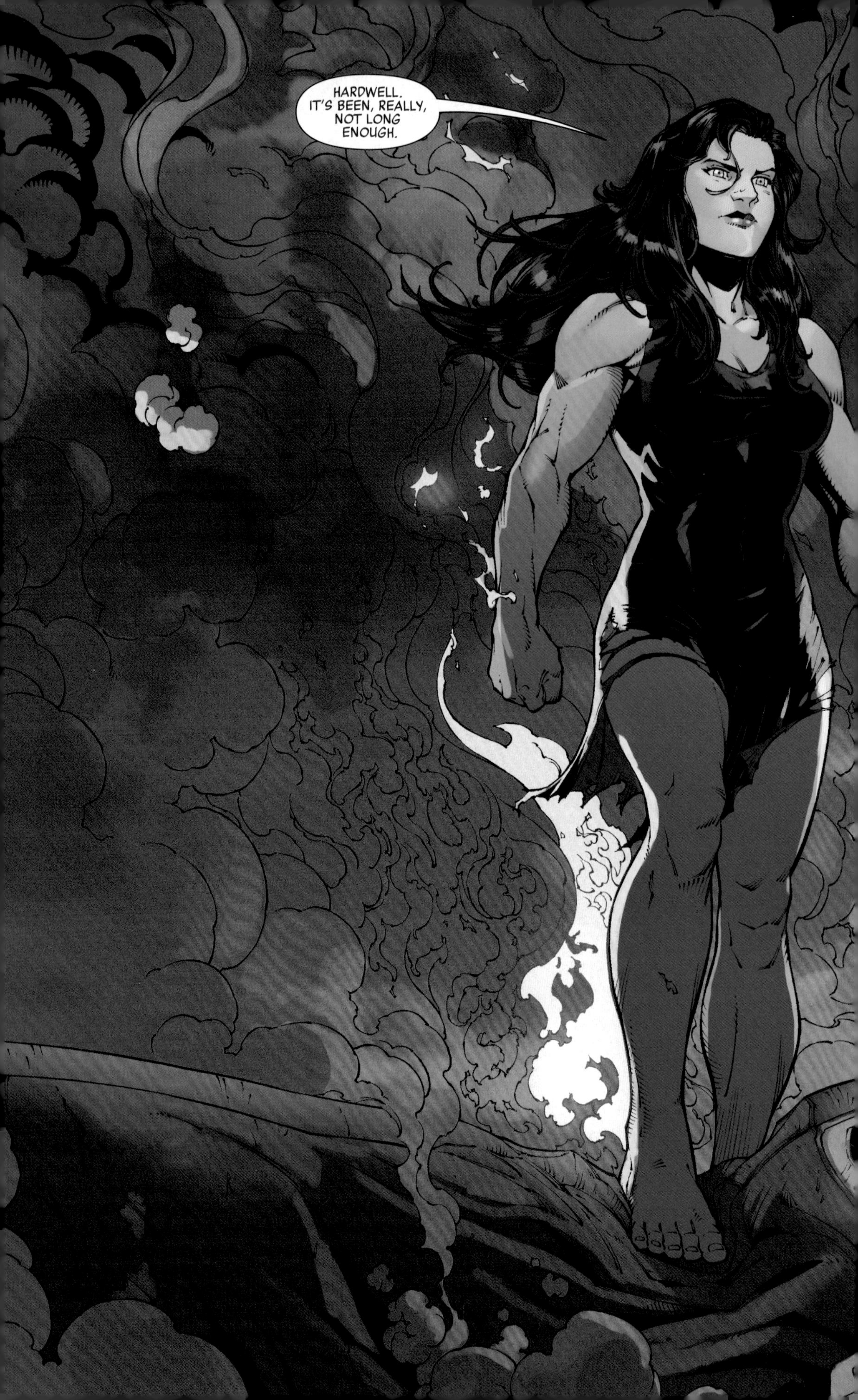
HARDWELL. IT'S BEEN, REALLY, NOT LONG ENOUGH.

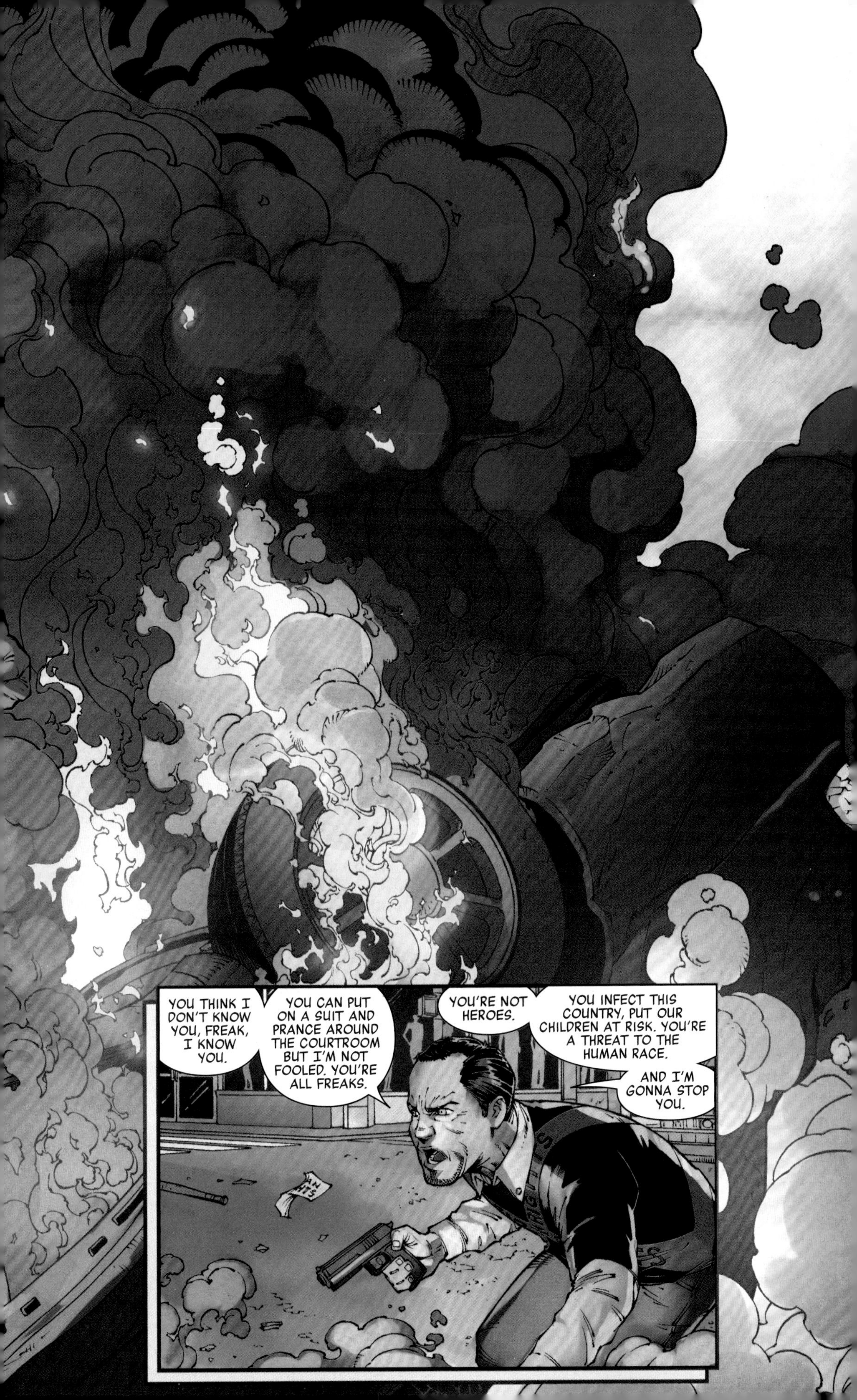
YOU THINK I DON'T KNOW YOU, FREAK, I KNOW YOU.
YOU CAN PUT ON A SUIT AND PRANCE AROUND THE COURTROOM BUT I'M NOT FOOLED. YOU'RE ALL FREAKS.
YOU'RE NOT HEROES.
YOU INFECT THIS COUNTRY, PUT OUR CHILDREN AT RISK. YOU'RE A THREAT TO THE HUMAN RACE.
AND I'M GONNA STOP YOU.

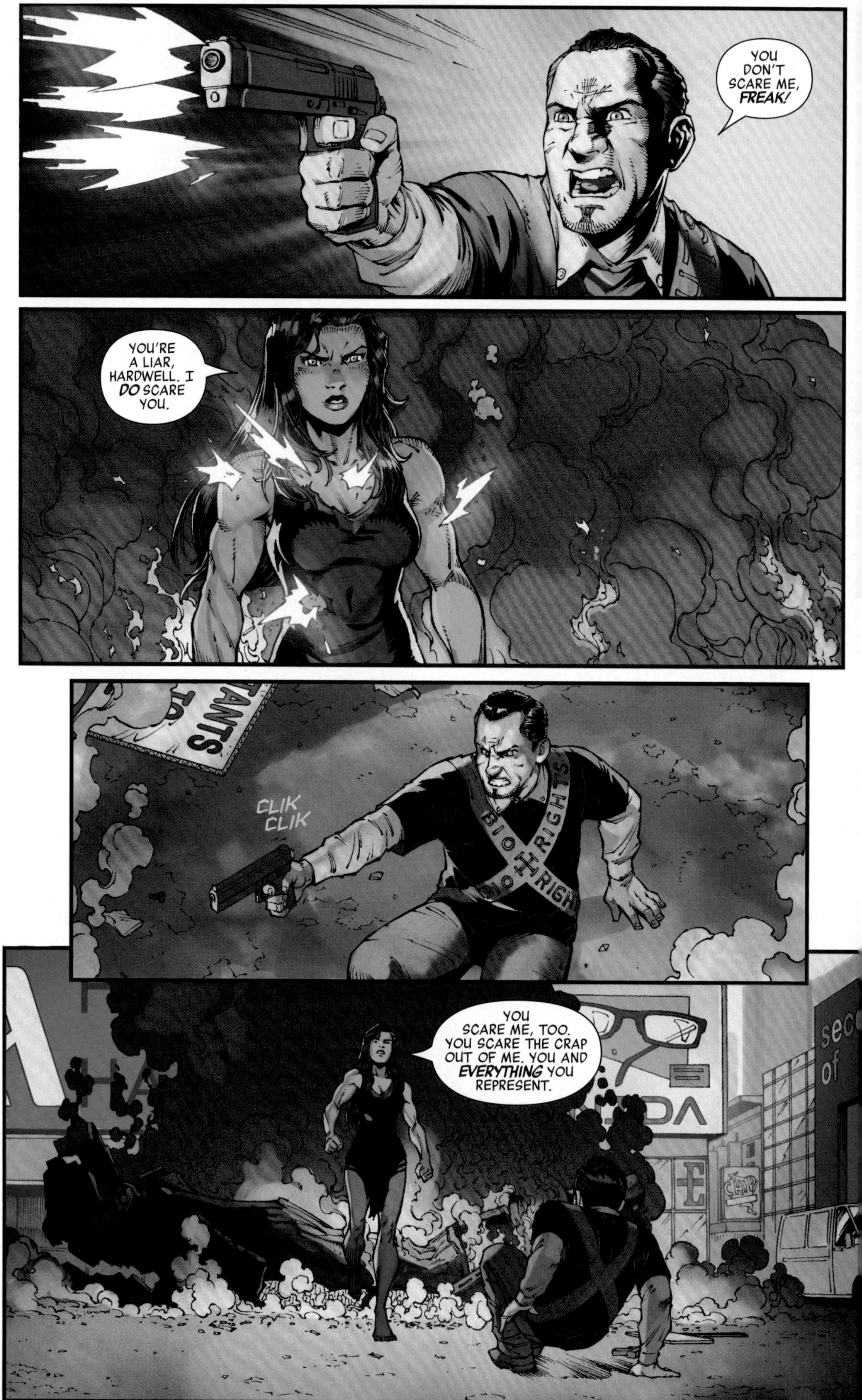
YOU DON'T SCARE ME, FREAK!
YOU'RE A LIAR, HARDWELL. I DO SCARE YOU.
CLIK CLIK
BIO RIGHTS
YOU SCARE ME, TOO. YOU SCARE THE CRAP OUT OF ME. YOU AND EVERYTHING YOU REPRESENT.

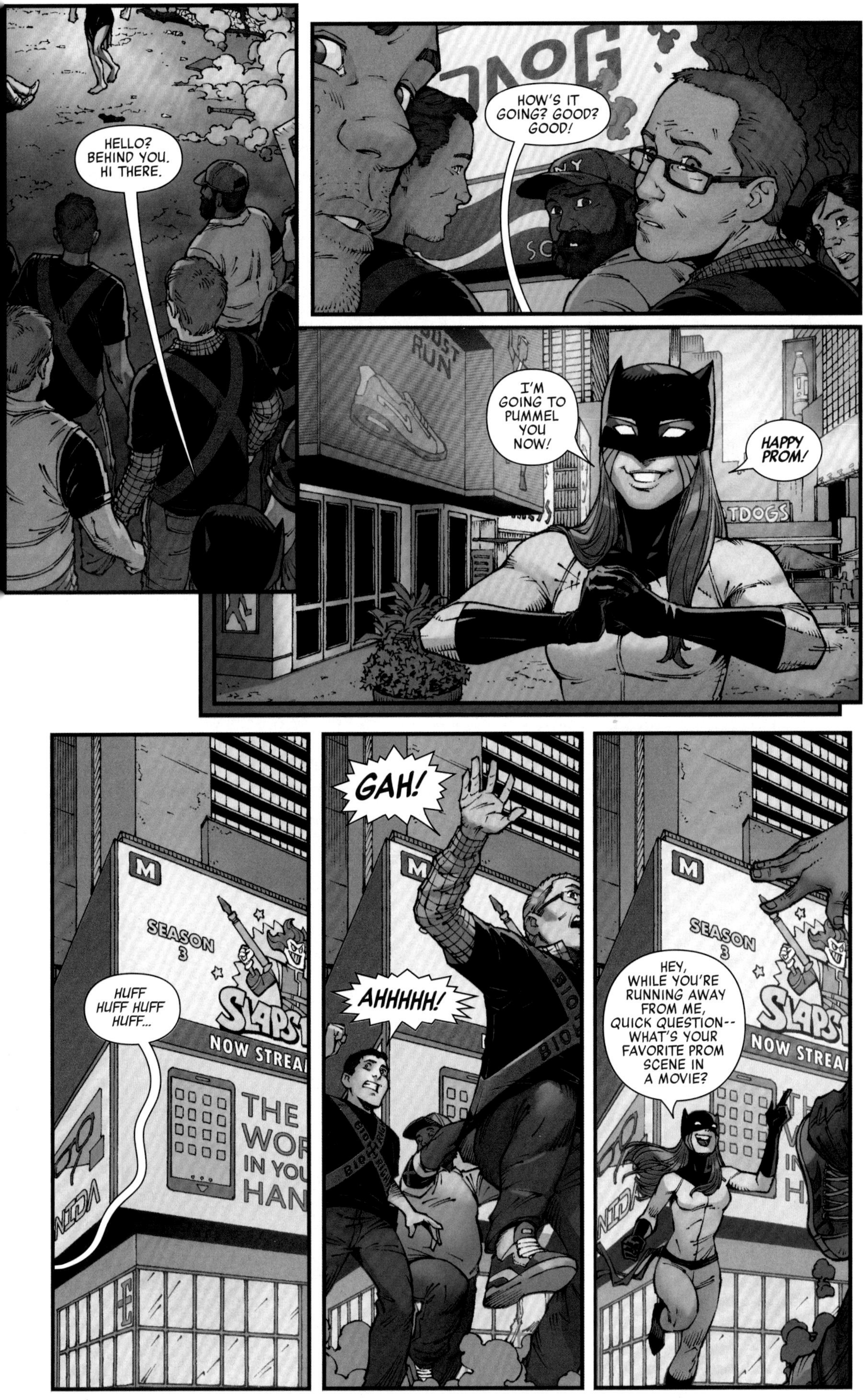
HELLO? BEHIND YOU. HI THERE.
HOW'S IT GOING? GOOD? GOOD!
I'M GOING TO PUMMEL YOU NOW!
HAPPY PROM!
SEASON 3
NOW STREA
HUFF HUFF HUFF HUFF...
GAH!
AHHHHH!
HEY, WHILE YOU'RE RUNNING AWAY FROM ME, QUICK QUESTION-- WHAT'S YOUR FAVORITE PROM SCENE IN A MOVIE?

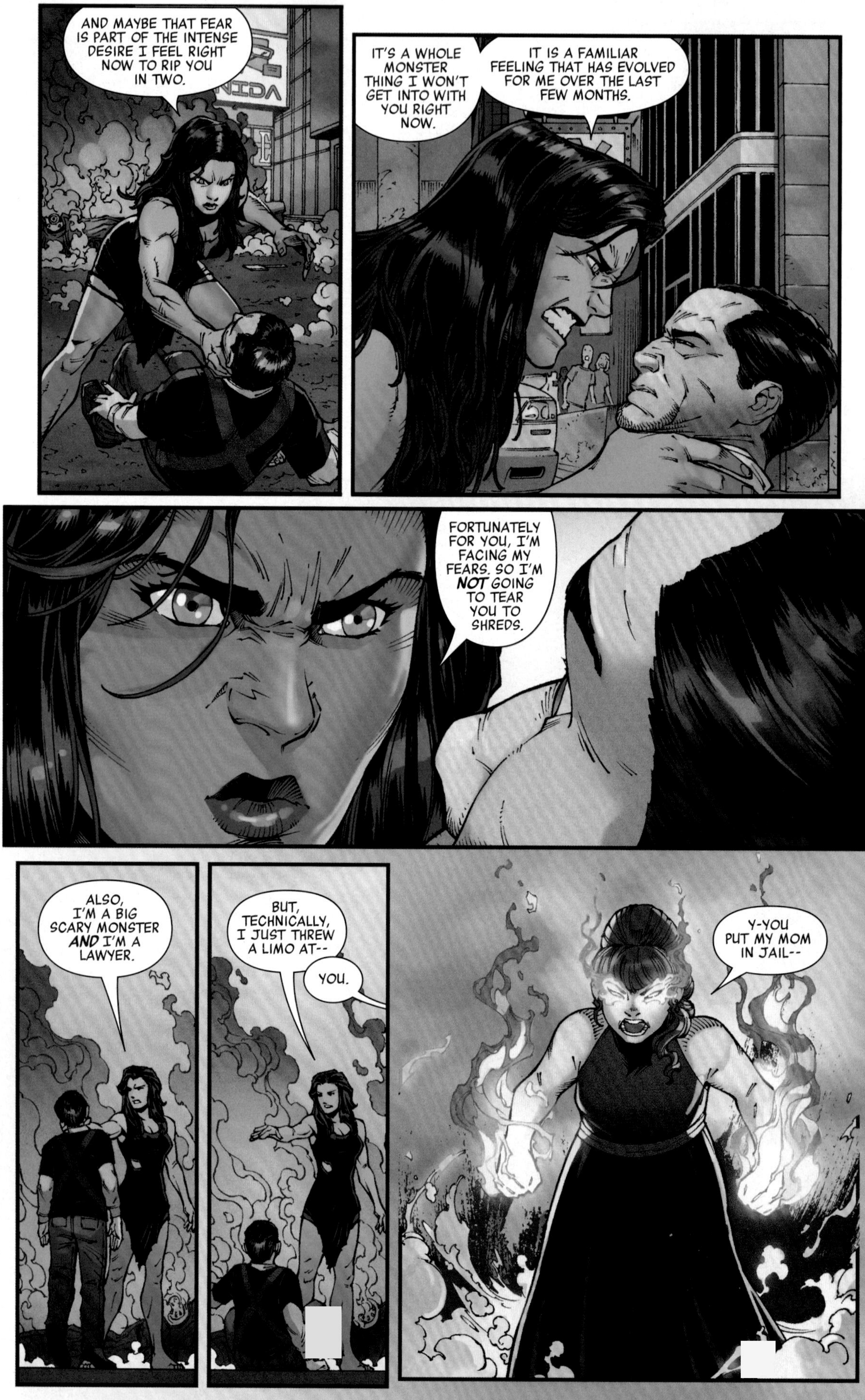
AND MAYBE THAT FEAR IS PART OF THE INTENSE DESIRE I FEEL RIGHT NOW TO RIP YOU IN TWO.
IT'S A WHOLE MONSTER THING I WON'T GET INTO WITH YOU RIGHT NOW.
IT IS A FAMILIAR FEELING THAT HAS EVOLVED FOR ME OVER THE LAST FEW MONTHS.
FORTUNATELY FOR YOU, I'M FACING MY FEARS. SO I'M NOT GOING TO TEAR YOU TO SHREDS.
ALSO, I'M A BIG SCARY MONSTER AND I'M A LAWYER.
BUT, TECHNICALLY, I JUST THREW A LIMO AT--
YOU.
Y-YOU PUT MY MOM IN JAIL--

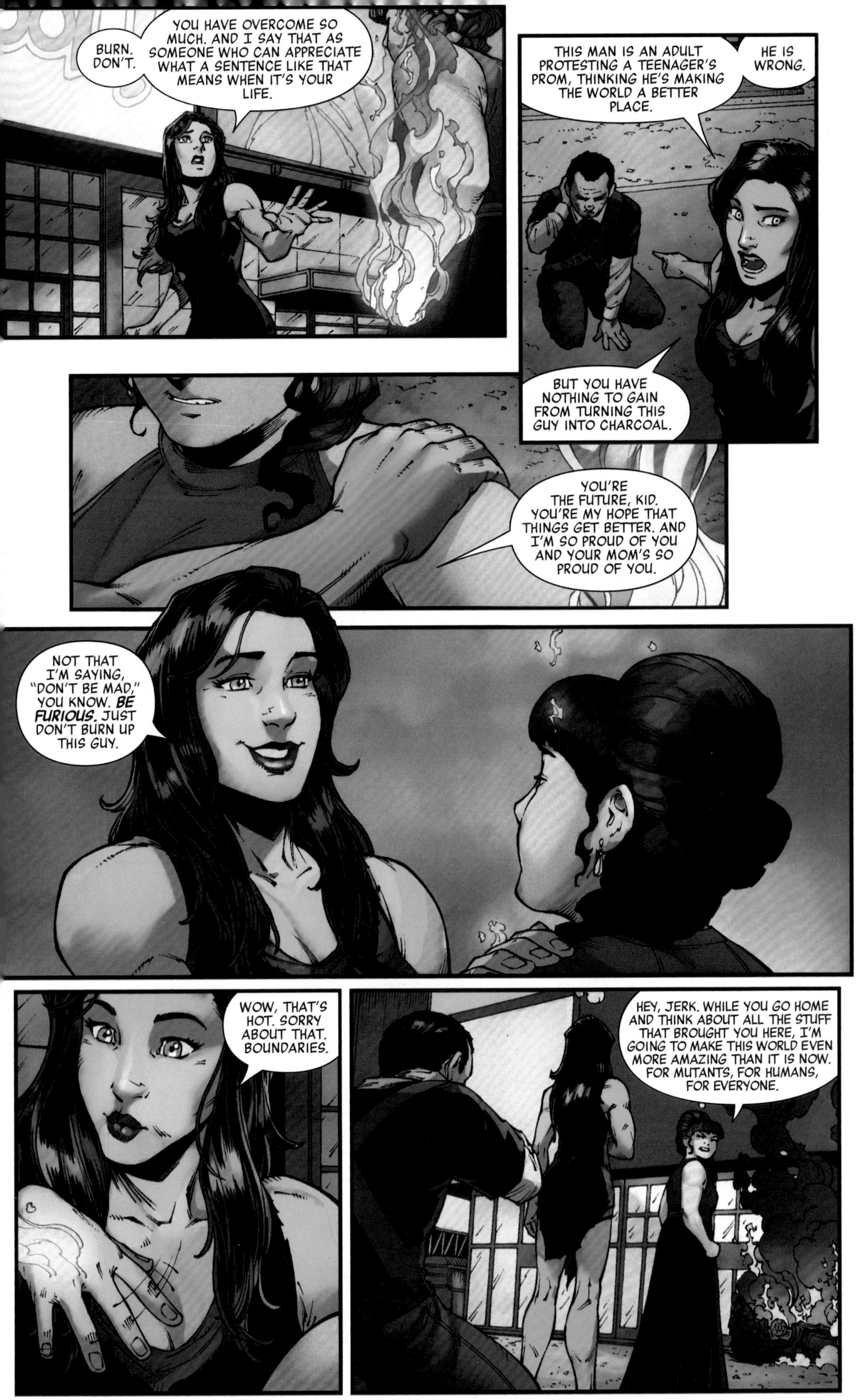
BURN. DON'T.
YOU HAVE OVERCOME SO MUCH. AND I SAY THAT AS SOMEONE WHO CAN APPRECIATE WHAT A SENTENCE LIKE THAT MEANS WHEN IT'S YOUR LIFE.
THIS MAN IS AN ADULT PROTESTING A TEENAGER'S PROM, THINKING HE'S MAKING THE WORLD A BETTER PLACE.
HE IS WRONG.
BUT YOU HAVE NOTHING TO GAIN FROM TURNING THIS GUY INTO CHARCOAL.
YOU'RE THE FUTURE, KID. YOU'RE MY HOPE THAT THINGS GET BETTER. AND I'M SO PROUD OF YOU AND YOUR MOM'S SO PROUD OF YOU.
NOT THAT I'M SAYING, "DON'T BE MAD," YOU KNOW. ***BE FURIOUS.*** JUST DON'T BURN UP THIS GUY.
WOW, THAT'S HOT. SORRY ABOUT THAT. BOUNDARIES.
HEY, JERK. WHILE YOU GO HOME AND THINK ABOUT ALL THE STUFF THAT BROUGHT YOU HERE, I'M GOING TO MAKE THIS WORLD EVEN MORE AMAZING THAN IT IS NOW. FOR MUTANTS, FOR HUMANS, FOR EVERYONE.

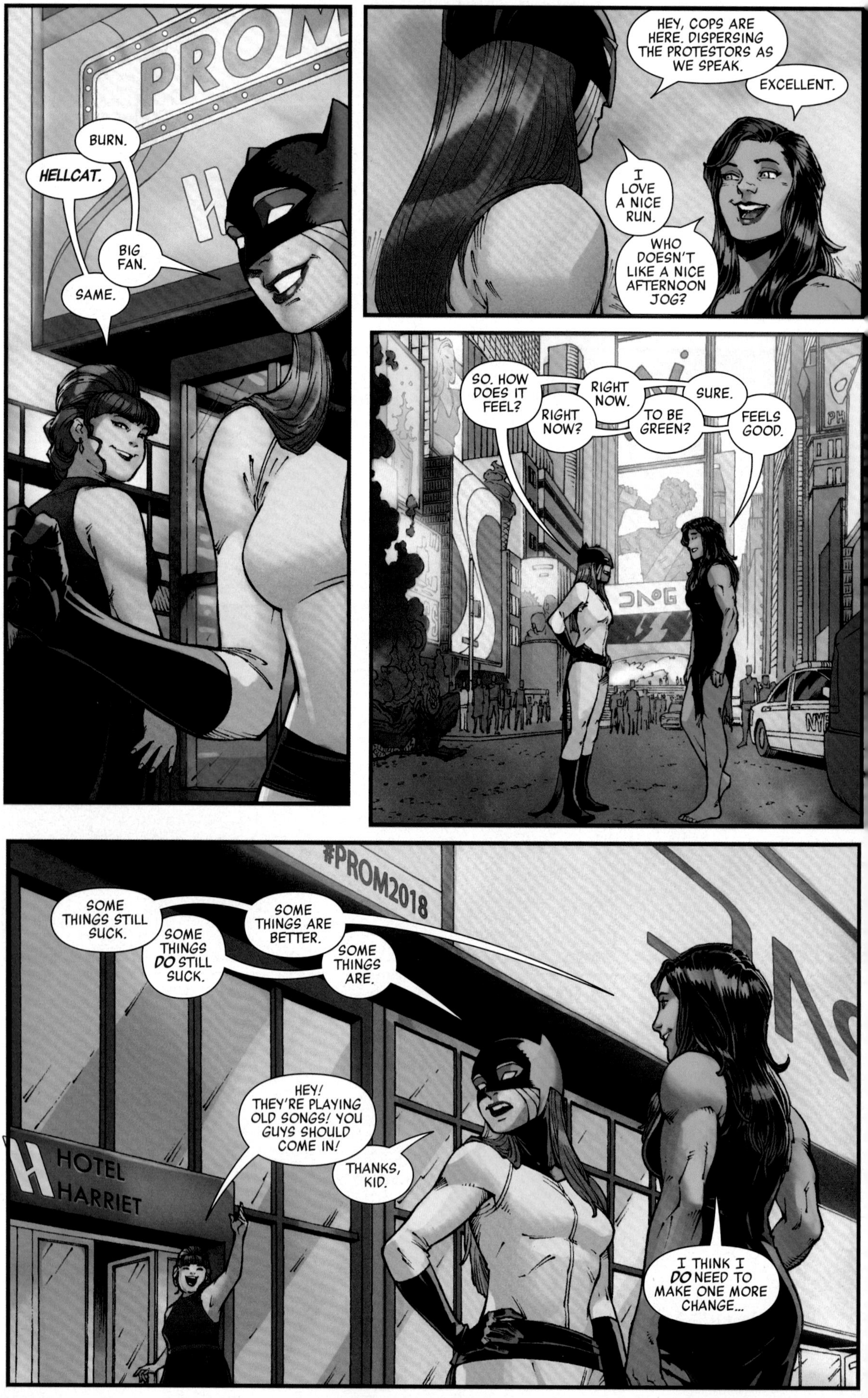
PROM
BURN.
HELLCAT.
BIG FAN.
SAME.
HEY, COPS ARE HERE. DISPERSING THE PROTESTORS AS WE SPEAK.
EXCELLENT.
I LOVE A NICE RUN.
WHO DOESN'T LIKE A NICE AFTERNOON JOG?
SO. HOW DOES IT FEEL?
RIGHT NOW?
RIGHT NOW.
TO BE GREEN?
SURE.
FEELS GOOD.
#PROM2018
SOME THINGS STILL SUCK.
SOME THINGS DO STILL SUCK.
SOME THINGS ARE BETTER.
SOME THINGS ARE.
HEY! THEY'RE PLAYING OLD SONGS! YOU GUYS SHOULD COME IN!
THANKS, KID.
HOTEL HARRIET
I THINK I DO NEED TO MAKE ONE MORE CHANGE...

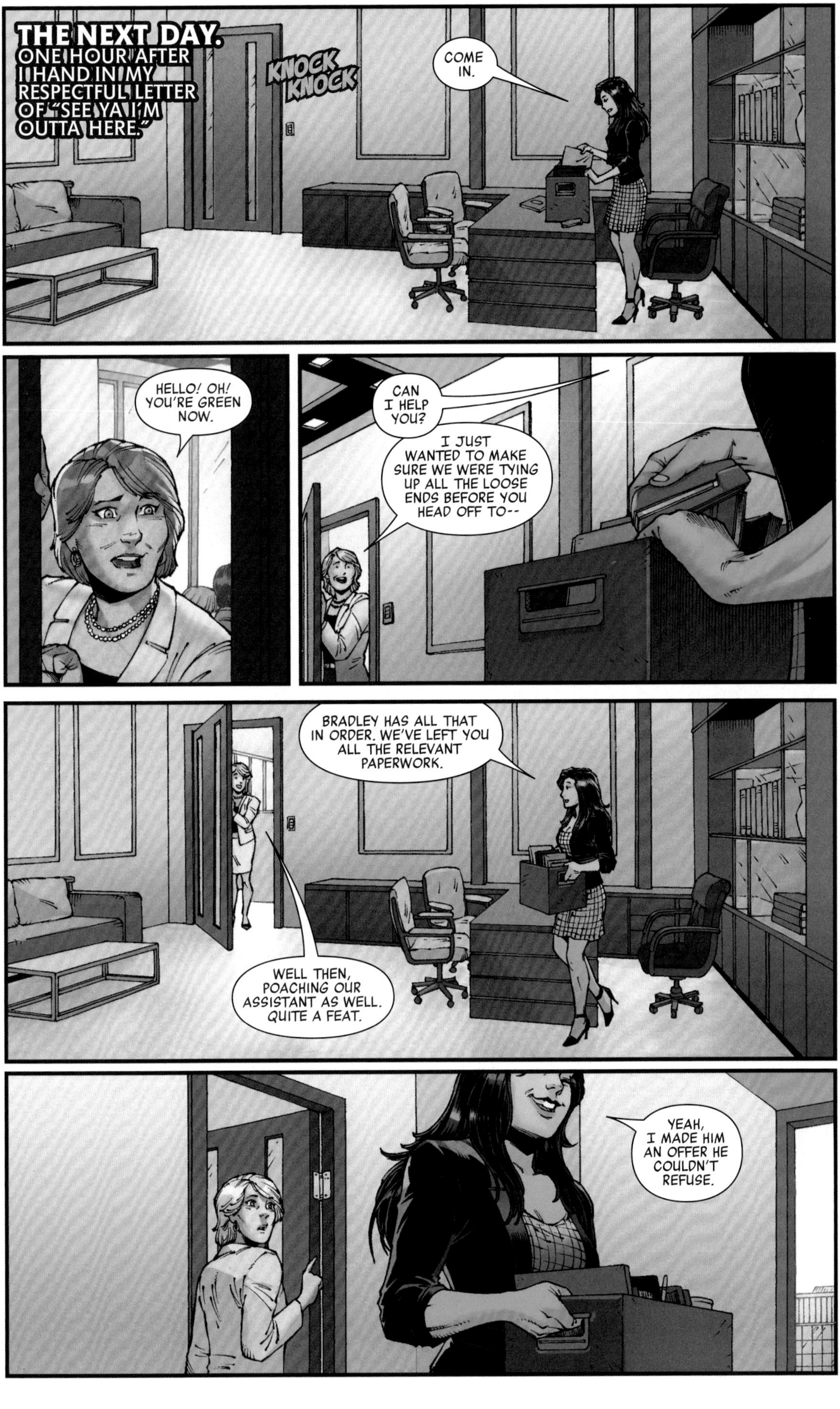
THE NEXT DAY.
ONE HOUR AFTER I HAND IN MY RESPECTFUL LETTER OF "SEE YA I'M OUTTA HERE."
KNOCK KNOCK
COME IN.
HELLO! OH! YOU'RE GREEN NOW.
CAN I HELP YOU?
I JUST WANTED TO MAKE SURE WE WERE TYING UP ALL THE LOOSE ENDS BEFORE YOU HEAD OFF TO--
BRADLEY HAS ALL THAT IN ORDER. WE'VE LEFT YOU ALL THE RELEVANT PAPERWORK.
WELL THEN, POACHING OUR ASSISTANT AS WELL. QUITE A FEAT.
YEAH, I MADE HIM AN OFFER HE COULDN'T REFUSE.

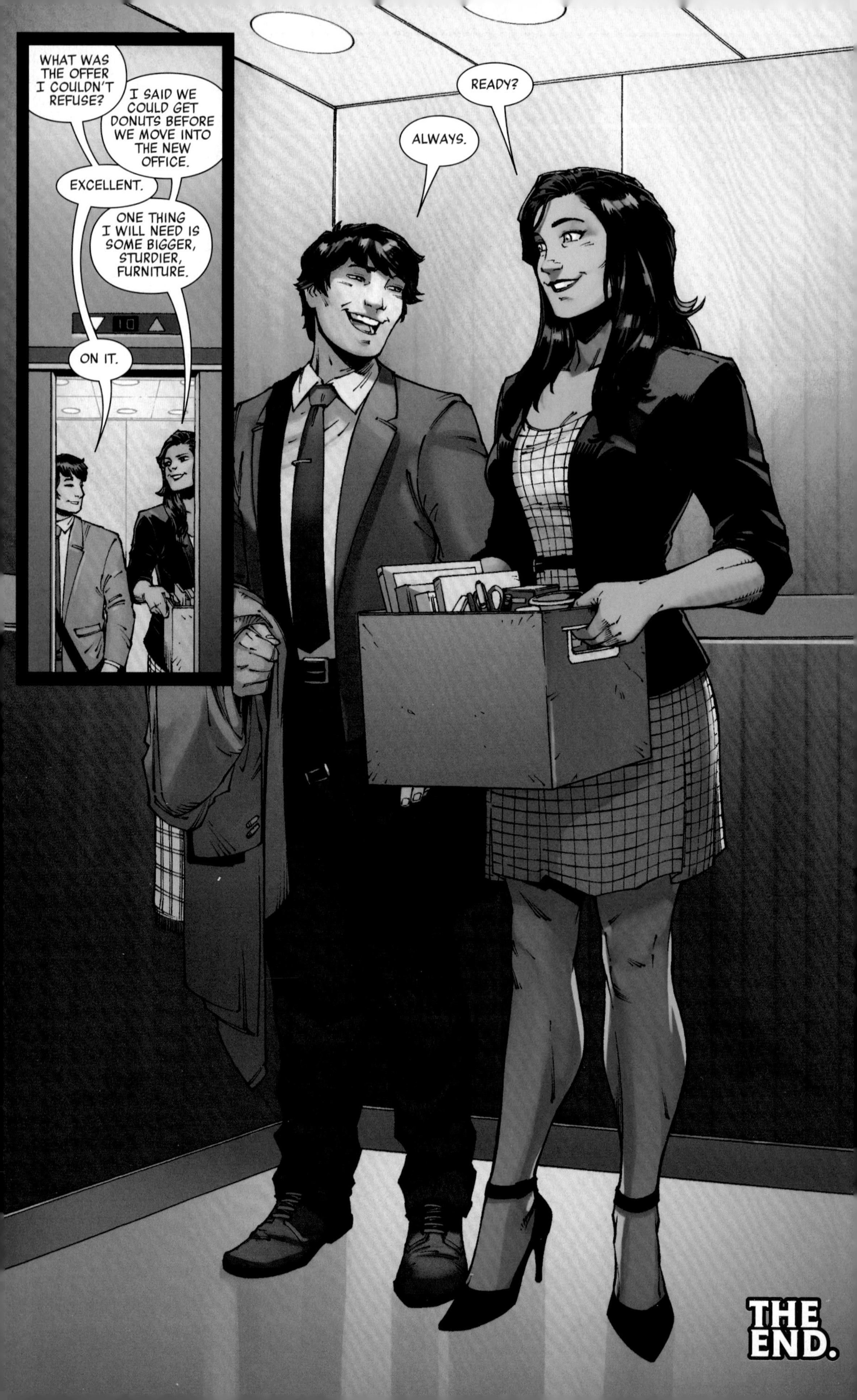
WHAT WAS THE OFFER I COULDN'T REFUSE?
I SAID WE COULD GET DONUTS BEFORE WE MOVE INTO THE NEW OFFICE.
EXCELLENT.
ONE THING I WILL NEED IS SOME BIGGER, STURDIER, FURNITURE.
ON IT.
READY?
ALWAYS.
THE END.

#159 LEGACY
HEADSHOT VARIANT BY
MIKE McKONE
& **RACHELLE ROSENBERG**

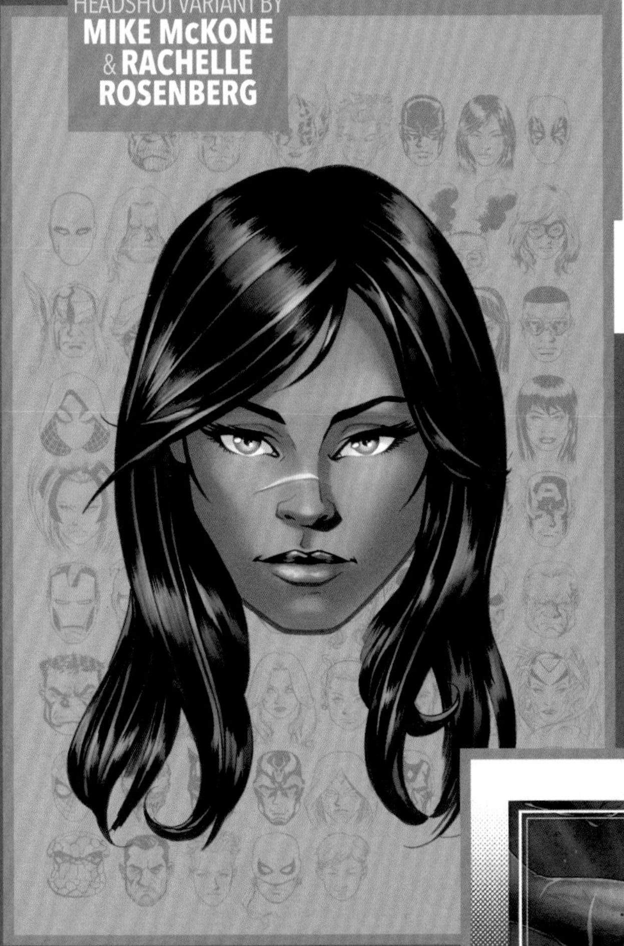

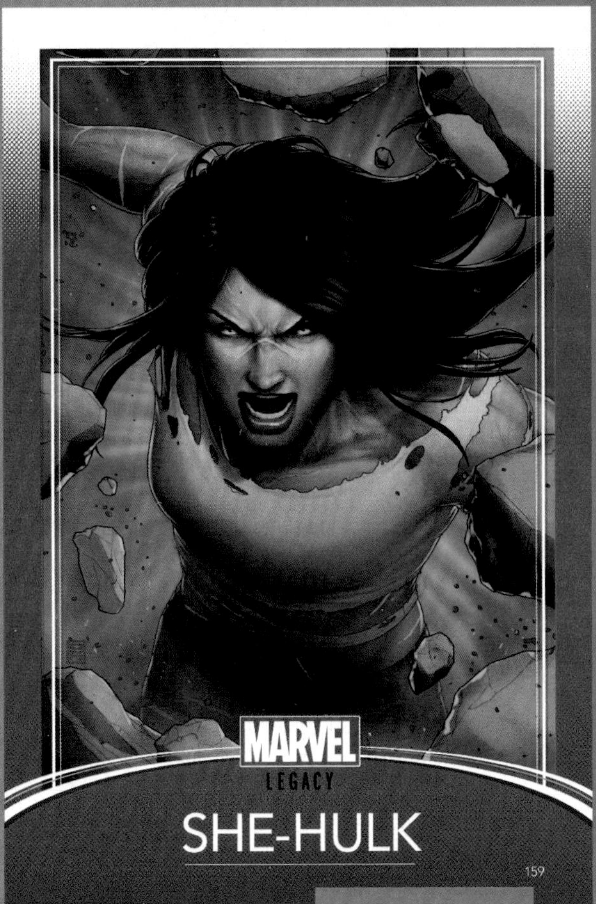
MARVEL
LEGACY
SHE-HULK
159

#159 TRADING CARD
VARIANT BY
JOHN TYLER CHRISTOPHER

#161 AVENGERS
VARIANT BY
MIKE PERKINS
& **ANDY TROY**

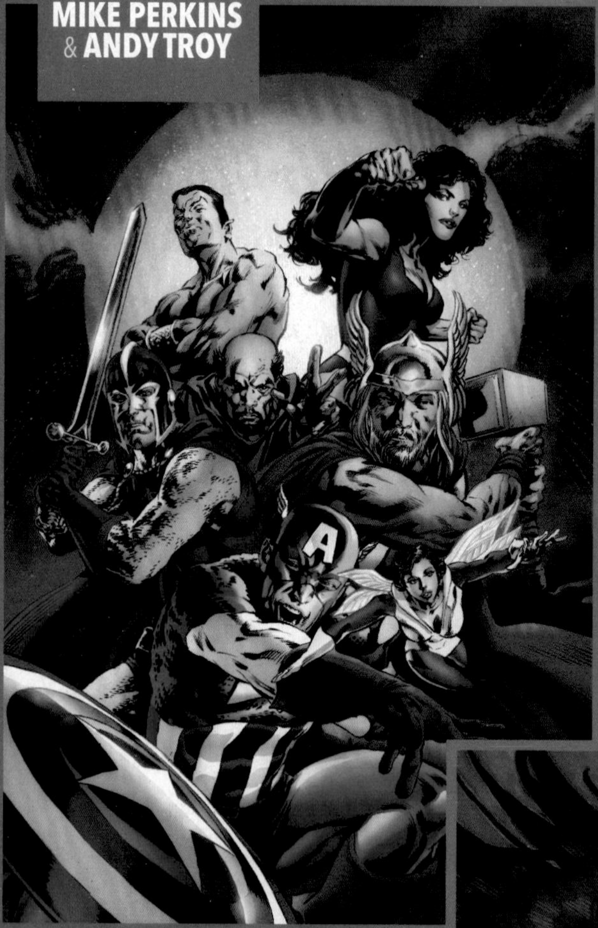
A

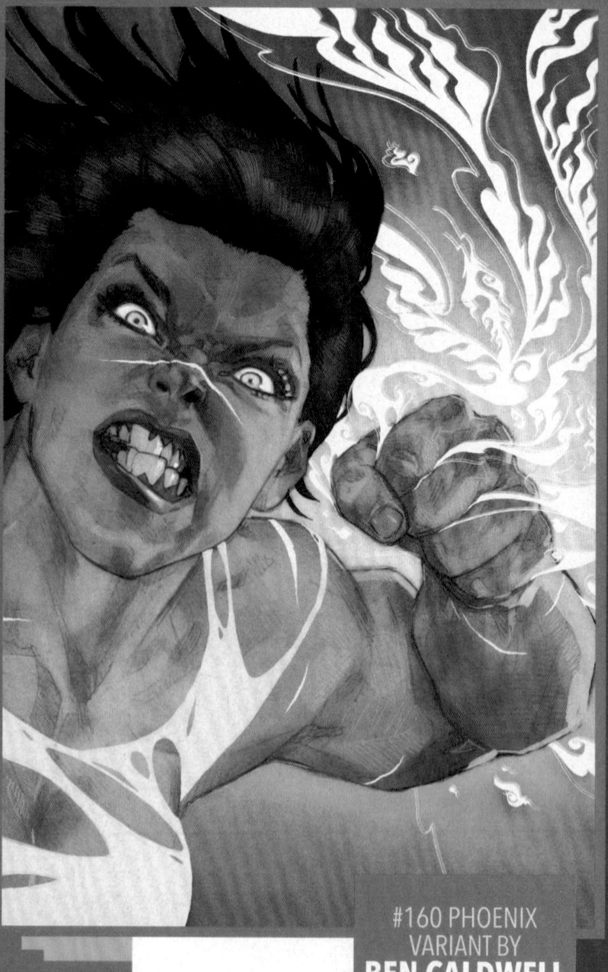

#160 PHOENIX
VARIANT BY
BEN CALDWELL